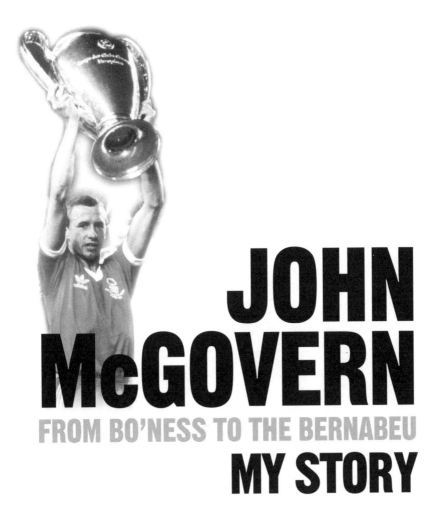

JOHN McGOVERN

FROM BO'NESS TO THE BERNABEU
MY STORY

To my mum, who has always shown me how to survive, and to Ann and Alek, who always remind me that I'm not the only person on the planet.

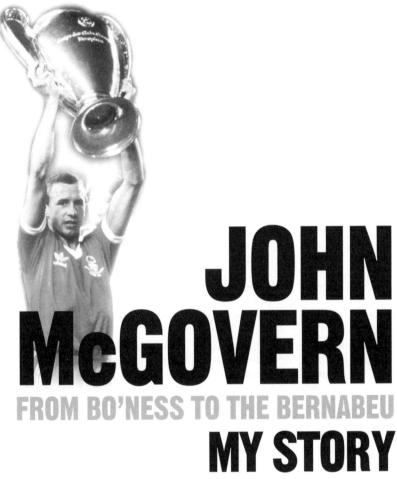

JOHN McGOVERN

FROM BO'NESS TO THE BERNABEU
MY STORY

VSP

Published by Vision Sports Publishing in 2012

Vision Sports Publishing
19–23 High Street
Kingston upon Thames
Surrey
KT1 1LL

www.visionsp.co.uk

ISBN: 978-1-907637-19-3

Written by John McGovern and Kevin Brennan
Copy editor: Alex Morton
Cover design: Doug Cheesman

Typeset by Palimpsest Book Production Limited, Falkirk, Stirlingshire

Printed in the UK by TJI International, Padstow, Cornwall

A CIP Catalogue record for this book
is available from the British Library

CONTENTS

ACKNOWLEDGEMENTS

Acknowledgements are as follows for help in completing this book:

Kevin Brennan for being patient with a novice writer – me. Steve Nicholson and the *Derby Evening Telegraph*. Paul Taylor and the *Nottingham Evening Post*. Gerry Somerton of the *Rotherham Advertiser*. John Lawson and Fraser Nicholson at Nottingham Forest FC. Neil Hallam, my friend and honest freelance journalist. Gordon Sharrocks from the *Bolton Evening News*.

To Jim, Toby, Alex and Henry from Vision Sports Publishing for all their enthusiasm and professionalism.

Special thanks to my good friend John Bilverstone for getting me and the rest of the super team on *Jim'll Fix It*, despite him being an Arsenal fan. And for being the only other person who, with myself, created the "orange dance".

To Fred Hunt and Dave Fox with their wives Marilyn and Esmie for superb nights in Belper, "We won't get fooled again."

To Burt Haimes in New York for our combined love of music, including The Radiators.

To Graeme and Eileen for being Graeme and Eileen.

To Dickie (big Forest fan) and Caro for their hospitality during our visits to the Cotswolds.

To my mates Chris Odell and Peter Day – who could forget the AC/DC concert at De Montfort Hall, Leicester?

Les Shaw for the best fish in the north in the country.

A special thanks to Kevin Keegan for taking the time to write the foreword.

To my family: Mum, for being superwoman at 89; brother Bert, for the competition when we were kids; sister June, her husband Bill and their lovely girls Robin and Becky – who roll out the red carpet when we visit San Francisco. Love you guys.

Kindest regards to my cousins Pat, Yvonne and Robert from Montrose, Tony and Leslie in Hartlepool and Eddie in Bo'ness. As a recently appointed ambassador for Mencap, a special thanks to Roger Grange from Nottingham for keeping his room tidy as promised.

To my stepsister Judy and stepbrother Roger for accepting me as family when my mum married their dad, Stan Wilkinson, while we were in Derby.

To my son Alek – I hope he manages to fulfil his dream as a musician as sometimes I find myself jealous of him for his ability to play the guitar. Anyone who is as creative and talented as he is at writing lyrics and composing songs shouldn't be allowed to fail. Are you listening Zane Lowe? Scrimtheband.com

And finally to Ann, who has put up with me for over 40 years. We have never married and, although she will hate me saying this, the sex is better when you aren't married.

We are opposites in many ways but united in many more. I told my son Alek he would never meet anyone in his life more honest than his mum. She will never lie to you, son. When he asked me the same question about me I couldn't say yes, only if I lied to him it was for his benefit and nothing else.

As always Ann, all my love for your honesty and for being one of the most genuine people on the planet.

FOREWORD

By Kevin Keegan

I have known John for many years and, both as a person and as a player, I have always had the utmost respect for him.

As a player he had a wonderful career, winning European Cups and league titles, as well as a host of other trophies, and was one of the lynchpins of two great sides which Brian Clough moulded, first at Derby County and then even more successfully with Nottingham Forest.

The first thing that struck me about John when I played against him was the fact that he simply didn't have the physique you would normally associate with a footballer, but when you saw him play all of that was pushed to one side. John could run forever and his ability to pass a ball and keep his team ticking was clearly something Brian Clough recognised in him at an early stage. It is no coincidence that Cloughie made John such an important part of his teams and also saw him as the ideal captain for Nottingham Forest during the most successful period in the club's history.

It's interesting that Brian saw something in John that made him want to sign him on three separate occasions. Believe me, when a manager takes over at a new club and then goes back to sign someone he has worked with before, it is a sure sign that the player is someone who will bring something to the team and who can be relied on. That was certainly the case with John, and their partnership as manager and player should not be underestimated.

John would leave nothing on the pitch, and when he played

the game he gave 100 per cent. I think that, like me, he tried to maximise his game as a player, supplementing the ability he had with sheer hard work and the sort of honest approach which earned respect not only from his own team-mates, but also from those of us who played against him.

The biggest game the two of us played in against each other was the European Cup Final of 1980 at the Bernabeu in Madrid, when Forest retained the trophy by beating my Hamburg side 1-0. It was a great achievement for Forest and they showed exactly what they were about that night. As usual John was at the heart of their play, keeping things ticking over and making sure that the simple things were done well, enabling his team to put in a thoroughly professional display to win the cup.

We played against each other on several occasions over the years and as an opponent I always knew that he would be there from the first whistle until the last. There was nothing of him, but as well as being able to pass the ball he was bone-hard and could certainly look after himself on the field.

Top players today have a wonderful time and of course earn huge amounts of money. I'm not saying it was better or worse in our day, but it was certainly different. It's not just the money that has changed, but the pitches, grounds and all-round technology that now surrounds the modern game. When we both started out long coach journeys were part and parcel of a footballer's life, and there weren't too many motorways around! I can remember eating packed sandwiches on a torturous journey to Exeter and back when I was playing for Scunthorpe, but it was all part of playing in that era.

We enjoyed and loved the game, and both John and I were fortunate enough to experience some huge highs during the course of our playing careers. What you always got from John was what it said on the tin. He never let anyone down. He was a reliable and solid professional, someone you could hang your hat on as a player and as a man, knowing exactly what he was about.

It was a pleasure to play against him during his distinguished career, and it has been a pleasure to remain a friend of his to this day.

PROLOGUE

It was the sort of moment I had come to savour during my footballing career. I had just played 90 minutes of hectic football and, although a communal bath in the dressing room at Preston North End's Deepdale stadium may not be the most luxurious of places, I wouldn't have swapped it for the world at that particular moment, because once again I was able to reflect on that wonderful experience for any footballer – victory in a cup final.

It's the most fantastic feeling and one I never tired of. The rest of the team were enjoying their moment of triumph just as much as me. We had won 1-0. And we were now the Dairy Crest Floodlit League Cup winners. Although I had won league titles and European Cups as a professional, I thought no less of the fact that I had just played in a match for Northern Premier League side Horwich RMI which had absolutely no financial reward for me. Football is football, and the feelings you get from being involved in a game are just the same. Winning a match is always wonderful and losing is always desperate. Just at that moment one of the other players jokingly shouted to me: "Hey John, this is much better than those European Cups you won!"

"It's a winner's medal, and that's all that matters," I said instantly and I meant it, as I held up the saucer-sized medal. It reminded me of winning my first medal, playing for a team called Central Park in Hartlepool. On that day as a 15-year-old, just as I was now as a 35-year-old, I had played for nothing, enjoying every minute. Today it stands with all my other winners' medals in my trophy cabinet at home. They are a reminder of all the good times I was lucky enough to have in my playing career – from Bo'ness to the Bernabéu.

Looking back, I suppose I was perhaps luckier than an awful lot of professional footballers, because along with the inevitable lows that any player has, I also experienced tremendous highs, more than most players could ever expect in a career. I worked hard and never gave less than 100 per cent in any match I ever played in, but I will always admit that I was fortunate in so many ways.

Perhaps the biggest slice of good fortune I had was having a couple of managerial geniuses around for much of my career. As a youngster at Hartlepools, Brian Clough and Peter Taylor spotted potential in me that others might have missed. I wasn't the sort of player who was blessed with great pace, and because of a missing muscle in my back my running style could best be described as ungainly, giving my left shoulder a strange shape that even to this day makes me feel slightly embarrassed when I catch sight of myself in the mirror. I was probably the slowest player in every team that I played in, but I could pass a football and whenever I took part in a match there was no more determined or competitive player than me. I also like to think that I am an honest person and that honesty has always been a part of the way I went about my business as a player both on and off the pitch.

Happily for me a certain Brian Clough saw an end product to what I could do on a football field and along with his partner, Peter Taylor, had enough faith in me to make sure they nurtured what talent I had and luckily I fitted into the style of football they loved to play and the sort of teams they wanted to create.

The two of them saw something in me when I was just a kid trying to make the grade with Hartlepools United and, although Clough seemed a frightening figure when I first met him, I very soon realised that here was a man who was not just a great manager, but also a genius. He had a presence about him. It was hard to define exactly what it was, but as soon as you met him there was no doubt in your mind that he was special. He made the game simple to understand and his common-sense approach to the way he wanted his players to perform and act struck a chord with me, and with his guidance my own game began to develop and flourish.

It's difficult to know exactly what Brian Clough saw in me and why we had such a long association as manager and player, but whatever it was I am grateful for it. There was an instant understanding and a mutual respect between us from the first moment we met. It began when he took over as my manager at Hartlepools, and our professional association ended when I left Nottingham Forest many years later. During that time we both enjoyed incredible success. I played for him at four different clubs, and with one notable and relatively brief exception I was able to experience some magical times and unique moments, playing in some great teams with great players and making football history along the way.

Brian had seen enough in me as a young player during his time with Hartlepools to want me in his team at Derby County as he and Peter Taylor built a side that took English football by storm, winning promotion and then the league title and rattling the cages of some of the biggest names in the European game. They were magical times for me, playing alongside and learning from the likes of the great Dave Mackay. That Derby side wrote a new chapter in the club's history and in doing so established Clough as a young and successful manager with the sort of personality that made him famous to a much wider audience than just football fans. There seemed no limit to what he could achieve with them, but along with his genius Brian also had an ego to match and it certainly played a part in him walking away from the team he had made one of the best in the country.

When he turned up as the new Leeds United manager some time later his short but eventful stay became one of the most infamous in the English game. He was ready to take on the team that Don Revie had built and mould a new side in his own image. Clough knew what he wanted and as part of his new plans he wanted me to join him at Elland Road. They were the current Football League champions, I was finding it hard to gain a regular place in the Derby team and it was also the chance to once more work with the man who had been the biggest influence on my career. The fact that the move turned out to be a disaster both for him and for me was not something I had bargained for. At least when Brian departed after a matter of weeks he did so with what was a huge pay-off package at the time. I, on the other hand, was left to contemplate life at a club where I clearly did not fit in, and where I was to have some of the worse moments of my career.

My nightmare ended with a move to Nottingham Forest, not a particularly fashionable or successful team and a club who were in the second tier of the English game. On paper it was a step down, but there were two significant factors that influenced me. One was the chance to play football again and enjoy the game I love, and the other was the opportunity to link up once more with Clough. Nobody, including me, could possibly have envisaged the influence and success he would have at the club in the years that followed. It was truly staggering. But I knew I would have success with him, there was absolutely no doubt in my mind about that, and I knew that I wanted to play for him again because I had always produced my best football when he was my manager. But the level of achievement was way beyond anything even he could have imagined.

At Nottingham Forest I became captain of the side and was part of a team that defied the odds and not only became kings of the domestic game, but also stormed through Europe to claim the European Cup in consecutive years. To be the man who collected that huge trophy and held it aloft on two occasions was something special. They were moments I will never forget and moments I could never have dreamed of when I started out as a professional. I have won promotions, League Cups, league titles and European trophies. During my career I played in all four divisions of the English league, from the bottom to the top in record time, and also tasted the game at non-league level. Football has been in my blood since I was a kid and the pure joy and pleasure I got from controlling a ball and passing it accurately to a team-mate never left me. I was able to earn my living from playing football, but that was a bonus. It was the game itself that always mattered most to me and still does to this day.

I'd had no intention of lacing up my boots again when I went to help with the coaching at Horwich back in 1984, but when I did start playing for them it was purely because of my love of the game. I'm not sure if the rest of the team believed me when I told them how delighted I was to get that winner's medal at Deepdale, but I certainly meant it. Winning football matches was always special for me and winning medals made the feeling even better.

Even before my love affair with the game began, my competitive instinct, combined with a passion for running and physical exercise, meant that sport of any kind was a natural outlet for the boundless energy and stamina I seemed to possess from a very early age. I was good at most sports, but it was football that captured my imagination like no other game and as soon as it had I was set on a course that was going to see me associated with the game for the rest of my life.

Hard work and dedication was always at the heart of what I did on a football field, because I knew that if I stuck to those principles they would allow the talent I had to flourish. I grew up and played in a completely different era to the stars of today's Premier League. Whether it was better or worse in those days is for others to debate, but what I do know is that I could not have had more satisfaction or fun from playing the game, I was able to meet some fantastic characters along the way and it has allowed me to collect some marvellous memories.

I have already mentioned that I feel my honesty served me well as a player, and in looking back I have tried to use that same honesty in order to tell the story of my life. I've enjoyed living it; I hope you enjoy reading about it.

CHAPTER ONE

LIFE IS A PLAY THING FOR YOU FOOLISH CLOWN

I was born on 28th October, 1949, in Montrose on the East Coast of Scotland, and our family of five lived in a two-room ground-floor flat in a three-storey tenement, at the end of Bridge Street on the outskirts of the town. It was a small, picturesque town, but it was a great playground for a kid, with plenty of places of interest to keep me occupied. I shared the house with my mum, Joyce, my dad, Robert, my sister, June, who was seven years older than me, and my brother, Bert, who was five years younger than her. The wash house and toilet were at the rear of the tenement, out the front door, along the close and up a few steps. Five into two rooms could be claustrophobic, but as the youngest and smallest everything seemed much larger than it really was so it never felt too cramped.

Across the road from our house was a long, narrow entrance to a public recreation area called the West End Park, while to the left was a long stone bridge that crossed the River Esk. Having a park so close to play in was a real bonus for us when we were kids, and so was living on the coast, as it meant we had a decent beach with large sand dunes that we would play on.

Jumping off the dunes into the cushioning soft sand was an adventure to be relished. My dad worked as a labourer, but had been a paratrooper, and he taught me to bend my knees when I landed on the sand, to break the impact.

My earliest memories as a five-year-old are full of adventures on the beach, the shore, or jumping out of a monkey-puzzle tree in West End Park. The winter also provided us with ready-made entertainment because it always snowed. There were snowball fights and, following some meticulous construction, we would produce a snowman which stood proudly at the entrance to the park and was visible from our front window.

My first school was the Southesk Primary where I distinguished myself academically, regularly topping the class, while my sporting inclinations were nurtured by typical children's games, such as playing "King of the Castle" on a shallow brick wall close to school. This involved battering other pupils with your schoolbag, until you were the last man standing on the wall. I had good balance and reveled in being a regular King of the Castle. I would often get cut and bruised in the process, but never used to complain. Instead, I got a great buzz of satisfaction from making sure I was the "King", and it was probably an early indication of the competitive side of my nature that I would stand up there fending-off all-comers in order to make sure I retained my title. The knocks and bumps I received as a consequence were quickly given a name by my mum.

"What are you complaining about?" she'd say, before pointing to the cuts and scrapes on my legs and knees. "You've just got another medal."

So my battle scars were the first-ever medals I won, and they were a source of pride because it was a reminder of the fact that I had been a winner.

In the winter my competitive spirit also went into overdrive when it came to sliding on a large frozen pond which was called the "Curly". It was a real favourite of mine, but I wasn't just content to slide on it, I wanted to make sure I slid the furthest. I wanted to beat everyone and show them that I was the best. If somebody beat me I would go back again and again until I finally managed to slide further than they had. Sometimes the other kids would go home, but I would stay there on my own until I had the satisfaction of knowing I had beaten their record and gone the furthest.

I was also pretty good when it came to playing marbles and was the unofficial Montrose junior champion, amassing so many of them that Mum had to stitch together a large oblong cloth bag two feet long, to hold the growing collection.

My winning instinct was very much part of the way I played and, even at that young age, if I lost it would really hurt me emotionally. I seemed to have an inner competitive streak, and I'm sure that was helped by the fact that I had an older brother. We got on well, but I wanted to be better than him, and perhaps the age difference between us acted as an extra spur.

One other instinct or habit I did develop was the inclination to run everywhere. Whether it was to school, the park, or beach, this compulsion always seemed to be there, as if a motivational voice inside was inciting me to run. I would compete against myself, seeing how fast I could run to different locations, having great fun at the same time. I loved running, and the sheer exhilaration I got from it was something that never left me in the years which followed.

I had a very stable, happy home life with my family and loved those early years in Montrose; it was a lovely place to be when I was a very young boy, and I will always hold very positive memories of my Scottish hometown. At the age of seven, however, I had to contend with the first major change in my life, when the family relocated across the border and set up home in Hartlepool on the north-east coast of England. It happened out of necessity when Dad had to try and find work. He was doing some home-study courses in an effort to become a civil engineer, but that never brought in any money, and when the labouring work began to dry up in Montrose he knew he had to do something about it. My mother had a couple of sisters who lived in the Hartlepool area, and I think it was through the two of them that Dad came to hear about the possibility of work. At first he went down there on his own, but once he had obtained a secure job he sent for the rest of the family and we all moved permanently to be with him.

Although it meant uprooting from Montrose, the move not

only gave my dad the chance to work, but we also benefitted as a family because our new home was considerably larger than the one we'd left. We had two bedrooms, a lounge, hallway, kitchen and a toilet in the back yard, which was real luxury. We even graduated from the tin bath in front of the fire, when a bath area was added at the back of the kitchen, so we were really living the high life.

Across the road from the house was an old cement works. It took up an area about the size of four football pitches, and the undulating surface of small hillocks made it look as though there were ant hills everywhere. My new junior school was called Throston and it was about a mile from home. The shortest and easiest way for me to get to the school was to come out of my house and walk down the road, but I couldn't resist running across the cement works on the undulating land, dodging all the hazards. I lost count of the number of times I went over on my ankle as I darted in and out, trying to avoid the hollows, lumps and bumps in the ground, but I also think that it helped to improve my balance.

If I thought I would miss the sand dunes of Montrose, I was pleasantly surprised, as the Hartlepool ones were infinitely larger. An added bonus was the promenade, where playing chicken with the waves as they pounded in from the North Sea provided a game with a real edge to it. You had to wait until the wave hit the breakwater and then run for your life. If you got a really big wave it could be more than a bit dangerous, and I once saw a huge piece of tarmac ripped from the promenade by the sheer force of the plunging water as it came crashing down just yards from where I'd been standing only seconds before.

The family soon settled into life in Hartlepool, and Bert and I quickly acquired two pigeons and a dog. The pigeons were relatively easy to care for, and their home was an old wooden tea chest customised with wire meshing at the open front, which sat proudly on top of our coal cellar. The only problem came when the two of them tried mating, prompting Dad to regularly chase our large grey one with a brush when it woke him early in the morning with its continual cooing.

Not long after we had moved to Hartlepool, my dad then made the decision to move much further away to take up a job opportunity when he was offered the chance to become a junior engineer on a dam project in Ghana. It was obviously a great opportunity for him, and financially he must have seen it as a chance to make decent money for the family, and so he left for Africa when I was about nine. He did it for all the right reasons, but it left a bit of a hole in my life, which I'm sure was true for the rest of the family.

I never imagined my mum would allow us a dog, but I think she did it knowing that I would miss my dad. Like any other son who hero-worships his father, I really missed him when he went abroad. Whether it was cleaning his work boots, which I got a penny for, or setting up toy soldiers for him to shoot down with my double-barreled cork gun, I loved his company. He even used to have June, Bert and I sit next to him, making us guess when a minute had elapsed on his pocket watch, with the closest shout from any of us winning a penny.

We called the black Labrador-cross dog we got from the kennels Kim. By coincidence the old cement works across the road had been flattened by the time she arrived and turned into a superb grass playing field, complete with a full-sized football pitch in the middle. So my mum had no problem in getting the dog out for a walk, as the newly prepared Central Park playing fields became a second home for Kim and me, allowing us to run and run to our hearts' content.

I was good enough academically to be able to follow my brother to grammar school. I had, however, received a severe rebuke from my teacher, as I was a lowly 12th in my class at the time I passed the 11-plus exam. Perhaps it was the audacity of wearing my brother's grammar school tie before the exam results were announced that annoyed him, but I was still at that cheeky stage.

I enjoyed my time at Throston, but never got involved in playing football there, not even in the school playground because the game had been banned after a couple of windows were accidently broken. I suppose some people might see it as strange, but I was never really interested in kicking a ball around at just the time most other kids would have been obsessed with the game.

Another distinctive memory of my time at Throston was playing the Pied Piper of Hamelin in an end-of-term school play. My vivid yellow-and-red costume hand-crafted by my mum was certainly bright, yet it was my raucous, extremely loud animated vocals that even had the teachers laughing. I think I had a love of music and singing from an early age and it has never left me.

Having passed my exams, I was in my last days at Throston and all set to take up my place at Henry Smith Grammar School when the family was hit with a bombshell. My dad was due to return to England from Ghana but had been involved in a motoring accident and subsequently died.

I found out when I came home for lunch one day, and it was a devastating blow. He had been away for two years, and during that time all I had were the happy memories from the time I had spent with him. Like so many boys, my dad was someone I worshipped and, even though he hadn't physically been around for two years, I knew he was always there. He might have been working abroad, but I knew he would be coming home, and although I never actually spoke to him during the time he was in Ghana – because we didn't have a phone – he would write regularly to my mum and we were able to keep up with what was happening with him.

I shed many tears when I heard the news of his death, and the realisation of what had happened began to sink in. I have never cried since.

The saying that bad news travels fast proved true when I went back to school that same afternoon. They all knew, barely an hour after I had been told. The reason for going back that after-noon was a very personal one. I think it was my way of trying to deal with the shock of losing my hero. I wanted to try and eliminate what had happened, but of course that wasn't possible, and instead I had to try and get on with the rest of my life as best I could, coping with the loss of someone who had meant so much to me. The kids at school didn't really know how to treat me when I went back that afternoon. They knew what had happened but we were all so young that having to cope with something like death was a new experience for all of us.

My dad was buried in Ghana and that possibly helped me to move on. He had died and I was never going to see him again. But even though I was still a very young boy, I retain some wonderful memories of him to this day.

Soon after the death of my dad, my sister June went to live in San Francisco, leaving my mother to look after Bert and myself. Weaker people might have faltered under such a cloud, but Mum set about making loose covers for three-piece suites and selling ladies' support corsets which helped women like her with back ailments. All of this was done with a prodigious energy, which she still retains to this day, even though she is now 89 years young. A glowing example of how the strong survive.

Henry Smith Grammar school had a proud sporting history in both rugby and cricket. Having graduated from jumping off giant sand dunes, running everywhere I could and chasing a mongrel until I was exhausted, these seemed the kind of games I might enjoy, and enjoy them I did as I went on to captain both teams. This was where my sporting life really took off, and I was even offered a trial at Durham County Cricket Club. I was a medium-fast bowler, which proved to be almost impossible during the trial on a rain-soaked wicket. Walking in the wet conditions, never mind running up to bowl, was difficult. The added handicap of having to wear flat-soled sandshoes because I couldn't afford cricket boots proved a bit too much to cope with, and I don't think the selectors were too happy with my grey school trousers either! They looked scornfully at me as though I was a piece of dirt, and it proved to be my first real experience of snobbery. I could imagine them making disparaging remarks about the kid from the wrong side of the tracks. I never won another trial, but I did win one trophy in cricket, while playing for West Hartlepool Juniors.

My introduction to West Hartlepool Juniors had been through a schoolmate and friend called Keith Gardner, who played regularly for them. I used to go along and watch him play and practise with the team, and on one occasion someone didn't turn up, so I had the chance to get involved. I didn't bat or bowl that day, but I claimed my place in the team with some acrobatic fielding and catching. My best bowling stint came during a match on 12th May, 1965, against Preston Juniors, and that was when I won my first-ever trophy. I was awarded an engraved cricket ball for my performance that day, after taking a hat-trick of wickets. The trophy still sits proudly in my trophy cabinet, reminding me that it was achieved with a pretty unorthodox over consisting of medium pace, spin, a bouncer, a full toss and a yorker. This purposeful variety proved too unpredictable for the bemused victims. Even the umpire commented on the mixture as he repeatedly raised the finger to signal out. I thank Keith for his friendship and for the fact that he helped pave the way for my only cricket trophy.

By the age of 13, there was one other sport I still had not tried yet, and my introduction to football was to happen away from Hartlepool.

With Mum being the breadwinner of the house, I was willingly whisked off to my grandmother's for the duration of the Christmas, Easter and summer school holidays. My grandmother lived on her own in Bo'ness, West Lothian, Scotland. Her top-floor tenement flat in East Castleloan had a great view over the River Forth. My main duties when I stayed with her were to chop wood, fetch coal up from the coalhouse and run to the Co-op for groceries. I revelled in my new-found independence, and after making sure Grannie was stocked up I would be out all day, either in the nearby Kinneil Woods or the local park. I spent hours making spears, bows and arrows or climbing trees, as I explored all the neighbouring woodlands, pretending to be Trailer Black, an Indiana Jones-type character from the *Wizard* comic. I was quite content on my own for a while, I savoured my independence, but it soon became repetitive. I needed the competition I got from playing cricket or rugby, but I was in Bo'ness on my own.

There simply isn't a decent cricket game involving one person, apart from catching practice of repeatedly throwing a tennis ball against a wall. And no one offered to join in as I spent hours kicking and catching a rugby ball, even with my schoolhouse name of "Barbarians" emblazoned on the back of my tracksuit top. Fate, however, soon unearthed a new attraction.

One lonely day a white plastic round ball, with the brand name of "Frido" written on it, came bouncing my way from the large corner house whose garden fence bordered my granny's coalhouse. Without hesitation I volleyed it back over the fence, which must have impressed the participants in a three-a-side game being played on the other side, because they momentarily stopped. An invitation immediately followed to join in, and the fun and chat that followed had me in stitches with laughter.

The immediate acceptance of a stranger by the other six lads was quite surprising, especially when the majority of our kick-about involved back-biting, mickey-taking and tripping, both accidentally and deliberate, which constantly interrupted the flow of play. The main protagonists appeared to be two neighbours, Jim Fleming and Ronnie Syme, whose nose-to-nose confrontations over all manner of things were hilarious in their outlandish animation. Ronnie's face would turn redder than a beetroot, his right foot stamping furiously in time with his waving right arm, with Jim's contorted face strained to bursting point as he stood on tiptoes in front of his much taller adversary. One minute it was all was calm, and the next all hell would break loose as an argument erupted. Amazingly, the shouting and gesticulating never progressed to blows, with the game ending in friendly banter and laughter.

When that first kickabout finished I was thankfully invited back the next day, so my play must have been okay. Then I was asked whether I was a blue or green. Not having a clue what they were talking about I said blue, simply because I liked the colour. I have followed Rangers' results ever since. It was only later, following an impromptu game, that I was informed of the importance of the Old Firm clubs in the football world. What did I know?

I will never forget the friendship shown by these boys. Honest laughter, coupled with running after a ball, were two things which were difficult to better. When my summer holiday in Bo'ness finished, following many informal games with Ronnie, Jim and the gang, I returned to Hartlepool heavily infected by the football bug.

From then on, I stayed behind at Henry Smith School every night after lessons had finished to play football with two friends, John Gretton and David Latimer. I would get home so late that my mum thought school finished at six o'clock. We were allowed to play football with a tennis ball in the school playground, and pretty soon I would carry that ball everywhere with me in my pocket as an absolute priority. I also started performing as an emergency linesman in support of my local team, Central Park FC, in the second division of the Under-18s Church League. They played literally across the road from my home. It was during these games that I befriended a boy called Kenny Jessop, whose dad Bob helped run the team. I asked if I could play for them but was told to try again the following season when I was 15, when I would be bigger and stronger. And, following Christmas, Easter and summer holidays spent in the Bo'ness football education department, practising daily for hours without fail, there was a massive improvement in my ability.

During this time I also met another boy called Patrick Duffy who became, and still is, a close friend. At the time I respectfully thought he was the greatest player I had ever played against and with, apart from Kenny Jessop. As teenagers, Patrick and I belonged to a group of lads who would travel anywhere in the Bo'ness area to play football. If transport was required, it was usually provided by Tony, the dad of Patrick's friend, Bert Corvy, or Ronnie Syme's elder brother, the legendary John Syme. John can only be described as a football nut. He was probably in his thirties yet ferried us all over the local area whenever there was the sniff of a game on offer. I can remember him once buying a brand new Ford Corsair and we set off in it for a game at Polmont, with 13 players somehow crammed in his car. Along the way we passed a police car going slowly in the opposite direction.

"Make yourselves inconspicuous!" John shouted suddenly.

We were wedged in like sardines, with our noses squashed against the windows and our faces resembling red gargoyles. There were also three more unfortunates in the boot, so his vocal instruction was something of an impossibility, but somehow we got away with it.

The good players, of course, never had to go in the boot. I was eternally grateful for that, suffering as I did from acute travel sickness, something that stayed with me even when I turned professional. We would turn up anywhere at any time for a game, playing against each other if we found no opposition. Ronnie, Jim Fleming (or "Flea" as he was known because he was very small) Bugs, Ian, Thornton, Eddie, Paddy, Bert, Taffy, Fuzzy and "Lugless Douglas" (who had very small "lugs", or ears) were all part of our youthful football band. We played on most days, with my own energy limitless. They say practice makes perfect and so, when I got back to Hartlepool from my summer holidays as a 15-year-old, I signed to play for Central Park.

The thought of playing with my friend, Kenny Jessop, gave me all the confidence I needed and when the season got underway I reveled in every minute of it, playing at outside-right. I was still pretty small and frail-looking, so the manager, "Miffy", Clifford Stubbs, and Kenny Jessop's dad Bob thought I might not get hurt as much playing out there. The wide position gave me the opportunity to test my much-improved ability in crossing and passing the ball. I did develop one trick, however, inherited from my rugby-playing days, which was the body swerve. I used it over and over again to throw the opposing full-back off balance and then knock it past him. When I became a professional I realised that in the professional game you could only use this move once. Pros remember and rarely fall for the same trick twice.

I could hardly wait for Saturdays to come around and for a while played rugby in the morning for Henry Smith, then football for Central Park in the afternoon. It seems strange to me now when people say that kids get too much football. Maybe I was fortunate in having an abundance of energy, but my sheer love of playing superseded everything else.

Being as keen as mustard, we all hated missing a fixture, especially through bad weather in the winter. One Saturday there had been a real blizzard, which had left four inches of snow covering the pitch. Although it seemed a mission impossible, we set about attempting to clear the whole playing surface. There must have been someone connected to our team who had brains, and they suggested simply clearing the lines, plus the penalty areas. We worked non-stop shovelling snow for over two hours, which must have impressed the referee. Having inspected the result of our Herculean efforts, he bravely allowed the game to be played. There is a saying that you only get as much out of a job as you are willing to put in and that day we got a well-earned victory both on and off the pitch.

As the season progressed, my play improved and when Miffy announced that Hartlepools United, as the club was then known, were going to start a youth team, both Kenny Jessop and myself were delighted when we were picked to play a trial match in Hartlepool. We must have done okay because both of us were asked back for training on Tuesday and Thursday nights, along with a few other boys and some of Hartlepools United's reserves. One Thursday night, after finishing our session the trainer, Tommy Johnson, asked us to stand in a line.

"The new manager of the club wants to say hello to you," he told us.

A slim man young enough to be a player was walking towards us together with another older-looking man. The last time I had seen the younger guy he had been wearing the red-striped shirt of Sunderland playing against Bury and had sustained an injury which would eventually lead to him having to end his career as a player. His name was Brian Clough, and he had just joined Hartlepools as their manager with his assistant Peter Taylor. As I looked along the line the first thing which struck me was the fact that Clough looked smaller than he had when I'd gone to see him play at Roker Park, but that thought was soon forgotten as the pair reached me and Brian suddenly spoke directly to me.

"Stand up straight, get your shoulders back, and get your hair cut – you look like a girl," he barked at me.

I gulped, swallowed hard, and took a pace back. I attempted to stand up straight, but I had never been properly able to because my left shoulder was badly rounded. I only found out many years later when I was examined at Nottingham Forest that I had been born with a muscle missing from my back. This abnormality threw my left arm across my body when I ran. With my right arm going forward it was counterproductive, producing an unusual, ugly running style, eliminating any chance of running really quickly. The deformity deeply embarrassed me in my teens and still does now. Living with this handicap is something of a burden you can never alleviate, and would in the future have me switching off the TV when watching myself on *Match of the Day*. I always thought that if I couldn't bear to watch myself play then why would any of the fans, which led me to believe that I could never be a fans' favourite. The one thing it did teach me, though, was how to adapt to and overcome problems.

Finding an answer to a personal problem is simply self-management, and it's better than feeling sorry for yourself. As a compensation for this handicap I seemed to have the ability to run forever. Not quickly, but I could run all day. Learning to kick with both feet was another way to compensate for my lack of pace, and I perfected this skill through incessant practice. Placing a ball a few inches from a wall then side footing it hard to simulate a block tackle gave me confidence when it came to making physical contact on the pitch. Tackling was initially never one of my greatest skills but, like lots of other things, I worked hard at them in order to make myself the best player I could possibly be.

Another example of how I made the best of what I had was a little heading practice routine I devised for myself. There was a sloping roof on the coal cellar in our back yard, and I would attempt to head balls as they rolled off of it at different heights and angles.

I wasn't sure what to make of my first meeting with Brian Clough, apart from the fact that he frightened the life out of me. He hadn't made any comment about the way the other lads in the line-up looked, but perhaps that was because I was the only one with long hair. Even at that age, I had another obsession as well as football, and that was music. The Beatles and Rolling Stones were without doubt the two greatest bands of the time and most pop fans were devotees of one or the other. I liked the Rolling Stones, due to the blues influence in many of their songs, and Mick Jagger was my hero. My long hair was a tribute to his anarchic bad-boy image, but it was obviously something Brian wasn't very keen on.

Despite my locks, soon after Clough and Taylor's arrival I found myself playing in the reserves, graduating very quickly from the youth team. I remember turning up at the club's Victoria Ground on a pushbike for my reserve-team debut. One of the ground staff found me eagerly waiting at the locked doors two hours before kick-off.

"Clear off," he said as he brushed past me. "We've got a match on here tonight."

I had to wait for Tommy Johnson, the trainer, to arrive before I could get into the ground, and my bike had to stand just inside the dressing room, attracting some inquisitive glances from the team. Hartlepools' strip in those days consisted of blue-and-white-striped V-neck shirts, with blue shorts and white socks. As a 15-year-old who only weighed 10 stone wet through, the kit posed a problem for me. Everything was "large" size, which meant I played that night with a dozen safety pins holding the massive shirt and shorts together with nips and tucks everywhere. When I first put the shirt on the V-neck came down to my navel, and you could hear a clinking noise as I ran out for kick-off!

Clough and Taylor kept a careful eye on me and the progress I was making. Playing for the reserves at such a young age was clearly an indication that things were moving in the right direction, but I was still astounded to read a comment from Peter Taylor which appeared in the local paper. After watching me in a game, he apparently turned to Brian and commented on my performance.

"Lock the doors to the ground and don't open them again till we sign that skinny kid playing at outside-right," he was reported to have said.

It was a great compliment for me, and obviously it was nice to read that they thought something of me.

I had already signed amateur forms for the club, which allowed me to play for them while I was still at school. I also continued to play for Central Park, and one of the tournaments we took part in that season featured pretty much every team in the town, but although we were all pretty young under-18s, the competition itself was open age, which in effect meant that we were playing against men. It was a seven-a-side tournament played on full-size pitches, and we managed to reach the semi-finals before being beaten. I was absolutely distraught at getting so far and yet missing out on reaching the final; it didn't matter that we had done well against teams who were much older than us, I felt utterly dejected and on the point of tears as I sat with my team-mates on the side of one of the pitches. Suddenly, I heard the voice of Brian Clough.

"What are you lot crying about?" he asked.

"We've lost," I told him quite forcefully. "We don't play to lose!"

I carried that same hatred of defeat through my career. I think it was something Brian recognised in me from an early age and he certainly always went out of his way to recruit players who desperately wanted to win.

Football was now playing an increasingly big part in my life. My studies had been pushed well aside as football began to dominate my every thought, and as my first full season with Central Park drew to a close I had another footballing experience that had a huge influence on me.

During my Easter break in Bo'ness I was invited by Pat Duffy and Bert Corvi to accompany them to a Celtic match, and it wasn't just any old game because they were playing at home against Liverpool in the first-leg semi-final of the 1966 European Cup Winners' Cup. Having climbed through a hole in a fence to see my first Hartlepools game, this match was infinitely more prestigious, and even before kick-off I was amazed by the intense, noisy, claustrophobic atmosphere.

We stood amongst the Celtic fanatics, packed in like sardines on the famous terrace known as "The Jungle", opposite the tunnel. As the players warmed up before the game, I witnessed a cheeky piece of showmanship from Peter Thompson, the Liverpool left-winger. As Thompson went through his warm-up routine, he received volley after volley of verbal abuse, but he produced a superb response. He stopped his football and then faced his detractors, before rolling the ball on to his instep, gently flicking it up, and deftly balancing the ball motionless on his forehead, as he raised his arms sideways in salute. For an instant The Jungle was silenced, and then he dropped the ball to his feet and jogged away. I stood open-mouthed at the audacity he had shown and at his ability to carry out the trick itself.

Despite the ferocity of the game, which ended in a 1-0 victory for Celtic thanks to a goal from Bobby Lennox, delighting my travelling companion, the image of Peter Thompson balancing a ball on his head produced a new challenge for me. How could I repeat the trick? It took me a couple of weeks to master the technique, and I also had a few rollickings from my mum along the way as I fell clumsily over settees and chairs indoors practising in our lounge on rainy days, but eventually I mastered the trick.

"Seals do that in the circus, not footballers," my mum scolded as another chair went tumbling.

I was also waiting nervously as the day I would get my O-level exam results drew near. Having always appeared near the top of the form, my mum was shocked when I only achieved two passes. I was pretty ashamed but pleadingly tried to convince her I was going to be a professional footballer. My brother had got five O-levels and he had been in the "B" class at school. I had always been in the "A" class, so it was assumed that I would do well when it came to my exams. My mum said that my dad had always wanted me to have an education, but as far as I was concerned when it came to academic matters they just didn't provide me with the sort of challenges I wanted and got from sport. It wasn't a case of me being thick, it was just that anything which involved me having to run about immediately engaged my interest and I had already made the decision in my own head that football was going to be the career I wanted to pursue.

After winning our Church League Division Two Cup and finishing runners-up in the league, my first football season was coming to a successful conclusion. An even bigger achievement was imminent, but it almost never happened.

Brian Clough picked me to play in Hartlepools' last game of the season. But to comply with Football League regulations he had to have the school's permission. Before Brian ever spoke to anyone at the school the headmaster, Mr Georgson, had me in his office for over an hour. He was soundly decrying the game of football in general, and also berated me, as captain of the rugby team, for somehow tarnishing the reputation of a rugby-playing school.

Brian told me some years later he had endured a similar conversation with the stubborn Mr Georgson, yet managed somehow to acquire the signed form, allowing me to play. A cartoon in the *Hartlepool Mail* newspaper showed a caricature of me, complete with schoolboy shorts and bag, running with a number seven on my back as I was watched by two of the team's supporters.

"Is this his team number or his age?" read the caption.

Only one person at school, my English teacher Don Brotherton, wished me good luck, which restored my faith in human nature. Some years later, on a visit back home I spotted him jigging away on the dance floor of a nightclub, giving it some cool moves. My respect for him definitely went up another notch, as he was really enjoying himself, totally uninhibited as he danced the night away. My kind of guy.

My first league game was a slightly less-than-impressive debut at home, the Victoria Ground, which ended in a 1-1 draw against Bradford City. My only clear recollection of the game is of the opposition full-back having a word with me before kick-off.

"Good luck today son," he told me. "But if you go past me I'll break your fucking leg!"

In 1966 this was no idle threat, and the same welcome was often repeated to me the following season.

With my failure to pass all my O-levels, after a frank discussion with my mum a decision was made that I would either go back to school or look for a job. That decision, we agreed, would be made after my summer holidays in Bo'ness.

So the summer of 1966 saw me once again in my element, playing football all the hours of the day with Pat Duffy, Bert Corvi, John and Ronnie Syme, Jim Fleming, Fuzzy, Taffy and the rest of the gang. We would, of course, play in all weathers, on many days arriving home caked from head to foot in mud. My grandmother had the greatest solution of all time for muddy bodies. It involved a scrubbing brush, her deep porcelain bath and DAZ washing powder. I swear it's the reason I have lovely soft skin to this day. It certainly removed all traces of mud, especially when applied with that scrubbing brush!

One morning a letter arrived for me from my mum. In it she explained that the manager of Middlesbrough, Stan Anderson, had invited her and my brother to watch a World Cup match at their ground, Ayresome Park, which was being used as one of the venues for the group stages of the competition England were hosting that year. Anderson wanted to discuss the possibility of me signing for the club. They had also been invited to another World Cup game at the ground, and she said that Mr Anderson would contact me when I got home. The news spurred me on to even greater effort, which upset the man living on the ground floor of my grandmother's tenement, because the coalhouses were only yards from his door and my practice of hitting a football over and over against the end wall used to drive him into a rage. I used to sprint past his window as a safety measure every time I returned to Grannie's top-floor flat.

When I got back to Hartlepool a representative of Middlesbrough FC took me over to Ayresome Park to meet Stan. First he shook my hand, then, surprisingly, apologised as he told me it had been a wasted journey. He explained that Hartlepools still had me registered as an amateur player, which meant that Middlesbrough couldn't actually approach me. At least my mum and brother got to watch two World Cup matches for nothing.

This incident certainly triggered some action from Brian Clough and Peter Taylor, as they became regular visitors to our house in Arch Street after the holidays. My mum wasn't sure what to do about my future, but fate again played its part. My grandmother was staying with us when Clough and Taylor turned up for yet another chat. Clough's charm worked its spell on my grandmother and she in turn convinced my mother that I should become a professional footballer. So, on 3rd September, 1966, I became Hartlepools United's first apprentice professional on wages of £8 a week. Shortly after that I signed a full-time professional contract on 7th November, taking my wages to £18 a week, plus £2 a week for being part of the first team, with £3 more for each match I played. I was rich!

At this point I feel I must give special mention to my grandmother, who was a typical Scottish housewife. She was 5ft 5in tall and about the same width, with a million sayings to help you through life. "A little is sufficient and enough is too much," she would tell you or, my favourite, "Life is a play thing for you foolish clown, whether you're up or whether you're down." She usually quoted this to me when I came home depressed after losing a game, and if I confided in her with a problem she would say, "It just goes to show you what it lets you see." Now don't ask me to explain that one . . .

CHAPTER TWO

LEARNING MY TRADE

At the Victoria Ground the "weights room" consisted of an iron bar with oil cans filled with cement at each end. The treatment room contained one heat lamp, plus a tub of all-purpose cream, which was a dubious mixture of heat-inducing snake oil that was more likely to kill than cure. The training area was a 20-yard wide piece of grass running down the side of the pitch. On rainy days Peter Taylor would send us on a run to the bus depot, down the town, then to the docks and back. This usually included a quick stop for the smokers in our group to have a fag.

My first season as a professional taught me many lessons, one of which was the art of survival in a man's game. The body swerve, the dummy, the backheel, the stepover, were not tricks in those days, they were survival tactics. When the opposition full-back said he was going to break your leg, he meant it. So I learnt quickly and my ability to spray the ball around with both feet stood me in good stead.

Another great lesson, the first of many during my career, came from Brian Clough. During one training session, he beckoned me over.

"McGovern, get the ball and bring it over here," he told me.

"What do you want me to do?" I asked him.

"I want you to dribble the ball around the corner flag and back as fast as you can," he instructed.

So off I went with his words of encouragement ringing in my ears.

"My grandmother runs faster than you!" he shouted, and when I returned to where he was standing he had another instruction for me.

"Now run round the corner flag again without the ball," he said. So off I went, slightly bemused by what he had asked me to do, and when I got back to him again he had a question for me.

"Tell me what was easier, running with the ball or without the ball?" he asked.

"Without it boss," I said.

"Well why don't you pass it on a bloody Saturday then?" he bellowed. "If one of your players is closer to the opposition goal than you are, why wouldn't you pass the ball to him?"

Manager 1, Apprentice 0.

What he said illustrates the simplicity of the game and how he liked it to be played. This was one of the many attributes Brian Clough possessed as a manager; he was able to make the game simple for footballers. If you transferred these lessons to any profession such as teaching, business, or even politics they would retain their value. The things he would say when he was coaching us were little gems, and I quickly decided that if I listened to what he said it would be of benefit to me. I took them all on board and put them to work within my personal ability as a player. I wanted to be the best I possibly could be and knew instantly when I started working with Clough that he was the sort of manager who could help me achieve that. He had an appealing manner that I liked and responded to, but he was always able to keep you off balance with the way he went about his job and what he said to you, even if you'd played well. Some years later when I was playing for him at Derby we had a match against Everton, who had Alan Ball in their midfield. Bally was a great player and had been a World Cup-winner with England, but I wanted to let him know that I could play a bit myself, and had a really good game against him.

As I came off the pitch feeling pretty good about my

performance and the fact that I had helped the team to an important victory, Brian was in the tunnel waiting for me.

"Who told you to mark Alan Ball?" he asked.

"Nobody boss," I replied. "I just wanted to show him I could play a bit as well."

"Well you did a great job for the side because he never got a kick," said Brian.

As I walked past him on my way to the dressing room, wallowing in the rare praise he had thrown my way, I got hit with the punchline.

"And he's a good player," shouted Clough. "You're not!"

I learned so much during my early days at Hartlepools. Peter Taylor, who brought nearly all the players to the club, had signed a defender called Tony Parry from Burton Albion. During a training session, when I was up against Tony, I threw him my customary body swerve, going left then jinking right. To my surprise Tony was already waiting, taking the ball from me like candy from a baby. Once again it was important to learn quickly, and the next time I came up against him I dummied left, followed by a second dummy to go right and then veered passed him on the left. When the session paused we both had a laugh together having both learned that good pros don't fall for the three-card trick twice.

Results that first season with Hartlepools were pretty good, but my travel sickness never made it easy for me because of the distances we had to cover for away matches. Trips to Barrow, Luton or Exeter were marathons, especially when there was no developed motorway system. It could have been a lot worse. I had suffered from travel sickness from childhood, yet found a remedy recommended by a pregnant American lady on one of my train journeys to Bo'ness. She witnessed my plight and persuaded my mum to let me take one of her prescription tablets, which she took to alleviate her morning sickness. Having tried every pill and remedy under the sun, I was delighted to find that they worked, so long as they were taken an hour before a journey. Although I still felt uneasy on long trips, these pills stopped me from vomiting, making travel almost bearable.

During half time in an away match at Exeter, I went to the toilet and dutifully took one of the pills in anticipation of the journey home, just as Peter Taylor came in. He saw me with the pill in my hand and instantly went berserk.

"What the hell are you taking?" he asked looking shocked and angry. "What bloody drugs are you on?"

It was only when Clough joined him after hearing the commotion, that my explanation was accepted. My mum told me my sister suffered in a similar fashion, and I realised it was just something I was going to have to learn to live with.

There were some good players at Hartlepools, who were all willing to help me in different ways. Goalkeeper Ken Simpkin used to get me free bus rides around the town, as he knew most of the "clippies", or fare collectors. Although it wasn't a fortune saved it felt like being a VIP, even if Ken had to inform them who I was as I still resembled a schoolboy.

Ken had a successful run in the side which saw him chosen to play for Wales at under-23 level. Weighing in at around 14 stone, he also had a weight problem. During one away match at Bradford, as Ken trundled towards his goal before kick-off, a section of the Bradford supporters chanted, "Billy Bunter, Billy Bunter," in time with his lurching steps. He had also won an advertising contract from diet health drink company Complan. Ken's normal training routine would see him don a couple of plastic covers from a dry cleaners under his kit in an effort to sweat off some of his excess weight, but the regime seemed to have little effect, and as the company monitored Ken's progress they were disappointed to find that he'd actually put weight on. After a thorough investigation, they discovered that Ken had been taking their drink with his favourite meal of fish and chips, instead of using it as a substitute for his meals!

Les Green was another goalkeeper who would go back with me in the afternoons for extra training. He still is the best goalkeeper I have ever played with for throwing the ball. He would position me next to the touchlines, where I would deliver crosses of different types, some lofted, some driven, in-swingers and out-swingers. As soon as Les caught them he would bowl them out to me cricket style at rocket pace, with pinpoint accuracy. He was also one of the most comical players I ever met, who kept team-mates amused for hours on end with superbly inventive humour. He was always able to find the funny side of pretty much any situation and was always making us laugh. Sadly, Les recently passed away after fighting a losing battle with cancer.

Hartlepools also signed an Irish international player from Sunderland, named Ambrose Foggerty. "Amby" was the only player I came across in football who wore a collar and tie to training. He apparently had a business interest outside of the game, so he wore his suit constantly, along with an old scruffy pair of brogue shoes. One day he was late for training and Clough made him join in immediately, giving him no time to change. It was quite comical, watching Amby run round in his suit, but I ended up more embarrassed than him when I was teamed to run against Foggerty in the finishing sprints, and he beat me in every one, despite wearing his suit, collar and tie, as well as those bloody brogues.

Playing with experienced players accelerated my own progress, despite the vast difference between junior and league football. I was also chosen to play in a trial match for Scotland's youth team at Dunfermline. My mum drove me up there only to discover the match had been postponed to the following day because of the state of the pitch due to some torrential rain. We stayed with relatives overnight before going back to Dunfermline's ground, only to be told the match had been transferred to Dundee. After a rapid 35-mile journey to Dundee, we arrived with only half an hour of the game left to play, but despite getting on for only 20 minutes I was promised another chance in a later fixture at Tynecastle, Heart of Midlothian's ground in Edinburgh.

For the match at Tynecastle we stayed overnight at the North British Hotel in Edinburgh. My mum packed everything but the kitchen sink into a battered old suitcase that looked as if it was ready for the tip. I carried my boots in my old Army and Navy stores rucksack, complete with Fred Flintstone and Barney Rubble cartoons painted on the closing flap. The rest of the rucksack was covered with names of my favourite bands, such as the Stones, Kinks, Beatles, Yardbirds, The Who and The Creation.

As I walked through the front door of the hotel I was met by one or two of the selectors. The warm greeting cooled as I told them I was from Hartlepools United, and when they looked at my highly decorated bag, the polite welcomes dried up completely and were replaced by some exaggerated stares, leaving me feeling decidedly uncomfortable. Despite the petty snobbery, I knew that once I got onto the pitch it would be up to me. Over the 90 minutes of the game, I thought my performance was pretty average, with no disastrous mistakes and at the same time no inspirational touches of brilliance. Back in Hartlepool, Peter Taylor questioned me about my performance.

"It was okay," I told him.

"Okay!" said Pete. "Didn't you put the centre-forward clean through on three occasions?"

"Yes Pete, but he missed all the chances."

He then told me to my surprise that he had sent a scout to watch the game and he'd given me a glowing report. The Scottish youth team selectors must have been distracted by my Fred Flintstone rucksack though because that was my second and last trial for the youth team.

Training sessions with Brian Clough were always varied, which kept you constantly on your toes. You never knew what was coming next. In the absence of a real training area, our six- or seven-a-sides took place on the slither of grass at the side of the pitch, and these games were a key part of our preparation.

Occasionally, "training" took an unusual turn. For instance, we spent one day unloading corrugated asbestos sheets from the back of a lorry. Brian had persuaded a local builder to supply them to cover the popular "Rink End" of the ground, where the 'Pools' diehard supporters congregated. I can remember getting home late in the afternoon with my aching arms dangling in front of me following the lifting marathon.

"What's wrong with your arms?" asked my mum.

I explained.

"What's that got to do with football?"

She had a point.

My fitness in those days was at a peak, and even though I was a full-time professional my appetite for simply kicking a ball remained undiminished. I would train in the morning with the other professionals, often returning for an extra afternoon stint. In the evenings I would meet my friend Kenny Jessop, walk the mile or so down to the sea front in Old Hartlepool and we would kick a tennis ball about using the sea front benches as goals. When it got dark we would walk back to Central Estate and visit the local fish and chip shop.

"Have you got any fish left?" we would ask.

"Certainly have," the delighted fish fryer would answer.

"Then you shouldn't have fried so many!" we shouted as we ran out of the door with torrents of abuse ringing in our ears. Only when we retraced our steps, entering the chip shop with big grins on our faces, would the owner appreciate our juvenile humour.

I had also become involved with my friend Kenny's sister, Kay, a vivacious brunette and lovely person, with whom I had a very close relationship. Kenny had not signed as a professional for Hartlepools, despite my much-repeated declaration to Brian Clough and Peter Taylor that he was a really good player. He never made it as a footballer but I'm pleased to say Kenny and his wife, Dot, are still great friends of mine. Genuine people are hard to find, but I've been so lucky to have them around in my life.

That first season as a professional was immensely educational, because I was effectively a boy working with men. The mature sense of humour, never mind the adult language, would often find me out of my depth, but I survived it. I think it was only my indisputable fitness and total dedication to football that earned me respect and credibility. For all the mickey-taking and friendly bullying that was hurled my way, I was accepted very quickly as a player who could contribute to the success of the team.

My fitness level also once prompted Brian Clough into directing a cutting comment at our right-back, Tony Bircumshaw. As an outside-right, my role was mainly an attacking one, but with energy to burn I tracked back every time we lost possession. In one match I had tracked back and then dispossessed the opposition's winger on numerous occasions.

"You should be giving young McGovern half your wages today," Clough barked at him. "He did your job as well as his own."

"I'm teaching him everything he knows boss," Tony responded quick as a flash, which almost brought a wry smile from Clough.

Whether players blend together tactically or get on with one another is totally down to the manager's man management skills. Clough's were second to none, with the wisdom and an erudite ability to give an explanation of exactly how he wanted his team to play. His simplification of tactics made players' jobs easy. Who wouldn't thrive in that environment? I certainly began to under his management, and my football education continued.

He was a very charismatic figure even at that stage in his career and, from the very first time I heard him talk, I listened intently. What he said would go into my head and I would throw out the bits that I didn't think were relevant, or which were for effect, and retain what I thought was important for me.

He treated everyone pretty much the same and he was always looking for high standards from the players he worked with. Some managers might be happy if their midfield players made four good passes out of seven during the course of a match, but he always used to say that if you made seven out of seven you might stand a chance of staying in the side.

He could be ruthless with his comments sometimes, but he was always able to do it with a certain charm. I very quickly began to listen to the words and not the way he said them. I realised later in my career, particularly in my days at Nottingham Forest, that if he had a go at me sometimes it wasn't actually for my benefit it was for the player sitting next to me in the dressing room. By that time I knew him so well and he knew me. He was aware that he could say something to me and I wouldn't be upset by it, but what he was really doing was making a more general point about the way the team was playing or what needed to be done.

In those early days at Hartlepools he said things to me which I knew were spot-on about what was required of a professional footballer, and I think we quickly established a relationship which would continue for many years at various clubs. It was the perfect relationship in many ways. Brian quickly assessed me as a player who unselfishly focused on trying to help the team win football matches. He also appreciated that a personal rollicking, or occasional praise, wouldn't affect my application one bit.

I'm sure the fact that having my dad die when I was 11 also played a significant part in my development in those early Hartlepools days. Brian probably represented that senior dominant male figure I never had at home, and I listened intently to this fascinating man who had suddenly come into my life.

I knew what he said was right. It sounded right, felt right, and I was positive in my own mind that it was right. Everything he said seemed to be exactly what I wanted to hear, even if it was criticism at times, because I was trying to be the best I could and always gave him total loyalty. He was educating me, and I think he could see an honest response in me. I learned good habits early on, and having Clough and Taylor at the club was like having a comfort blanket for me because I instinctively knew they were superb at what they did.

It was also obvious from a very early stage that Brian relied heavily on Peter when it came to making the right choice about which players would be right for the team. Clough would tell Taylor he needed a left-back or a striker, or a midfield player and Peter would go out and buy him. This system worked so well throughout the time they were together. One thing is certain, they were better together than they were when they were apart, as experiences in later years would go on to prove.

Peter Taylor was also a calming influence on Brian, and he would occasionally adopt the role of good cop, to Clough's bad cop. He also had a very dry sense of humour and gave me a taste of it one day when he sat me down and had a quiet word.

"John, do you realise that you have got an advantage over any other professional in the game of football?"

"What is it, Pete?" I enquired eagerly.

"Well," he said slowly. "When professionals reach the age of 30 they all lose a yard of pace, but you'll never have that problem."

He then turned and left, leaving me scratching my head, chuckling as I began to appreciate his sarcasm. Thankfully my lack of pace never stopped me having a pretty decent career.

Apart from his quiet demeanour and wit, Peter could also be quite ruthless, as I experienced during a home game against Halifax. I had gone over and badly twisted my ankle after five minutes of the game. Despite limping badly I played on until half time. In the dressing room Peter told the trainer to strap up my ankle, insisting I would be fine. Brian looked at the size of it, which was twice as big as the other one and was clearly concerned.

"Peter there's no way he can play on," insisted Clough.

"There's nothing wrong with him, get it strapped," barked Taylor. It was only when I couldn't get my boot on that he conceded I couldn't play on. An X-ray later showed I had played for 40 minutes with a broken ankle.

Because our training was carried out at such a fierce tempo, playing football that way became second nature. There was no need to motivate players on a match day. If you trained and tackled like tigers during the week, matches became merely an extension of everyday training. Confidence grew throughout the team during the season, which ended with the expectation of promotion the following season. Clough inspired the players both on and off the field as we sat beside supporters in working men's clubs on numerous nights, with Brian going out and begging for local support. His speeches were captivating and his energy prodigious, as he literally pleaded for the whole town to financially support the team. He actually used to pass the hat around, inspired by this Pied Piper figure who knew exactly what to say and how to say it, to get them on his side.

But despite all that he did at the club and with the supporters, at the end of my first full season Clough and Taylor left Hartlepools to take charge of Derby County.

Before they left, the two of them made it clear that I would be part of their future plans. I had been substitute for our game against Bradford Park Avenue one day and sat next to Clough on the bench.

"When Peter and I leave here you are going with us," he had told me. "There's a centre-half playing for Tranmere who is also coming, because you're the only ones in this league worth taking."

"Okay," I said, and took it with a pinch of salt just like most 17-year-olds would have. It didn't really make much sense at the time.

CHAPTER THREE

CLOUGHIE'S BLUE-EYED BOY

Despite Clough's promise, come the start of the 1967/68 season I was still a Hartlepools United player, looking ahead to my second year in professional football under a new manager. Hartlepools' incoming boss was Angus McLean, and as a friendly gesture I went in to the ground during the summer break to introduce myself. His opening line was incredible.

"So you're Cloughie's blue-eyed boy are you? Well I'm going to change all that."

The animosity was instant. From the first day in charge of the team, all he did was criticise me, ably supported by his assistant, John Simpson, who was the new trainer. In their eyes I could do nothing right.

"You can't run," McClean declared after one sprinting session. "Well I'm going to make you run."

The way in which he attempted to make this happen was by making me wear spikes or sprinter's shoes every day for a week, before playing against Notts County on the Saturday. When I turned out for the match my calves seized up during the game, making even walking agony.

McLean would have been better off employed by the Gestapo. He almost destroyed my love of the game, as did Simpson, who was a sadist, and someone who would have been at home working for the Spanish Inquisition. Taking a scrubbing brush to clean out cuts or scrapes was one of his party pieces. He actually tried to use this method on me once. Despite my tender years, I told him in no uncertain terms exactly what he could do with his scrubbing brush, which only aggravated an already poor relationship. I'm sure their persecution of me had something to do with their jealousy of Clough and Taylor's well-earned respect. Players were afraid of Brian, yet respected him. They may have been afraid of McLean and Simpson, but they simply loathed them.

When my normally controlled temper reached boiling point at the beginning of one training session, I decided to prove a point. The object of the training session was to run five laps, then walk one, in order to recover. Then run four laps, walk one, then three laps, down to a single last lap. A lap was the perimeter of the pitch. When we started together all the experienced pros tried to keep a rein on the younger fitter players, in order to maintain a manageable pace. I started at what could only be described as a suicidal pace. With my ability to run forever I literally lapped the whole squad on the first five circuits. By the time I had finished the total exercise, the other players were miles behind. McLean and Simpson, their red faces contorted with rage, then started shouting at the players. Revenge, they say, is a sweet thing and I savoured mine immensely that day as I patiently waited for the others to finish. Some of them did have a go at me for making it a hard session, although McLean and Simpson seemed to back off with their verbal intimidation from that day.

As the season progressed we were performing with greater consistency, although I was left out of the team whenever McLean needed a scapegoat. We adopted a man-to-man marking system when we were defending. Each defender was told who he had to stay with when the opposition had possession. In theory this sounds fine, yet in reality it becomes unworkable as soon as one of the opposition beats or loses his marker. This system was instantly scrapped after we lost 7-0 at Reading. Two players got the blame, a striker called Bobby Cummings and me as outside-right. I can vividly remember our right-back Tony Burcumshaw standing alongside "his" man allowing the Reading striker to run straight past him and smash in two goals.

"My man didn't score," he cockily told me at the final whistle.

I looked at him in amazement, then after a quick bath sneaked out of the ground for the team bus, totally ashamed, and it was a very long and lonely trip home. But not as long as the one we had to Luton.

We were told to report to the Victoria Ground at 6.30am for the journey because, these being pre-motorway days, you needed an early start. With the help of the driver, who got lost, we turned up at the hotel in Luton for our pre-match meal almost six hours later at 2.10pm. With fillet steak, tea, toast and rice pudding to follow, there was no way I could eat so close to the 3pm kick-off. I am not quite sure how well the other players were fed at home, but they scoffed the lot and mine as well, before turning out less than an hour later. Unfortunately we lost 1-0, to a Bruce Rioch 25-yard rocket, after a surprisingly good performance.

Long away trips were still pretty hard, as I fought the travel sickness, but learning to drive seemed to gradually lessen the severity. The only reason I had a car to drive was because my mum had decided to buy one with the insurance money from my dad's death some years before. The car was a Mark One Ford Cortina, registration number NEF 959, in dark blue. I passed my test first time, although I did have to repeat my emergency stop three times to convince the examiner. What a feeling of confidence and importance I got from being able to drive, but I realised it would be quite a considerable time before I could afford to buy a car of my own.

During the 1967/68 season, because of continual criticism from the management duo of McLean and Simpson, I began to question whether or not I really wanted to continue playing professional football. Something that had been an inspiration and desire from the very first time I was invited to have that kickabout on holiday at my grandmother's. These doubts were partly tempered by the fact that football was the only qualification I had, but my love of the game was slowly being drained from me.

On reflection, Brian Clough and Peter Taylor had spoiled me by filling me with enormous confidence, something which McLean and Simpson had no apparent intention of repeating. My form suffered, yet somehow my natural enthusiasm and a few encouraging words from some of my team-mates kept me going. By the end of that season, due to a tremendously consistent late run of form, we managed to win promotion to the Third Division. Our last two matches were both against Swansea, away on Monday night, 6th May, and at home for the last game on the following Saturday, by which time we had already clinched promotion. I played in both matches, but because of my hatred for the management I was a reluctant participant when it came to the press photograph after we had clinched promotion at Swansea on the Monday night. Immediately after the photograph I went into the toilets, where I was violently sick because of the tangled up mix of emotions I was feeling. I despised playing for the manager and, although we'd won promotion under him, the whole time playing for him was very stressful. After our post-match celebrations in the dressing room, followed by a marathon bus ride home, we arrived back at the Victoria Ground in the early hours of the morning. Suffering from my usual travel sickness too, I looked and felt like death warmed up.

The fatigue was immediately lifted by an offer from Tyne-Tees television to travel straight up to the Newcastle studios for an interview, which would pay us £5 each. How could we refuse such riches? We splashed water on our faces, ran combs through our hair and off we went.

So in May 1968 Hartlepools had won promotion for the first time in the club's history. A civic reception followed, giving joy to the whole town, except for one inexperienced outside-right, who wasn't in the mood to join in the celebrations. Our final game against Swansea was played in front of over 11,000 celebrating fans, and they were able to enjoy the sight of us winning 2-0. Despite crossing a ball which eluded their goalkeeper for the second goal, my celebrations were thoughtfully subdued.

However, that summer, my disillusionment soon gave way to a renewed determination to practise as much as I could and improve beyond recognition. I was spurred on by an approach from Len Shackleton, the former Sunderland player who was a sports writer for one of the national Sunday newspapers. He told me Brian Clough and Peter Taylor were still very interested in taking me to Derby County, and he suggested that if I asked for a transfer it might speed up the proposed move. Using a reporter as a go-between when it came to trying to get a player to move was pretty common practice, but being tapped up was new to me just like so many other things. I had no experience whatsoever, but when I informed my mum of my decision to ask for a transfer, she backed me all the way, adding that when I moved she would go with me. Perhaps she saw it as an opportunity to move out of the house she had been living in at the time of my dad's death, or the fact that she didn't particularly like Hartlepool, I don't really know, but the decision was made and I couldn't wait to get away.

Angus McLean went berserk, of course, and tried to extract a confession from me saying I had been illegally approached, then tried to frighten me, but by now I was used to the way he carried on. This man had made my life hell during the time he was in charge, and there had been times when I had been physically sick on the pitch before matches because of the nerves I'd suffered under his regime. It had been tough for me to continue under the sort of pressure he seemed to delight in forcing upon me, but I had come through it. He might have been a bully, but in the end I had stood up to him and hadn't been beaten by his tactics. Despite his anger at me handing in a transfer request and his belief that I had been tapped up, I never gave him the satisfaction of owning up to it and now I had a way out of my nightmare. In truth, I would have been prepared to walk to wherever Clough and Taylor were to play for them again in order to regain my love of the game.

CHAPTER FOUR

GOOD-TO-BE-ALIVE DAYS

The new season started with Hartlepool chairman, Mr Curry, congratulating all the players and informing us that in appreciation of us winning promotion we would be rewarded with club suits, sporting gold thread badges bearing the club crest. We had been given a promotion bonus of £40 each and, true to form, the club then took £20 back from each of us the following week to pay for the suits. I estimated they were only worth 10 quid in the first place!

Having put in my transfer request, I couldn't wait to get away. I'd hated my time under McLean, and the prospect of breaking free from his style of management and teaming up again with Brian Clough and Peter Taylor filled me with a mixture of relief and excitement. I had been given a sample of what I could expect from them, and I knew that they were the sort of people I wanted to work for and who would also help make me into the best player I could be. The only problem was that things didn't happen as quickly as I had hoped. In fact, it was only after about six or seven games of the new season had been played that Derby eventually came in with an offer of £7,500 for me. Happily, it was accepted and with a feeling of grateful anticipation I made my way down to Derby's Baseball Ground where I was due to meet Brian and Peter before putting pen to paper and signing for my new club.

On the way down the A1 road was flooded and I was delayed

by about four hours, making me late for our meeting. I had driven down with my mum, and when we finally got to the ground Peter joked that they thought I might have changed my mind. The way he said it made me laugh, and then I realised that it was about the first time for a year that I had laughed about anything to do with football, because there had been precious little to smile about under McLean.

Brian just put a contract down in front of me and I signed it. The whole thing was as simple as that, and it was a process which would be repeated on other occasions during my time playing for him. I had trust in him and didn't even ask what was in it, and so on 12th September, 1968, about six weeks short of my 19th birthday, I became a Derby County player earning £25 per week, which was exactly the same wage I'd been on at Hartlepool. There was no increase in salary, although there was the possibility of an extra £5 if I played in the first team. I must admit that I had expected a bit of a rise in wages considering I was swapping the Third Division for the Second, but it wasn't to be, and I was just overjoyed to have made the move and be working with Clough and Taylor again. When I spoke to Peter I couldn't help asking him why it had taken them so long to actually sign me after I had handed in my transfer request.

"I came to watch your last Hartlepool game at Bristol Rovers, because I never assess players in home games," he told me. "Away from home is where you judge a player. You had an easy option of a pass, but ignored it to take on the full-back at the edge of the penalty area, beat him and cross the ball. If you had chosen the easy option, you would still be playing for Hartlepool!"

It was a reminder for me that I should never take things for granted, and Peter's brutally honest explanation was typically short, sharp and to the point, which was typical of the way he and Clough operated.

Having moved away from my home in Hartlepool, I had to live in digs for a time, staying first with the Notley family, in St Giles Road, Normanton, and then with a lovely Polish couple, in Dairyhouse Road, where I was the only tenant, and that suited my dedicated lifestyle perfectly. For company I ended up knocking about with the reserve-team goalkeeper Alek Ludzik, who was a great lad but as mad as a March Hare. He would do some very random, off-the-wall things – on one occasion we had been for a night out in Derby, and sometime after midnight Alek suddenly insisted we went and got some chips from somewhere. Nowhere near was open, and in the end we had to drive all the way to a service station on the M1 so he could get some. There were also some other really good youngsters I mixed with, such as Tommy Kane, Kenny Blair, Tommy Mason and the striker Barry Butlin.

Eventually my mother and brother moved down to Derby and we lived in a three-bedroom semi-detached house in Birchover Way, Allestree, just on the outskirts of Derby. It offered a very settled environment and there was no hint of homesickness with Mum around, who along with my brother soon found a job at the Rolls-Royce factory. In some ways I had been sorry to leave Hartlepool though, because of things like my friendship with Kenny Jessop. Sadder still, I ended my close relationship with his sister Kay, feeling I had to sacrifice everything to establish myself again as a footballer.

Not long after joining Derby, I went to a snooker hall in Babington Lane one afternoon after training. Albert Mays, the hall manager, was also an ex-Derby County player.

"You're young McGovern from Hartlepool aren't you?" he said. "Are you going to get into the first team?"

"I most certainly am," I replied, as quick as a flash.

He allowed me a free session for my cheek, but in fact I wasn't being cheeky I was just being positive and confident, even though I hadn't even seen the first team play.

The first time I did watch them, their performance and result gave little indication that my confidence was justified. They played Chelsea in a League Cup replay, which meant a full house at the Baseball Ground and a buzzing atmosphere. Following an emphatic 3-1 win, which had seen Dave Mackay score from 30 yards, with Alan Durban and Kevin Hector getting the other two, the players left the pitch to a deserved standing ovation. As I watched them leave the field I reflected on Dave's performance and realised just how far I was from being as good a player as him. It was a sobering thought regarding his sublime ability, which was remarkable, disproving media criticism that he was past his best after suffering two broken legs.

I knew the only way I was going to make progress was to make sure I played out of my skin for the reserves. It sounds simple really, but the reserve-team trainer was another major stumbling block to my progress. His name was Jack Burkett, who had captained Nottingham Forest to FA Cup success in 1959 when they had beaten Luton Town 2-1. He took one look at me, my then puny body and awkward running style, and dismissed me as having no potential whatsoever.

"You can't run, you've got no strength and you can't head a ball," was his considered opinion of my ability as a player.

I'd heard this sort of comment so many times I wasn't fazed. He kept telling me how good some of his reserves were, saying I would never be as quick as Peter Daniel, or as aggressive as John Richardson, or head the ball like Barry Butlin. But I knew I was still an outside-right who had the ability to pass the ball accurately with both feet. I also had good ball control and the vision to see and understand the game.

Trainers like Jack Burkett were blinkered as far as I was concerned. They saw only pace, strength and aggression as attributes, instead of the numerous other things players require, things such as control, temperament, vision and the one ability which nobody can teach you, which is when to play the ball. You can show a player how to hold their feet or legs to improve or maintain balance, but knowing when to play the ball is pure natural ability, which develops through an informed football brain which improves with experience. If someone ever tells you they can coach a player into knowing when to play the ball, then spit in their eye and tell them it can't be done.

Jack Burkett was also someone who thought that physical strength was an absolute necessity. He used to embarrass me by teaming me with the strongest apprentice during circuit training then laugh at me in front of the group when I struggled with the heavy dumbbells. He never appreciated my simple question when it came to training with heavy weights.

"What has lifting weights got to do with passing a ball?" I wanted to know.

As a result of all this my early reserve career at Derby was not brilliant and eventually reached the stage where Peter Taylor questioned me after a game, demanding to know why I had been given a bad report. It had said I never got a kick during the game.

"I never got the ball Pete," I told him.

Peter left the meeting immediately without further discussion, leaving me a little uncertain about the outcome, but it wasn't long before he returned and asked me a question.

"Do you fancy moving inside and playing in central midfield?" he asked.

"I'd love it," I replied. "I can make sure I get enough of the ball playing there."

Peter's intuition about my ability to adapt to a central midfield position was justly rewarded, as I revelled in the change and the chance to show Jack Burkett and anyone else who doubted me what I could do.

I was picked for Derby County's first team a little more than eight weeks after my September arrival, making my debut at home against Charlton on 9th November. I played in central midfield alongside the likes of Dave Mackay, Roy McFarland (Roy was the Tranmere centre-half Brian Clough had told me about at Hartlepool and subsequently snapped up), Kevin Hector, John O'Hare, Willie Carlin, Ron Webster, John Robson, Jim Walker, Alan Hinton, Frank Wignall, Alan Durban and Les Green, who I had played with at Hartlepool. We won 2-1. So at the age of just 19 my Derby career was up and running, but I had to learn quickly how to hack it with the big boys. I did have a head start on most players breaking into the first team, as collectively the players in the side were a superbly talented and experienced outfit – John Robson at full-back was the only real youngster apart from me. But with the massive confidence already in the camp, the blend of youth and experience propelled us towards the top of the league.

My new role in midfield meant perfecting new skills, so with tackling being one of the weaker elements of my game who better to ask for advice than Dave Mackay? After one training session I talked to Dave, telling him I was desperate to stay in the first team, and asked him if he could teach me his superb tackling technique.

"I like to slide tackle, so I go in low," Dave explained.

"What happens if you miss the ball?" I asked him.

"I punch them in the bollocks," he replied with a shrug of his shoulders. "Get a ball and I'll show you right now."

"Er, no thanks Dave," I said backing away hastily.

Brian Clough happened to overhear our conversation and shouted over to Dave.

"You're wasting your time – my grandmother tackles better than McGovern!"

Thankfully, even without a personal demonstration from Dave, I learned to "put my foot in" when required.

Playing in Derby's first team also meant training with Jimmy Gordon, who Brian knew from his days at Middlesbrough. Jimmy was definitely old school. He had a sergeant major style, but his knowledge and enthusiasm were infectious and, although he gave out compliments sparingly, I enjoyed every training session under his perceptive eye. On a cold winter's day Jimmy would turn up with shorts on, take in a huge gulp of the freezing air, breathe out and then share his thoughts with the rest of us. And those thoughts hardly varied.

"A good-to-be-alive day," he would declare in a loud voice and he really meant it. Jimmy loved his job and I loved training with him.

Besides Jimmy Gordon's work-outs, training under Brian was an absolute joy; short, sharp sessions to keep us on our toes always ending with a five-a-side match or a small-sided game in a confined area to sharpen up all your ball skills. The games were played with a passion and ferocity that was the equivalent pace and tempo of a league game, with full-blooded tackles demanded of everyone, including the manager.

"If you don't tackle like tigers in training how can you do it on a Saturday?" was one of Brian's favourite sayings.

There is no harm in repeating good habits. Hartlepools and Derby might have been in different leagues, but the same theory applied. There was always an end product to these fiercely competitive small-sided games. A yellow jersey was awarded to the worst player on the losing team, voted for by the winning team. The nominated player had to wear the jersey until the end of the next game, and the stigma of wearing the dreaded booby prize guaranteed 100 per cent effort from us all.

One person who did bring a temporary halt to the tradition was Dave Mackay. Dave was so fiercely competitive and proud of his ability that he boasted he could never play badly enough to be voted the worst player. So when that day duly arrived he ripped up the jersey with his bare hands, verbally threatening the players who had voted against him to beware in the next game. This provoked an outbreak of stifled laughter, with all the players, thinking of self-preservation, secretly hoping they would be on Dave's side for the next five-a-side game.

Dave Mackay was the ultimate competitor, whose attitude and commitment to winning at anything was an inspiration to every player in the club. His experience, allied to that of Willie Carlin, another brilliant example of "true grit", provided the rock-solid foundation the team was built on. Training, playing, travelling and living with players of their ilk can only enhance your own ability, unless you are a mug. I made sure it was an experience I never wasted.

Having arrived at Derby County from a newly promoted Third Division team, my own expectations were boundless, partly due to the blinkered approach I possessed. I developed an obsession with trying to make a football do exactly what I wanted to do with it, no matter how the thing was delivered to me. I knew I didn't possess the sort of pace which would allow me to run past players, so I realised that instant control of the ball could give me an edge. No one reaches perfection in anything, but I believed the ability to control a ball with either foot would give me the advantage over my opponents.

I was able to hone and enhance that ability when I got to Derby by means of a very simple device that had been at the club for some time. We used to call it the "shooting box". The box was situated under the main stand at the Baseball Ground, about 20ft in length with sloping sides and a back wall and a flat chicken-wire mesh roof. When the game started the first player would whack the ball against the back wall, and because of the sloping sides the ball would rebound at all sorts of angles. As it cleared the front of the box the next player in line had to return the ball, with only one touch allowed. If his effort failed to hit the back wall and return over the entrance line he was out of the game. With restricted standing room, plus the handicap of some steps on the left-hand side of the box entrance, balance and technique were essential.

My two-footed ability kept me up alongside the claimants to being "King of the Shooting Box". A certain Dave Mackay, as expected, also laid claim to the title – and even Cloughie joined in with the competition. Dave also helped teach Clough's two sons, Nigel and Simon, how to kick a football in there.

Derby hadn't started the season particularly well, but after that victory over Chelsea the potential quality of the players in the squad that Brian and Peter had assembled began to shine through. With Dave Mackay driving us forward and setting an example for everyone, the team began playing very good football and in the process started to string together some wins. By the time Christmas came around we were at the top of the league, and come the New Year we really began to motor, finishing the season with a real flourish by winning our last nine games to ensure the Second Division title. It was no surprise that we won the league by seven clear points considering the quality of the side, nor that Dave Mackay was named the joint Football Writers' Footballer of the Year (with Tony Book of Manchester City).

I had kept my place in the team since my debut in November. Our last home game against Bristol City was particularly memorable for a warning from Brian before we took to the field. His instructions were crystal clear:

"If any of you flick the ball when you should get hold of it, if any of you backheel the ball to show off, or if any of you try anything fancy rather than playing the ball the way it should be played, I will not only take you off to expose you, we will play without a substitute to replace you," he told us. "By the way I will also fine you, because the supporters that have come to watch you today have come to see you play the way you have played all season. They also pay your wages. Good luck."

Needless to say, we won that fixture and did it in style with a 5-0 scoreline. The spectators were also treated to a certain Dave Mackay, flicking, backheeling, back-heading (jumping and turning 180 degrees in mid-air before throwing his head backwards to connect with the ball), nutmegging people and generally stunning everyone with his sublime ability. Had any other player in a Derby shirt attempted any of the tricks Dave completed that day, they would have been hauled off the pitch in disgrace. Such was Dave's confidence he never put a foot wrong and when we came off the field Brian just smiled and shook his hand. It's called respect, which Dave as a player and Brian as a manager went through their lives automatically earning from virtually everyone they met.

Winners are easy to recognise, even when you're only 19 years old. I have never seen a player back-head the ball as Dave demonstrated during the Bristol game. It ranks up there with the Pelé scissor kick, the Cruyff turn or the Maradona cross, with one leg striking the ball from behind the other, as supreme acts of showmanship. What an experience to witness as a mere mortal.

The club held a celebration dinner with players and directors mixing together as we all enjoyed the achievement. The club chairman, Sidney Bradley, thought it would be a nice time to introduce his wife to the club's Captain Marvel and so he tapped Dave on the shoulder.

"Dave, would you like to say hello to my wife?" he asked.

"No thanks," said Dave turning away. The open-mouthed

Bradley gasped as his embarrassed wife turned red in the face, but then Dave immediately turned back, and took her hand.

"Delighted," he said with a smile bringing the chairman's pounding heart rate back to normal. The captain's comic timing was as precise as his tackling.

You couldn't help being impressed by Dave, both as a player and as a person. When I arrived at the club he was coming up to his 34th birthday, and had already earned legendary status as part of Tottenham Hotspur's famous Double-winning side in 1961. He had also come back from breaking his leg twice during his time with Spurs and, not only was he as hard as nails, he was also one of the most skilful players I have ever seen, with unsurpassable competitive spirit. My first impression of him when we met was that he was smaller than I had imagined, but his huge barrel chest used to give him a presence on the pitch that nobody else had. He had a huge passion to be a winner, and that rubbed off on everyone at the club. It used to hurt his pride if he lost a tackle or even gave the ball away. That sort of search for perfection drove him on, and it was a pleasure to play with someone like him. He encouraged me all the time, but also let me know what was expected of me within the framework of the team. Dave, along with Willie Carlin, would always give me advice and they both helped me develop my own game, as did Brian Clough.

Although Derby was very different to Hartlepools, Clough's methods stayed pretty much the same. There was no set time when it came to the length of a training session. It could last for two hours or 20 minutes, but the one consistent factor was that everything we did was done at full pace. Jimmy Gordon would come out and do the warm-up exercises with the team and then Clough would appear.

"Right, last pair mounted!" he might shout, which meant that you had to jump on someone's back. Or he might tell you to get down, slide through your partner's legs and then jump on the back of the next man. All this had to be done at speed and with agility, and if you ended up as the last person or pair to complete the task he'd asked you to carry out it would mean getting down on the ground and doing five or 10 press-ups. Everything was short and sharp, but it was also very competitive and nobody, least of all Dave Mackay, wanted to come last. It was comical at times seeing Dave push and shove people in order to make sure he wasn't going to be the one who had to do the press-ups.

We'd finish up with a five-a-side game which was nearly always two-touch, so the pace was once again very quick. Sometimes we also played five-a-sides where we weren't allowed to shout to each other, and it was amazing how much running you had to do in order to get in front of the man in possession so that he could see you to pass the ball. Clough would often join in these games, and of course he would insist on playing centre-forward. When he did play the game would rarely end until his side had won – once we ended up playing for about an hour!

Everything Brian did was based on common sense and making sure things were kept simple. He never really bothered too much with the opposition and instead preferred to concentrate on his own team and what we could do. We each knew our jobs and he filled us with a lot of confidence because he believed in all of us.

Brian wasn't the sort of manager to bombard you with facts and figures, but he always seemed to know the right things to say and the right time to say them. He believed that the most important time for a manager was the five minutes before you went out to kick off and the period he had with you at half time. There was no clenching of fists, shouting or slapping of each other's backs as we went out to face the opposition, it was all very business-like, calm and collected.

"You've done it during the week," Clough would say. "Now go out and do it on a Saturday!"

With a Second Division Championship medal to add to the promotion I'd got with Hartlepools, I was thrilled at the prospect of competing with the stars in the First Division. Before the excitement of a new season in the top flight, though, we were all treated to a close-season trip to Cala Millor in Mallorca, to wind down.

Visiting this spot was to become an annual occurrence for the players, who thrived on a few days without wives, girlfriends or family to worry about. We certainly let our hair down. An end-of-season break was always enjoyable, but when we had some-thing to celebrate it tended to end up as a non-stop party. Having a drink, or 10, was practically expected, but there was always one provision when you worked for Clough and Taylor – any trouble and you were on the next plane home.

During all the years I went partying to Cala Millor with both Derby and Forest, I usually stayed out of trouble. It was only this one summer of '69 when I got arrested . . .

The arrest followed a normal peaceful evening out with the lads. As we strolled back to our hotel, walking along dimly lit streets, we suddenly had to jump for our lives as a swerving, speeding car almost ran into our group. When the driver screeched to a halt just ahead of us Les Green ran over to him and furiously banged on the roof of his car, letting him know exactly what he thought of the guy's dangerous driving. We dragged Les away following a heated verbal exchange of opinions with the driver. For everyone concerned the scuffle should have finished there and then, but during the incident we hadn't real-ised that Les, who was a strongly-built goalkeeper, had left a large dent in the car roof, and shortly before arriving back at our hotel we again had to jump onto the narrow pavement as a police car pulled up, sirens blazing. An officer got out and, without provocation, immediately knocked Willy Carlin over a small retaining wall. Willie, who was a tough little Scouser, picked himself up ready to respond but a few of us grabbed him, preventing the situation from escalating further. Then, just to add to the drama, the young policeman drew his pistol and pointed it straight at us.

Never has a group of men sobered up so quickly.

A police chief then arrived and we were escorted back to the hotel, where four of our passports were confiscated. Ironically, Les's was not one of them, but mine was! Peter Taylor, who along with Brian always stayed in a different hotel to the players, then arrived and was fully informed about the incident. He agreed that we were the victims of an overreaction both by the wayward driver and then the police, so we didn't get sent home.

It was, however, another lesson learned: when in a foreign country, tread carefully. There were even headlines back home in the British papers screaming "Football Stars Under Arrest", but I was more worried about my mum giving me a clip around the ears when I got home.

The following day the four of us who'd had our passports taken appeared in the local court. We were informed by a translator that the judge didn't really know what to charge us with. He eventually settled on fining us, before taking us all to the nearest bar and spending the fine buying drinks and extolling virtues of Real Madrid and their history. The guy whose car had been damaged was also there, invited along by the judge and, to crown a farcical episode, he gave us a lift back to the hotel afterwards!

CHAPTER FIVE

"BORDER" AND THE BIG BOYS

A fter a typically short pre-season we prepared for life with the big boys in the 1969/70 season, our first in the top division. Clough and Taylor believed that long pre-season training programmes were never beneficial because they shortened players' summer breaks. Their philosophy was that a football season lasted a tough non-stop nine or 10 months, making the summer rest period crucial. Training in pre-season is always hard, but once you have reached a peak, short sessions are all that is required to maintain your fitness. Playing two or three games a week during the season maintains all that you have achieved in pre-season.

As the big kick-off approached, my enthusiasm was as high as ever, partly due to the fact that I had signed a new contract during the summer – my new basic wage was now £40 per week. At 19 years of age I also had four valuable years of experience under my belt.

In our first match of the season we drew 0-0 at home against Burnley, which was a slightly disappointing start in front of our own fans. I did notice a distinct difference in the playing style of our visitors compared to teams in the Second Division. Burnley gave the ball away less frequently and showed control and patience in playing numerous square passes as part of their measured approach play.

As you might expect, Brian was confident even before a ball

was kicked, and he made a very good point about there being no real pressure on us.

"They're not expecting you to do anything," he told us. "You've just got promoted."

Playing in the First Division never overawed us, and we made a really good start to the season. Following the Burnley game we collected wins against Ipswich both away and at home, with a 1-1 draw at Coventry sandwiched in between the two wins. After the Ipswich home win we had another match at the Baseball Ground against Stoke, and there were a few of us who didn't exactly cover ourselves in glory during the game, which ended 0-0. It included a comical incident when Brian decided to make a substitution. This was obviously long before the electronic boards used today, and it was left to Jimmy Gordon to beckon the unfortunate player being withdrawn. But such was our lacklustre performance that four of us, with heads down, started the walk of shame, before it became clear that in fact it was crowd favourite Kevin Hector being surprisingly taken off.

We continued our good start and after 10 games found ourselves proudly sitting at the top of the First Division, with all of us finding the experience of playing against the best in the country incredibly exciting.

One of our best wins was a 2-1 home victory over Everton, the game during which I had taken it upon myself to mark Alan Ball and Clough had paid me that "and he's a good player, you're not" back-handed compliment. Despite the quip at the end, his praise made me feel like a million dollars, and I was beginning to think I was a half-decent player after all. We also had a fantastic 5-0 win against Dave Mackay's old club Tottenham at the Baseball Ground. My first reaction at the final whistle was to run over and shake hands with Jimmy Greaves. Jimmy had been one of my boyhood heroes, and I had kept a scrapbook of him, which I still have today, so after shaking his hand I refused to wash mine in the bath afterwards. I went out for a celebration drink that night with the dirtiest hand in Derby.

It was an incredible time for me, and I think I probably

appreciated it even more because of the fact that it had all happened so quickly. A couple of years earlier I had been playing for Hartlepools in front of about 6,000, and now I was playing in front of nearly 40,000 at the Baseball Ground with the prospect of visits to places like Old Trafford, Anfield and Highbury.

The bubble burst in our next game, however, as we subsided to a 1-0 defeat at Sheffield Wednesday. But it was our first loss in 12 league matches, which was a tremendous start for any side, let alone one that had just been promoted from the Second Division.

Regardless of my work rate, I never managed to score many goals during my career, but I did manage my first one for Derby that season when I netted against Liverpool at the Baseball Ground with a 20-yarder with the outside of my right foot in a resounding 4-0 victory. The confidence generated by the manager and Peter Taylor carried us through that first season in Division One with few difficulties. Playing alongside good men with tremendous ability and a dedicated work ethic guaranteed a happy, competitive and enjoyable environment which we all thrived in.

Clough was the same as ever, so you could never be complacent, despite the fact that the move up to the First Division had gone so well. He maintained his ability to keep everyone on their toes, whether it was on the training field or just walking down the corridor. Occasionally Peter Taylor might see you and say the words that often had me feeling like a guilty schoolboy.

"The boss wants a word with you in his office," Pete would say. Suddenly you would be wondering what you had done wrong, but quite often it would be nothing at all. I remember on one occasion I knocked on his door and poked my head into his office.

"You wanted to see me boss," I said.

"You do know it's your mum's birthday coming up?" he replied. "I take it you have bought her a card and present?"

Luckily, I had already bought both, so I avoided an ear-bashing.

We weren't really allowed to talk to the press or do newspaper articles unless Brian gave his say so, and then it was really only with the local paper, but the boss did enough talking for the whole team anyway. It was also good for the players, because there was no pressure on us and we could concentrate on what he wanted us to do, which was win football matches. He was also very keen to make sure that as a team we stuck to the principles he'd laid down, things like not arguing with the referee or disputing his decisions.

"You don't swear at referees," he would tell us. "Why? Because he makes fewer mistakes than you do, and if you keep having a go at referees and then you're involved in a 50-50 tackle in our penalty area in the last five minutes of a match, he'll give a penalty against you . . . and then I'll fine you!"

One of Brian and Peter's firm beliefs when it came to having a successful team was to make sure the players stayed fresh, and there were often little breaks arranged whenever it was possible. Frequent visits were made to training centres such as Lea Green in Derbyshire, or Bisham Abbey in Buckinghamshire. Sharing dormitories was stipulated to improve team bonding. These trips helped introduce variety during a week free from fixtures.

Bisham Abbey was situated at the end of a long tree-lined drive, conveniently within walking distance of the local pub, The Bull. There was training, of course – the normal short, sharp sessions – plus a chance during rest periods to indulge in a game of tennis. Les Green kept everyone amused and on their toes with his hilarious brand of observational humour, or straight-forward practical jokes. One of his favourites was jumping out from hidden spots to scare the life out of you.

One night we'd been given permission by Brian and Peter to go out, and as the evening's enjoyment at The Bull was coming to a close we realised Les was absent. This could only mean one thing. He would be waiting in ambush between the main road and the Abbey. It was 11 o'clock at night, with barely enough light to make out the Abbey at the far end of the drive. As soon as we began the approach, moving gingerly forward, the tension began to mount. Then suddenly ghostly shouts of "HOOOOOOOOO!" and "AAAARGH!" brought us to an immediate halt.

"Where is he?" someone asked.

"He must be in the trees," someone else suggested.

"Come on Les, stop messing about," one of the other lads said, as the shouts got louder. Suddenly, as we all tentatively edged towards the Abbey, there was the ominous cracking noise of an overhead branch breaking. This was followed by a panic-driven sprint towards the Abbey. Les had fallen out of his ambush tree, but landed on Alan Hinton, giving the rest of us time to reach safety.

On another night, after curfew, Les left our downstairs dormitory to terrorise the upstairs dorm. As we discussed what he might be up to we heard the noise of someone or something rolling down the stairs. The upstairs dorm had ambushed the ambusher, tied his hands and feet with training socks and bowled him down the stairs. We untied Les then pleaded with him to get some sleep. Despite our pleas, Les stormed back upstairs, where the noise of furniture being moved around filtered down. Some minutes later Les reappeared rubbing his hands together.

"That will teach them to tie me up," he beamed.

It transpired that Les had barricaded the upper dorm door with various massive wardrobes. Only someone with Les's strength and ingenuity could have completed such a task, which led to more uncontrolled laughter the next morning when the upstairs occupants couldn't get out of their room.

All the players shared in and enjoyed these pranks, although the same could not be said of the manager, especially if he got woken up.

Trying to get Les to switch the lights off in the dormitory was at times impossible. The problem was that he always chose a bed within reach of the master switch. Just as you were beginning to drift off for a good night's sleep, you would be woken with the sound of Les playfully strangling one of his victims, as they struggled to escape his vice-like grip. His other favourite was to imitate a German air raid, complete with flashing room lights and a running commentary from the German bomber commander.

During one extended bout of frivolity the sound of creaking

stairs interrupted Les in full flow. Just before the dormitory door opened, Les jumped onto an overhanging ledge directly above the door. Brian Clough pushed the door open and scanned the room, with the players laughing uncontrollably as Les, unseen by the manager, did his chimpanzee impression above Brian's head.

"Where is he, that bloody goalkeeper?" shouted Clough, as he looked towards Dave Mackay, hoping for a sensible answer. Unfortunately Dave was bent double laughing and wheezing, incapable of reply, as Les continued his impression.

"That bloody man!" added Clough as he turned to leave, slamming the door on the way.

If keeping the players laughing had been financially rewarded, Les Green would have been the best-paid employee at Derby County football club.

I must also credit Les with my nickname, which I was "christened" with on a pre-season tour to Germany. We were staying in a small town called Biberach, enjoying a well-earned night out. As usual there was a curfew, which we had exceeded by a couple of hours. Returning en masse to our hotel, I was trying to get the lads to reduce the noise level, knowing a fine was imminent. Despite my pleading, the bedlam continued, instigating my departure from the more than merry band. I sneaked into the hotel and my room via the back stairs, creeping into bed undetected as I had anticipated the management's old trick of waiting patiently in a secluded spot, to surprise the latecomers. From my room I heard them arrive, but they were so noisy the whole hotel must have heard them.

The next morning there was the inevitable post-mortem, with the manager questioning the culprits. He turned to me and asked what time I had got in that night?

"It was 12 o'clock boss, just before curfew," I said amid some disbelieving looks from the rest of the lads. When the manager's inquiries were completed and the guilty parties severely reprimanded, Les shouted over to me.

"You lying bugger!" he said. "I'm going to call you Border Mask from now on, a man with two faces."

I eventually found out that Border Mask had been a losing racehorse in one of Les's accumulators. Obscure it may have been, but the name stuck, although the mask part disappeared, leaving me known simply as "Border".

There was a tremendous feel-good factor throughout the town that season with us in the First Division and doing well. We gratefully received perks, such as free cinema tickets, which were very much appreciated, particularly as I was now going out with a new very attractive girlfriend called Ann Sharman. I think it's often the case in Britain that when the local team is buzzing, the whole town follows suit.

Dave Mackay obviously played a big part in the success we had in that first season after promotion. He had a leading role on the field and was also a big part of our activities when we went out as a group. When that happened we would usually end up at the Iron Gate Tavern, and more specifically in the downstairs cellar bar. It had a low ceiling and bare brick walls, with a certain corner which we christened "The Captain's Corner" because that was where Dave would sit and hold court. He would be the life and soul of the party. At times it seemed as though the whole town was down there wanting to shake hands with Dave and the rest of the team. We used to mix and mingle with the supporters all the time, which just added to the vibrant atmosphere generated by the positive displays of the team.

We ended the season with another great run of form, remaining unbeaten in our last 12 league matches and winning eight of them. Had it not been for some mid-season inconsistency, we might well have been up there challenging for the title itself. That was eventually won by Everton, with Leeds in second place and Chelsea finishing third. We ended the season in a very credible fourth spot, qualifying for Europe. But we were tragically denied participation in the UEFA Cup, as the club was banned due to some administrative irregularities regarding the 1969 accounts, where the club was found guilty of gross negligence. Derby County were fined £10,000 and banned from playing against any foreign teams for a year. It was no fault of the players, who also missed out on the contractual £500 incentive bonus for qualification, after deservedly earning it.

Despite missing out on Europe, I looked back on that first season in the top flight as overwhelmingly positive. I had gained invaluable experience in midfield, played against my boyhood heroes, Jimmy Greaves and Dennis Law, scored my first goal for the club and could pretty much call myself a regular for the first team, having made 32 full appearances in the league with another as substitute. I'd played in all four of our FA Cup matches and all six of the games we had in the League Cup. I also, at the age of 19, had become the youngest player to play in all four divisions of the Football League, when I appeared in that first game of the season against Burnley.

It was all heady stuff in many ways, but I wasn't about to get carried away. I'm not that sort of person, and any team that Clough and Taylor were in charge of knew that there was never any room for complacency. I knew we had a good team that could only get better, and was confident of the fact that we would. We had more than held our own in the top division and surprised even the sceptics. Being a successful team, however, isn't defined by what you do in one season. It's having the quality to maintain and build on what you have achieved. Improving was what we all wanted to do.

CHAPTER SIX

COSTING CLOUGHIE A CUP FINAL

The 1970/71 season started with a pre-season trophy win when we beat a star-studded Manchester United side 4-1 on 8th August at the Baseball Ground to win the Watney Cup. It was considered a minor trophy by many people, but not the players or the management of Derby County. The first team to a man played in every round as we beat Fulham 5-3 away from home after extra time and then Sheffield United 1-0 at the Baseball Ground before taking on Man United. Brian and Peter's philosophy was simple: if Derby County were playing a fixture the best players all turned out, whether it was a cup-tie, friendly or testimonial, the first team played. This was greatly appreciated by everyone who was raising club funds, receiving a benefit or having a testimonial match.

As a player in those days I wanted to play in every game, regardless of who it was against. As an exceptionally fit 20-year-old, playing three times a week was a doddle. My enthusiasm for chasing and controlling a ball never diminished, although there was one occasion where I should have turned down the offer to play. It was against a team of Leicester press men, and I'd gone along to watch them play against the press boys from Derby. I went there to support my friends, Trevor East, Patrick O'Connell, John Barton, Roger Smith and Paul Ham. The Derby team was a man short and I was waiting for kick-off, wearing jeans and trainers. Then someone asked me if I fancied a game, so I played despite having turned out for Derby in a First Division game the day before and then having a late night on the town. I enjoyed the game and thought no more of it. When I reported for training the following morning, Peter Taylor called me over and questioned what I had been doing the previous day. When I confessed to having played in the game, he went berserk.

"Don't you know the club could get fined because of you playing in that game? And what if you'd broken your leg or been injured?" he asked.

Apparently one of the opposition had been miffed at the "ringer" playing in midfield and complained to the referee. The ref mentioned it to a league representative, who in turn phoned Peter to warn him of possible repercussions, which thankfully never materialised.

"Don't ever do that again," Peter warned me.

Playing with your heart, not your head, is still a fault of many young players. In my case, on that day I just couldn't resist having a kickabout.

Working for Brian was a constant education. He didn't ask you to do things you weren't capable of, but he was very keen on emphasising the basics of his footballing philosophy. Things like making sure a forward held onto the ball when it was played up to him. He hated it if a striker tried to flick the ball on and didn't allow his team the possession needed to construct an attack. Years later when I was playing for Nottingham Forest, our centre-forward, Peter Withe, flicked the ball three times in about the first 15 minutes of the game and Brian substituted him.

"I've told you before about doing that," Cloughie said to him. "If you'd done it once I might have let you get away with it, but three times! You might as well come and sit next to me."

He would tell full-backs that it was vitally important for them to make sure the opponents' wide players did not get crosses in, and for a midfield player like me there were always little reminders of what he expected.

"If you're not playing well, pass the ball five yards and make sure we keep it," he would instruct me. "Once you get your touch you can pass it 10 yards, and when you're really on form pass it any distance you want."

Alan Hinton was a terrific player with two great feet, and he also had a bullet of a shot on him. Brian liked him to hug the touchline and give the team its width, but sometimes Alan would come inside.

"If you come inside you balls-up everything we're trying to do, so stay wide," Brian insisted. "I want to see chalk on your boots. Those other nuggets [this was a frequently-used Clough expression] in midfield can tackle and run around, but they can't do what you do, so stay wide!"

He also hated it if a striker missed the target from relatively close range, and would really let them know all about it if they did so.

"You've missed the target from 18 yards and the goal is 12 yards wide – do you know how bad that is?!" He would shout at them, although having been a striker he did understand the mentality of a forward player who was always looking to score goals. He was at pains to point out their thinking to me sometimes, particularly if I'd been frustrated by a piece of play and thought the striker should have passed the ball.

"As a midfielder you think he should have passed the ball to you from that angle, don't you?" he would ask me. "But he's a striker and he has to be selfish . . . sometimes."

There was always a feasible explanation for why he wanted you to do something. Quite often it was said with a cutting edge and a touch of humour, but the point came across loud and clear. If you were sensible you took note and acted on the advice. I lost count of the number of times he talked to me about my own game, but all he was ever trying to do was make sure I did the right thing for the team and at the same time that also helped improve me as a player.

"My grandmother can run better than you, tackle better than you and pass better than you" he shouted at me once during training. "I don't expect you to tackle like Dave Mackay, but I do expect you to try!"

Brian's comments, like his training methods, were short and

sharp, and he was probably the only man with the charisma to operate in the way he did. Some managers know what to say, some know how to say it and some know when to say it, but Brian could do it all. There were no grey areas, he told you what he wanted and expected and the rest was down to the players. He allowed you to express yourself, but when it came to things like defending it was all about what you did as a unit. He also had great faith in his own beliefs and in each player's ability to carry out his ideas. I remember us being 3-0 down away from home in a game once, but Brian didn't panic.

"It doesn't matter because he'll get us a goal," said Clough pointing to our striker John O'Hare. "But he'll only get us a goal if we stop their midfield player running the game."

The result was that John did get us a goal, after we had done exactly what the manager requested and stopped the danger in midfield. Brian expected to be listened to. If you didn't, you wouldn't last long.

"You can tell a player once and you can even give him the benefit of the doubt for a second time," he told me. "But if he does same thing again, he's out of the club. Football's a simple game. If players can't learn a lesson that I've given them after three attempts, get rid, because he won't benefit you or any of the other players."

Not only did Brian like things done quickly in training, he also wanted the same to happen on the pitch during games. If we got a free kick he wanted it taken quickly, because he knew that some of their players would be running back to their own goal and not be facing play. We often used to catch teams cold, and it worked time and again.

It was a great learning process for me, and I knew that my own game was improving all the time – how could it not? I was playing under Brian Clough, against the best players and teams in the country, and our own side was full of quality.

Because I was surrounded by so many stylish and talented players, I got used to the fact that if the team had a poor spell or game, I would be the whipping boy for disgruntled spectators. Coping with criticism forms part of your education throughout life, and you have to find ways of handling it. I was no different to many young players who wished they could play like Jimmy Greaves, Dennis Law or George Best. I was a basic midfield grafter with a developing knowledge of the game which complemented my ability to pass the ball, a quality that indirectly caused some upheaval at Manchester City.

We were due to play City whose assistant manager, Malcolm Allison, was almost as flamboyant in his manner and comments as Clough himself. "You got one of Malcolm Allison's scouts the sack," Clough reported to me during a pre-match meeting.

I stared back bemused as he explained what had happened.

"The scout gave Malcolm a report of our team saying they were all good players except McGovern. So Malcolm asked him why you were the only weak player and the scout told him that all you do is win the ball and pass it to the nearest white shirt."

"'So that's all he does?' asked Malcolm. 'Well you're fired, because if we had a few players like that we would be top of the league – and you don't know your job!'"

I took Brian telling me that story as a great compliment, coming from someone who was a believer in passing and how simply the game of football should be played.

Brian demanded that his players play the ball to feet whenever they could. For throw-ins you also had to throw the ball to head or feet, not into space, and when the ball was returned you should know where it was going next. If not then, in Brian's opinion, you shouldn't be playing in the first place. Players who threw the ball above head height, and down the touchline were instantly rebuked.

"I'll put you down the line and throw the ball in the air to you when we're playing Liverpool and Tommy Smith is marking you, then see how you like it," Clough would tell the culprit.

Throughout my whole career I learned a wealth of instructions from Clough which remain etched in my mind, like commandments cast in tablets of stone.

As a midfield player, not allowing the opposition a free shot was a number-one priority.

"Put your body in the way of the ball, I don't care if it hits you right in the balls, we've got good medical staff to take care of that," he would tell us. "Don't you dare turn your back when the opposition are going to shoot or I'll cut your balls off."

As a midfielder you were automatically in a defensive wall when there was a free kick against you on the edge of the penalty area. One Saturday we lost a goal because someone turned their back and left a gap. On the Monday morning Clough demanded we practise defending free kicks.

"Alan Hinton will take the free kicks," he informed us. Now Alan had one of the fiercest recorded shots in football, and when he let fly the ball could travel at over 70mph.

"If any of you move or turn your backs, I will personally cut your balls off," added Brian. Believe me, it was a wonder any of us had balls left after facing the full force of Alan's shooting, as Clough made sure none of us turned our backs or moved.

With cupped hands covering our assets, the first thought that goes through your head is the hope that the ball won't hit you but the guy standing next to you. Then "bang," the first shot smashes into the side of your head crushing your ear against your skull, and the sound of bells starts ringing loudly in your head as the ball flies harmlessly over the crossbar. Then just when you begin to feel grateful that the ordeal is over, Cloughie's voice booms out.

"Somebody moved – take another one!"

After you have been peppered by a series of bludgeoning missiles, you begin to threaten your own team-mates.

"If any of you move this time I will cut your balls off!"

The ordeal finishes with a few bruised body parts and a lesson hard learned. The golden rule of all ball sports is never turn your back; you can't see where the ball is.

Our league programme in 1970 began with a disappointment when we lost 2-1 at Chelsea, and this was followed by a midweek away game on the Wednesday against Wolves. Before the game I spotted Angus McLean, my former antagonistic manager from Hartlepools. He extended his hand as he approached me in the corridor at Molineux and, despite the narrow corridor, I neatly avoided the expected handshake as I gently sidestepped him and jogged onto the pitch to inspect the playing surface. McClean had been given a scouting job with Wolves, hence his presence at the ground where he had once been a player. How he actually dared to try and shake hands with me after his bullying at Hartlepools I will never know, although it certainly fired me up for the game. Before kick-off Brian had a less-than-quiet word with me.

"McGovern, do you know who you will be playing against in midfield?" he asked.

Before I had a chance to reply, he told me: "Mike Bailey is their captain and one of their best players. If he gets a kick tonight I am personally going to come on the pitch and kick you!"

I don't know whether it was the threat of being kicked or the unexpected sight of Angus McClean before the match, but I enjoyed a successful night, hitting two goals, although the first took a massive deflection. The second was a right-foot effort, after I had robbed Mike Bailey in a tackle, which flew into the top corner from 20 yards. We ran out 4-2 winners with Alan Durban and John O'Hare also getting on the scoresheet.

When it was all over, I couldn't help reflecting on what McClean had once said to me.

"Can't run, can't play . . ."

I wondered what he thought that night after seeing me score twice to help earn the win.

This was the second occasion I had deliberately man-marked an opponent. The first, against Alan Ball, had been done on my own initiative, but this time it had been under the manager's instructions. This tactical ploy helped to dictate where I would ultimately achieve my most successful role.

The win at Wolves was followed by home victories against Stoke and Ipswich, before we drew at Huddersfield and lost home games to Coventry and Newcastle. In many ways that little batch of games reflected the way the season would progress. We lost too many games and never put together strong runs as we had done in the previous season. In the end we finished ninth in the league, but looking at the bigger picture it was still a pretty good performance from a team which was playing only its second season in the First Division following promotion.

In May 1971 Dave Mackay left the club for Swindon Town. He may have been at the Baseball Ground for less than three years, but his legendary status was assured for the special leadership qualities and sublime ability he'd demonstrated throughout that time. It had been an absolute pleasure to be part of the same team as him, and in typical Dave fashion he ended his time as a player with the club by playing in every league game that season. Remarkably, it was the first time he had ever done that in his career, and it was fitting that he should bow out having been such a part of the success story which had seen the club promoted to the top flight and quickly establish itself as a force to be reckoned with in the English game.

Mackay-less, the 1971/72 season began with a 2-2 home draw against Manchester United, followed by wins against West Ham and Leicester and a 2-2 draw at Coventry. We then repeated that score at the Baseball Ground against Southampton, in a match which saw my frustration with the County fans boil over. I was playing really well, yet still being booed by a section in the "popular side" every time I touched the ball. I then received a ball on the right of the Southampton penalty area, dummied to cross it, and slammed a driven shot just inside the far post. Kevin Hector raced over and picked me up in celebration, turning me to face the "pop" side, where the fanatics were actually starting to applaud. I gave them a double "V" sign in return as my anger exploded.

"Fuck you," I shouted at the top of my voice.

"Not a wise decision," was a comment made to me after the game by a few concerned friends. I didn't give a monkey's and was determined they would never ever put me off doing what I wanted to do. The louder they criticised the more determined I knew I would be. But it still didn't stop me from chastising myself when committing errors I knew I shouldn't commit. Brian Clough set you standards of the highest level. Who wants average, who wants mediocrity? You will win nothing. Constant reminders keep you on your toes, and everyone needs nudges to keep performing at their maximum.

Occasionally, of course, the manager gave me a face-to-face rollicking, the human equivalent of being confronted by an erupting volcano. After disposing of Shrewsbury and Notts County, we were drawn against Arsenal in the fifth round of the FA Cup that season. Following a 2-2 draw at the Baseball Ground and a 0-0 draw at Highbury we lined up for the second replay against them at Leicester's Filbert Street. We lost the game 1-0, and I was responsible for the loose backpass which led to the decisive goal. Needless to say, the manager was scathing at the final whistle.

"McGovern you cost me a cup final, and don't you ever forget it!" he shouted.

I could not have been more dejected. Not only had I given away the goal, but finished the game with stitches in my head and was substituted. I felt I had let the whole team down and was miserable about what had happened. Such was Clough's anger that, despite being restored to the side, he did not speak to me for about four weeks. I was in the team, yet never mentioned during team talks.

He did eventually start talking to me again, but from that moment on, before every cup match, League Cup, FA Cup or European Cup, the routine was always the same. Before I took to the field of play the manager would approach me with his little reminder.

"McGovern, you cost me a cup final once and don't you ever forget it."

I never did, although the lack of communication during that four-week period began to get to me to the point where my mum questioned my ultra-quiet behaviour. Telling her the story was a relief in itself, but little did I know that she rang Brian personally to discuss the matter. She never mentioned it to me, and I only discovered what had happened years later when I was in Brian's house shortly before he died.

"Your mam gave me a bollocking once," he suddenly told me.

"She's given me one or two myself Brian," I joked.

"I mean she gave me a really big bollocking and not many people have done that," he insisted as he gave me the full story of what had happened.

My mum later confirmed that she had taken it out on Brian for the way he had treated me after the Arsenal game. I just laughed at the thought of one disciplinarian being soundly scolded by an even bigger one!

Despite the FA Cup loss to Arsenal, we maintained consistently good form in the league. Ironically, we began to play particularly well and pick up wins after losing 2-0 away to the Gunners in the league during the first half of February. We were glad to see the back of them in the end, as together with the league defeat we ended up playing Arsenal four times in the space of 29 days. Finishing ninth the previous season had been something of a disappointment, because we all thought we were better than that.

This time we started to show much more consistent form just at the right time of the season. Of the seven matches that followed the Arsenal game we won six and drew the other, so by the time we reached our 1st April fixture with Leeds United at the Baseball Ground we were really buzzing and in with a genuine chance of taking the League Championship. This was the great Leeds team of Billy Bremner, Johnny Giles, Peter Lorimer, Norman Hunter and Eddie Gray, who were as well known for their intimidating tactics as they were for their sublime ability to play football.

Clough had always preached against getting involved with referees, in any way, shape or form, and he openly criticised the tactics used by the Leeds players when it came to officials, because they would often surround them to put pressure on the referee when there was a decision to be made on the pitch. And there were other things about the way that particular Leeds team played which Clough did not like, for example their time-wasting. If they were winning 1-0 and it was near the end of the game a Leeds player would pretend to take a throw-in, then put the ball down for a second player to eventually pick up. In

Clough's eyes this was cheating. He totally respected the ability of the Leeds players, but he honestly believed they could have won more silverware by cutting out the cynical part of their playing philosophy.

During the game I was booked for kicking Johnny Giles, the little Leeds midfield general who, in my opinion, was a superb player. He was, however, just as adept at kicking the opposition as he was at passing the ball, so when the opportunity for revenge arrived I accepted it gleefully. After taking his legs away from him, I turned immediately to give my name to the surprised referee.

"You don't kick people!" shouted the prone Giles.

"I do now!" I growled.

When you played against Billy Bremner or Johnny Giles, you had to go into "battle mode". They were great players with a professional, ruthless streak who would intimidate you in any way possible to win the game.

This time, we won though – 2-0 with goals from John O'Hare and Norman Hunter, who put one into his own net.

Following this mature performance, we unfortunately lost 1-0 at home to Newcastle, but then drew 0-0 at West Brom, beat Sheffield United 4-0 at their place and then won 3-0 at home to Huddersfield. With an away fixture at Manchester City, followed by a final home game against Liverpool, we knew that two victories would almost certainly clinch the First Division title. But a disappointing 2-0 defeat in Manchester meant we needed a victory in our game against Liverpool at the Baseball Ground to keep our title hopes alive.

It wasn't just Derby versus Liverpool, who were also challenging for the title along with Leeds and ourselves. This was Bill Shankly versus Brian Clough, a veritable clash of the Titans. Even before the game kicked-off, Brian had made an inspired gamble, picking 16-year-old Steve Powell at right-back. He'd made his debut for the first team aged just 16 years and 30 days in a Texaco Cup tie against Stoke at the Baseball Ground the previous October and was a player with an old head on young shoulders. With so much at stake for both sides, the match was no classic. It was more like a boxing bout as each of us tried to punch then counter-punch. We were two evenly matched sides who showed the kind of commitment needed to win titles, and the packed Baseball Ground helped to produce a scintillating cauldron of tension worthy of the occasion.

I somehow managed to score the winner, falling backwards as I hit a right-footer into the top corner. Lots of people have since asked me why I was falling when I hit the shot. Well, it was because as the ball ran across the edge of the Liverpool penalty area Alan Durban went to strike it. He then dummied his shot, allowing the ball to come to me. Alan Durban leaving a shooting opportunity to someone else was unheard of, so you could have literally knocked me down with a feather, which explains why I was off balance as the ball screamed into the net. Off balance or not, I knew my connection was fine. The eruption of noise from the crowd confirmed I had hit the target.

At the end of the game there were no celebrations. Liverpool could still leapfrog us by winning their final match against Arsenal while Leeds only needed a draw to win the title in their last game against Wolves, with both games taking place on the Monday night after the Leeds–Arsenal FA Cup Final. No point in hanging around waiting to be disappointed, so as usual we packed up and shipped out to our perennial haunt, Cala Millor, in Majorca. Sun, sea, sand and a wing and a prayer required. Peter Taylor travelled with the players, enabling Brian to enjoy a family holiday in the Scilly Isles.

On the Monday night after Leeds had won the cup final 1-0, we all gathered in a lounge at the hotel where Peter Taylor was staying (as usual the management always had a different hotel to the players). It was all very restricted in those days, and there was no such thing as being able to watch live games from home as would be the case now. Peter had arranged for a telephone link from Madrid that would give us the final scores, and the reception from the phone was poor, but then he shouted out a score.

"Liverpool have drawn 0-0," he said and we all started to cheer.

"What about Leeds?" we all screamed as one.

"They've . . . they've," and then Peter's hands went up in dismay as the line went dead.

"I think they've lost but I'm not certain," he added leaving us all in limbo. There were muted celebrations, but the inability to receive confirmation proved to be a major party pooper.

That night was the earliest I ever went to bed in all our trips to Majorca. When we woke up in the morning the dream was realised then doubly confirmed as press men from all of Europe descended on our hotel, to inform us that Wolves had beaten Leeds 2-1, making us Division One champions. The celebrations began immediately, with one or two good-natured reporters and photographers very forgiving as we threw them in the pool, although we did let them put their cameras, pens and notepads down first.

I was 22 years of age, with a First Division Championship medal to add to my Second Division Championship medal, and yes, I was full of it. I remember thinking to myself, "It can't get better than this." (I was wrong.)

After countless celebrations and a civic reception, the highlight of which was an open-top bus tour ending in Derby's town square, my thoughts were already turning towards the upcoming season, when we would represent England in the European Cup. Another important item on my agenda was a new contract, and more specifically how much of an increase I might get. I actually needed a rise, having religiously saved up for the last 18 months and blown every penny I had on a brand-new, state-of-the-art 1300 Ford Escort GT. What a flashy motor!

Whenever you asked Brian Clough for a rise it was inevitable he and Peter would try and unsettle you. If you asked them after training you would always be delayed. "Tomorrow, come and see me tomorrow," Brian would say, giving him and Peter time to work out a few reasons for not giving you an increase.

We had won the First Division Championship for the first time in the club's history which should have simplified matters, but who was I kidding?

When I was finally granted an appointment, I entered the boss's office to find Brian and Peter sitting opposite each other as usual.

"What do you want?" asked Brian.

"I've come to ask for a rise, boss," I answered. Peter laughed out loud.

"Have you got a mortgage?" barked Brian, knowing full well I was living with my mum and stepdad, Stan, the man she had met and subsequently married after moving down to Derby.

"No boss," I replied.

"Have you got any payments to make on that new car of yours?" asked Peter.

"No Pete, all paid for," I explained.

"Are you married yet?" Clough continued.

"No boss," I said evenly, even though I knew he already knew I wasn't.

"Any kids yet," Pete asked cheekily.

"No Pete," I replied.

Clough then looked me directly in the eye.

"Then what do you need a rise for?" he asked.

"Boss, we've won the league and my contract is up, so I thought I deserved a rise," I explained.

"What, the way you were playing?" said Pete shaking his head and tutting at the same time. My confidence was slowly beginning to erode and I was starting to sweat, when Clough came face to face with me.

"How many games did you play for the first team last season?" he demanded.

My confidence soared. Finally I've got him. I'd played 39 full league games, five in the FA Cup, one in the League Cup and six in the Texaco Cup, which we'd won by beating Airdrieonians 2-1 on aggregate in the final. A quick piece of mental arithmetic brought the answer I was looking for.

"I played 51 games for the first team," I beamed.

Clough's reply killed me stone dead: "There you are, you're not even a regular member of the first team yet, now get out of my office!"

I was driving down the road following my brief audience, when I realised that of the 57 competitive matches the first team had played that season I'd only missed six and was injured for most of those – in the other game I had been substitute.

But the dismay during that journey was soon replaced by elation when I was offered a new improved contract pushing my wages up from £60 to £80 a week. I also received a bonus of £3,000 for winning the Championship, which after tax and deductions ended up being £1,200, all of which I later blew on another car exchange for a new Ford Escort Mexico.

Winning the First Division title allowed me the luxury of two breaks in Majorca, one with the team, the other with two friends, Patrick O'Conner and Paul Ham. Patrick and Paul were great lads, which meant no arguments or disagreements, making it a great holiday. We made friends with a couple we met out there, Jack and Sandra Mason. Sandra was pregnant and suffered morning sickness each day, so she obviously didn't fancy doing anything too energetic and preferred to take it easy, which in turn allowed Jack some free time to join our merry band.

When we first met I'd told Jack I worked in computers for Rolls-Royce in Derby. He believed me, or so I thought, until he watched me playing a game of head tennis over a sunbed against Paul and Patrick. When he mentioned how easy I made it look I had to confess all about my true career and we had a laugh and a drink about it. We had a great time with him. Having won the title after such a good season, I still remember that summer very fondly. I have also remained firm and faithful friends with Jack in the years that have followed, and also with his lovely second wife, Sue.

Jack's only regret that holiday was getting involved in an impromptu football match between the hotel's waiters and the guests. It was supposed to be a friendly kickabout, with the prolonged pre-match warm up conducted in the bar. Unfortunately the match turned distinctly serious once proceedings got underway. Dennis Rofe, the Leicester City player, who was staying in the hotel, had thankfully also volunteered to join our make-shift outfit. Spanish pride was definitely at stake as scything tackles produced one or two casualties, including my new friend Jack, who ended up with a swollen ankle. Before it got out of hand Dennis and I decided to even the score with a few bone-crunching challenges.

Suddenly our Spanish opponents became a lot friendlier, ensuring the game ended in smiles and handshakes. As for Jack, he ended up being helped by a few of our team as he limped his way back to the bar.

The close-season should have been a time to switch off and recharge your batteries after a hard season. Personally, I never stopped training during the summer, simply because playing with a ball was the best way for me to enjoy myself. So whether it was kicking around on Normanton Park, Markeaton Park or chasing a tennis ball, I was always fighting fit, and with Europe looming I was determined to make the most of yet another new experience in my football career.

CHAPTER SEVEN

JUVENTUS? LIKE A MID-TABLE ENGLISH THIRD DIVISION TEAM

Making club history by winning the league title was very special for everyone associated with Derby County. We had really put ourselves on the footballing map. In just our third season in the top division, we had come top of the pile with the likes of Leeds and Liverpool trailing behind us. The league win also meant we would be competing against the best that Europe had to offer. Unlike the present system, back then only teams that had won their league title could enter the European Cup. It was simply the champions from each country in Europe competing against each other in a knockout competition played over two legs in each round, until the final. Having seen both Celtic and Manchester United lift the trophy in 1967 and 1968 respectively, all the players were aware of just how prestigious it was to be England's representative in 1972, and we were all looking forward to the prospect of pitting ourselves against the best Europe had to offer.

Our league season started disappointingly, though, with draws at Southampton and Crystal Palace, before losing 2-1 at home to Chelsea. Happily, we bounced back with a win at the Baseball Ground against Manchester City, but consistency remained elusive as the side won just one and lost three of our next four games. It was hardly the sort of preparation we wanted for our first European Cup game, which was going to be played against FK Zeljeznicar from Sarajevo in Yugoslavia.

The atmosphere generated inside the old Baseball Ground for a night match was incredible and the occasion was memorable as we won that first-ever European Cup match 2-0, with goals from the immaculate Roy McFarland and Archie Gemmill, who had become such an important part of the team since his arrival from Preston a couple of years earlier. We finished the job off in the away leg, Alan Hinton and John O'Hare scoring in a 2-1 win, giving us a 4-1 aggregate victory.

We still couldn't really get things together in the league, however, as we kept winning one game then losing the next. By the time we lost 3-1 at Ipswich towards the end of October, we were in 16th place in the table, not good for a team who were the reigning league champions. Just four days after that defeat in East Anglia we took on the reigning champions of Portugal, Benfica, at the Baseball Ground. Their star player was the brilliant Eusebio who had become such a hero in this country for his performances during the 1966 World Cup. He had also been part of the Benfica team that had lost to Manchester United in the European Cup Final less than four years earlier. They were a quality side who we knew would be difficult opposition, and I don't suppose they appreciated the little surprise Brian had waiting for them when they arrived at the Baseball Ground for the first leg.

Brian would often pop down to the Baseball Ground before a match and water the pitch himself. "We play well on a wet surface," he used to say. "If you haven't got enough water, get the fire brigade in," he would often inform his bemused groundsman. We didn't have a sprinkler system and instead two huge hosepipes were used. Apparently on the night before the Benfica game he went down there to perform his watering trick and, having turned on the hoses, he then fell asleep. By the time he woke up he was soaking and the pitch had gallons of water on it. Sir Stanley Rous, the president of FIFA, who was at the game was later intrigued to know how the pitch could have been so muddy when there had been no sign of rain at the hotel he was staying at, which was just minutes away from the ground. In typical Cloughie fashion, Brian explained to the visiting dignitary that we often had torrential downpours at the Baseball Ground when they didn't get any at all half a mile away in the town!

Like the rest of us, Brian was obviously aware that Eusebio was a great player, but in the build-up to the game he never mentioned him once, instead it was all about what we were going to do.

"If we're on form we win the game," was all he said about what was needed.

When the Benfica players took to the field the look on their faces said it all. They were faced with the sort of tricky surface which we thrived on and the cranked-up decibel level of our supporters. And once the game got underway, they realised they were also up against a team who wouldn't give them a second to settle on the ball.

We ran them into the ground and during a pulsating first half scored three goals. I managed to notch the third with a left-footer from 12 yards, running onto a knock-down from our big young striker, Roger Davies, while Roy McFarland and Kevin Hector provided the first two. Once again, the atmosphere at the Baseball Ground was incredible and I think that the way the place was constructed helped enhance everything for a night game. The crowd was right on top of you because the terracing was so close to the pitch, and the stands were high and steep. When you added the bright floodlights and the fact that there were about 40,000 people screaming you on, it must have been like entering a bear pit for some of the visiting teams who weren't used to the ground.

The second half was scoreless as Benfica settled down and became more accustomed to the muddy conditions. At the final whistle the roar that followed seemed to last an eternity. It heralded one of the great occasions in Derby County's history. We had shown pride, passion and commitment both on and off the field.

Before the return leg in Lisbon we were walloped 4-0 at

Manchester City. Hardly ideal preparation, but completing an aggregate win in Lisbon looked relatively easy on paper.

Benfica's magnificent Stadium of Light was festooned with models of eagles, which was the club symbol. Despite our 3-0 head-start, the match itself proved to be a really stern test of character. For pretty much the entire first 45 minutes we didn't manage to get out of our own half. The Lisbon Eagles hustled us in all areas of the field. We were forced onto the back foot from the opening whistle and had to desperately defend in numbers. Complacency or conceding an early goal could have been disastrous, but the true grit and determination which often typifies British football earned us a 0-0 draw and a place in the next round.

A couple of weeks after that result in Lisbon we played the water trick to perfection once more when Arsenal visited the Baseball Ground. As usual the groundsman (or maybe Brian?) flooded the pitch the day before, but had obviously not taken note of the weather forecast, because on the morning of the match there was a huge downpour. I was standing in the tunnel before kick-off looking at the paddy field that was masquerading as a playing surface when Charlie George, the Arsenal forward who later played for England, came sauntering up round the passageway.

"Where's the pitch mate?" he chirped.

"There it is Charlie," I said hesitantly pointing at the flooded mess in front of me. As Charlie took one step on it he almost lost his shiny leather shoe in the Baseball Ground mud.

"You call that a bleedin' pitch!" he said hopping on his other leg and trying to extract his foot.

"Not easy to walk on is it Charlie?" I smiled. "Wait till you try and play on it."

Arsenal's ability to play football was severely compromised that afternoon as our team of mudlarks put them to the sword. The 5-0 scoreline was certainly no fluke as the Baseball quagmire claimed yet another scalp. One very obvious lesson Arsenal learned that day was that you can't play one-touch football in six inches of mud.

In February we travelled down to White Hart Lane for an FA Cup replay against Tottenham Hotspur, following a 1-1 draw at the Baseball Ground. With less than 10 minutes remaining our supporters were streaming out of the ground as Spurs led 3-1. What followed was one of the outstanding comebacks in FA Cup history. We not only scored twice in normal time to shock the Spurs faithful, but ran out 5-3 extra-time winners in what was a pulsating cup-tie. Roger Davies, our tall gangly centre-forward, weighed in with a hat-trick in a game which reminded us all of the old cliché that, "it's never over till the final whistle." We beat Queens Park Rangers in the next round with a 4-2 home win, but then went out at the quarter-final stage when Leeds came to our place and won with the only goal of the game from Peter Lorimer. Leeds continued their run, which would eventually see them go on to lose in the final to Second Division Sunderland.

The third round of the European Cup didn't take place until March, and we were drawn against the Czech side, Spartak Trnava, with the first leg being played away from home. Four days before the game we had a tough home match in the league against Leeds United who were third in the table. Following some erratic form early on in the season we'd settled down after the turn of the year and were just a couple of places behind Leeds going into the game. It was a big match for both of us, and it ended disappointingly in a 3-2 defeat. However, the thing I remember most about the day was getting concussion after a clash with their defender, Gordon McQueen. He actually headed my head as we challenged for the ball, and I ended up clattering into a wall at the side of the pitch. I had blood coming out of my ear and had to go for an X-ray to make sure I hadn't fractured my skull. Thankfully, I was given the all-clear with only concussion, but it left me with a very delicate head.

These days an injury like that would have seen me sidelined for some time, but not back then. We had the important European game coming up, and I was in the team for it. Every time I headed the ball against Trnava my head felt as though it was going to explode. It seemed like something had burst inside it and each header gave me considerable discomfort. I clearly should not have been playing, but people didn't think that way then – you just had to patch yourself up and get on with it.

We lost the game 1-0 but secured a place in the semi-final thanks to a Kevin Hector double and a clean sheet back at the Baseball Ground.

Our opponents in the semi-finals were the Italian champions Juventus, who Peter Taylor went to check out on a scouting trip. Brian consequently handed Peter the job of giving the team talk before the first leg in Turin. This role-reversal was unusual but understandable in the circumstances, as Peter had witnessed their strengths and weaknesses at first hand during his scouting mission. I never thought Peter was comfortable when it came to getting his point over to the players, although working with a master speaker as a partner must have been intimidating for him. As players we were used to sitting, listening and then digesting the words of wisdom that came from Clough's mouth.

So, as Peter prepared to talk to us we braced ourselves, expecting a report filled with news about their sublime ability, their flair plus the expected physical side of their game such as barging and obstruction. I don't know if Peter was trying to give us a psychological boost, but I think we were all astounded when we heard his description of the Italian champions.

"I would describe Juventus as good enough to be mid-table in the English Third Division," he said. "Maybe top half, but certainly no better than that."

We soon found out that Peter may have stretched his version of the truth a little too far, because Juventus were a very good side, but the manner in which they played the match surprised all of us.

As usual we had set off for the tie in Italy full of optimism. We knew we were a good side and there was a feeling that, despite our lack of experience in Europe, we were capable of going all the way in the competition. We always approached these big games in much the same way we would any other, but there was something which was slightly different about this particular trip. We had a guest travelling with us during our stay in Turin. John Charles, the brilliant Welsh player, who had previously played for Juventus, joined us. I'm not sure what the reasoning was behind him coming with us, but it could only have happened if it had been sanctioned by Brian and it was certainly wonderful for the rest of us to rub shoulders with the big man. He had been idolised by the Juventus supporters, and we saw an example of this when we arrived at the ground. One of the groundstaff knelt in front of John to kiss his hand, crying with joy, and everywhere we went people flocked to see him. They hugged him, kissed him or shook his hands. It was wonderful to witness such respect for one of football's all-time great players, and it was an honour to be in his company.

Joy turned into a sudden nightmare as we lost the away leg in Turin 3-1, with Kevin Hector scoring our goal and 72,000 spectators watching us being kicked from pillar to post. Roy McFarland and Archie Gemmill were the first two players booked, for inexplicable reasons, by the German referee, Mr Schulenburg, who we thought must have had some Italian relatives. I found it amazing that the referee could come to some of the decisions he did and there was no way that either Roy or Archie should have been booked. But as a result of his actions they were ruled out of the return leg.

Peter Taylor was nearly arrested at half time as he tried to intercept the referee who was shepherded into his room by the Juventus substitute, Helmutt Haller, the former German World Cup star. As we left the pitch at the end of the game I was almost in tears, astonished that such favouritism could happen during a televised game at which UEFA officials were present. They were a good enough side not to have to resort to the sort of tactics they did. I'm not saying they wouldn't have won the match anyway, but it would certainly have been a different game. The fact that it left us without two of our best players for the return leg clearly had an effect on the overall outcome of the tie. I don't remember it as a classic in any way, and they made sure that the play was constantly broken up with the sort of tactics they employed. Not only were the Italians prepared to foul us, they also dived all over the place, something which really appalled Clough, because he would never have allowed any team of his to do anything like that. Brian was never the type of manager to complain regarding referees or refereeing decisions, and he never allowed his players to disrespectfully talk back to officials, but the blatantly biased manner in which Shulenburg behaved that night upset all of us. After the game Brian emerged from the dressing room to tell the Italian journalists exactly what he thought.

"No cheating bastards will I talk to, I will not talk to any cheating bastards!" he spat, and then told a British reporter who spoke Italian to tell the waiting local media exactly what he had said so that the message came across loud and clear.

Giuseppe Furino, the Juventus midfield hatchet man who had kicked everything that moved in Turin, was earmarked for instant revenge at the return game. Unfortunately, during the match he expertly played every ball first time, never allowing us the chance to swing a kick at him. Amid an electric, pulsating atmosphere, generated by the tremendously vocal Derby fans, the Italians doggedly held us at bay until we finally won a penalty with 15 minutes left to play. The normally ice-cool Alan Hinton missed from the spot, which was a rarity for him, and we went tumbling out of the competition feeling totally and utterly dejected. I believe that, had we scored from the penalty, the impetus and confidence would have enabled us to score again. On level terms you would then favour the home team going into extra-time. But it was what happened in Turin that ultimately decided the tie.

Although we all smelt the distinct whiff of corruption concerning the conduct of Mr Schulenburg, nothing was proved despite an official investigation into the whole affair. The brutal lesson we learned as players, following our disappointment, was that the good guys don't always win in the end. The referee's suspension could never make up for the heartache of feeling cheated.

The league season finished with Derby in a disappointing seventh place, but I'd got an appetite for European football which I wanted to try and satisfy in the seasons ahead.

CHAPTER EIGHT

MAKING THE MOST OF A COLLISION

Goal of the month! It was a left-footed screamer which flew past Peter Bonetti's right hand and into the top corner, the only goal of our opening game of 1973/74 against Chelsea at the Baseball Ground, which earned me the award. Not a bad start. That win was followed by another 1-0 victory at home against Manchester City, a result which prompted thoughts of a promising and eventful season. That was exactly what it turned out to be, and we improved on the previous season's league position, eventually finishing third in the First Division behind the champions Leeds United and Liverpool in second place. But it was the events off the field early on in the season which really proved to be significant, because although we finished the season in third, we also ended it with a new manager in charge.

On 15th October, 1973, Derby County FC, our players and fans and the greater footballing world was rocked by newspaper headlines that screamed out from front and back pages: "Clough and Taylor Resign".

During their six years at Derby County the management duo had dragged the club from the Second Division doldrums to winning the League Championship for the first time in its history. Only the season before we had been competing against and beating some of the best teams in Europe as we reached the semi-finals of the European Cup and, but for the dubious refereeing in our first leg against Juventus, we might well have gone on to win the competition. Clough and Taylor had been a huge influence on my career, and with them at the helm I genuinely believed we could go on to be a truly great team. Brian was a unique manager and with Peter at his side they formed a perfect and formidable partnership. It was unthinkable that they would part company with the club, with the team they had built and with the fans who worshipped them. Or was it?

For some time there had been behind-the-scenes rumblings about Brian and the fact that he was becoming bigger than the club, and in many ways that was probably true. Not only had his success rightly earned him praise and credibility within the football world, but his personality and outspoken comments both in newspapers and more importantly on television had brought him to a much wider audience. He wasn't just a football manager, he was a character who transcended sport and had become a celebrity. He was impersonated by Mike Yarwood, he appeared on talk shows as well as acting as a pundit on football programmes, where he was superb value. The TV people always knew they were going to get a show when Brian was on the screens. He was brutally candid and that made him watchable, even to people who had no interest in football at all.

His relationship with Derby chairman, Sam Longson, was certainly not what it once was. It was no longer the sort of father-and-son relationship it had seemed when Brian first took over. Clough's outspokenness and his love of a TV camera had probably driven a wedge between the two men. After all, Longson was a self-made millionaire; he wasn't likely to take kindly to someone who gave the impression that he ran Derby County from top to bottom. I believe that Peter Taylor's position had also been under scrutiny by Jack Kirkland, who had joined the club as a director and wanted to know exactly what Taylor did as part of the Clough and Taylor package.

Clough and Taylor's last game in charge of the team had been two days before their resignation, when we went to Old Trafford and beat Manchester United, with the only goal of the game scored by Kevin Hector. Things apparently came to a head on the Monday following that match when Brian told the board that he and Peter wanted to resign. Whether or not he thought they would plead with him to stay, I don't know. But it seems he marched into the boardroom and told the chairman and directors that was what he and Peter were going to do, and Sam Longson promptly accepted the resignations.

The players used to love watching Brian on television and, despite the fact that many people seemed to think that his new-found national celebrity changed him, I can tell you that on the training pitch he was exactly the same as he had always been. People used to say that he missed training because of all the television work, but he didn't, and if he wasn't there because he was off looking at a player or a team, then Jimmy Gordon would take the session and it certainly had no adverse effect on the team. Whatever the truth was regarding the clash of egos between Brian and the chairman, the end result was that it disrupted the progress of a developing team who had been wholeheartedly worshipped by the Derby people. If the results had been awful and we had plummeted down the league, that would have been one thing, but it never happened. We were still one of the best sides in the country.

When the players found out that Brian and Peter had resigned and the chairman had accepted the resignation there was one question on all of our lips – "Why?" quickly followed by, "You must be joking". There was disbelief from all of the lads in the team and from the people of Derby in general. Clough and Taylor *were* Derby County for so many of them, and the shock-waves from the fall-out of his actions began to be felt immediately, with protest meetings and marches quickly organised by the fans, as well as a groundswell among some of the players to try and get Brian reinstated.

I doubt that the resignation of any other manager at any other club would have ignited the sort of scenes witnessed that week. He admitted in later years that his actions were a mistake, but having made the decision Clough was never the sort of person to back down, and he certainly wasn't going to ask for his job back.

I don't think he ever really stopped to think about his growing fame. The more successful he was, the more he would do in terms of his media work and the more outrageous he might appear to the public. He knew what he'd done as manager of Derby and he wanted to tell everyone, but I think that he perhaps over-stepped the mark with the chairman, and once his resignation was accepted there was no way back for either himself or Peter Taylor.

The players had some meetings and, despite various crazy ideas which included taking off for a holiday to Cala Millor instead of playing against Leicester, sanity prevailed, enabling us to go ahead with the match at the Baseball Ground in an emotionally charged local derby against the Foxes. An appearance by Brian in the directors' box only added to the volatile atmosphere inside the ground. Brian took his bow, followed by Sam Longson, in a visible duel meant to extract the maximum vocal response from the crowd. There was clearly only one winner and that was the ex-manager, who then left for London and an appearance that same night on *The Michael Parkinson Show*, which was watched by millions.

My own feeling at the time was that Brian had been unwise and very hasty indeed. He had been building something special at Derby and he was really only at the beginning of it. He'd gone in and said he was going to resign and the chairman had called his bluff. I had known Brian and Peter all my professional football life and I had tremendous respect for both of them, I admired them as people and I had a lot to thank them for, but once they had made their decision and walked away from the club I felt that we as players had to move on. We were professionals and as such all I ever wanted to do was play. I was contracted to do that for Derby County, not Brian Clough and Peter Taylor, and Cloughie would have been the first person to realise that. Going over old ground and attending reinstatement meetings just seemed wrong and pointless to me, and I never felt comfortable with it.

Thankfully we managed to win the match against Leicester 2-1, with yours truly heading the winner over Peter Shilton into the far corner of the net from an Alan Hinton cross, although I was actually trying to direct the ball to Kevin Hector. To the supporters Clough's departure seemed like the end of the world. For the players it was a confusing, unsettling time, with over six months of the season still to play. The sooner the situation was resolved, the easier it would become for everyone to return to some form of normality

There was talk of the club trying to get Bobby Robson in as the new manager. He had done a fantastic job with Ipswich and would have been top of the list for lots of clubs. It was rumoured that he turned the chance down, and I'm sure that part of the reason for him doing so was the fact that he would have been on a hiding to nothing in trying to replace Clough and Taylor, especially after all the protests and unrest his departure had caused.

Any manager coming into the job would have found it difficult, but at the same time the club realised that if there was anyone who might have a chance at replacing a Derby legend, it would be another. And so they turned to Dave Mackay.

After leaving Derby, Dave had gone on to Swindon, first as a player and then as their player-manager. For the previous 11 months before he returned to the Baseball Ground as our new manager, he had been in charge of Nottingham Forest.

It was a very astute move by the directors, in the face of enormous animosity and outrage from the Derby supporters. The constant rumblings of discontent, however, wouldn't subside, even after Dave was named as the new manager. He even got a phone call from our captain, Roy McFarland, telling him not to take the job because the players were still trying to get Brian back.

Typically, once Dave had decided to take the job he wasn't about to back down and, despite the clamour from so many people for Clough and Taylor to return, Dave knew that he was stepping into a potentially favourable situation. We were not a team who were bottom of the league and struggling for survival, which is often the case when a manager takes over a new club. Instead, we were a team who had won the Championship a little more than 18 months earlier and had completed a lengthy European Cup campaign. The truth was that we could only get better, and for Dave it was an ideal opportunity to manage a club that was improving with some very, very good players in its ranks.

One day, shortly after he became manager, Dave entered the dressing room and placed a sheet of blank paper on the table in the centre of the room.

"I know all about the meetings, and all I want to know is who wants to play for me as manager of Derby County?" He said placing a pen next to the paper before turning his back and walking out.

I have always had the courage to stand by my own convictions, so I immediately stood up, walked over to the table, and signed the sheet.

"I'm not signing anything," I could hear others saying as I left the room.

That evening Roy McFarland rang me at home, criticising my decision and claiming that what I had done was, "against the boss."

"It's not against him Mac," I explained. "All I want to do is play football and always have. Besides, Dave is the manager now, and I want to get on with my job."

Later that same evening Brian Clough rang me to ask why I had taken the action I had. I repeated what I'd said to Roy as he listened without criticising me in any way.

"Dave MacKay is the manager now, for better or for worse, and I just want to play. Besides, I'm not too good at club politics either."

"That's all I wanted to know," Clough said, and then put the phone down.

John O'Hare was the only other player I know who signed the sheet.

So Brian and Peter left Derby County, where the shell-shocked players, plus a worshipping local populace, yearned for some kind of miracle that might turn the clock back. It never happened, despite the continuation of an official protest movement that seemed unable to get on with life. We all go through traumas, break-ups, the loss of loved ones, business disasters or personal failures, and when these things happen my attitude is that all you can do is move on. As my mum still tells me, "You can't avoid what is coming towards you, just make the most of the collision." She's right, what else is there to do? You can sit and feel sorry for yourself or roll up your sleeves and deal with it.

The town of Derby and the club did just that. The team was strengthened by Dave Mackay's signing of three very good players – Francis Lee, the Manchester City striker; goal-scoring midfielder Bruce Rioch from Aston Villa; and Arsenal legend Charlie George. These players added a real positive edge to the squad. As for me, it was a case of whether my maturing defensive duties and general lack of scoring potential (my rare strike against Chelsea apart) would be accommodated within Dave's new tactics for the side.

Unfortunately, when Bruce Rioch arrived at the club early in 1974 it became obvious pretty soon that Dave preferred him to me in midfield, which meant I had to rely on players being injured or suspended in order to get a place in the side. After missing a game against Chelsea I was back in the starting line-up for our home game with Newcastle and ended up on the winning side as a goal from Roy McFarland gave us a 1-0 victory.

"John McGovern was the outstanding player on the pitch," Dave said after the game.

But although I kept my place for the next game at Manchester City where we lost by the only goal of the match, I was left out of the side after that and didn't play another first-team game for the rest of the season. Not being in the team was a new experience for me, and when it was obvious that Dave was always likely to put Bruce in the side ahead of me it didn't take long for me to start thinking that it might be better if I moved on. Some players can accept being a squad member who might be called on once every few weeks, but not me. I was not upset or angry with Dave. He was the manager and he had made his decision. He wanted someone playing in midfield who he thought could give him more goals than I could and I respected that. It is all part of being a professional footballer, and so too is making sure you protect your own interests. You have to follow that dream which, having played regularly for the first team, meant not taking a step backwards and playing reserve-team football. Towards the end of that season I was already dictating my transfer request when I got a call which might resolve my situation.

"I want you to come down to Brighton," said the familiar voice of Brian Clough.

He and Peter had surprised everyone in football once again by agreeing to travel south to take over at Brighton and Hove Albion, who were struggling in the Third Division. Having taken me from Hartlepool to Derby, they clearly liked the idea of repeating the exercise once more, but I was genuinely surprised when he called me out of the blue.

Normally I would have said "yes", without hesitation, so my reply must have thrown him.

"I might have considered it," I said. "But Brighton are in the Third Division."

Brian didn't say anything, but my ears were left ringing as the phone was slammed down at the other end of the line.

Having graduated through the four divisions of the Football League, then tasted the wonders of European football, I knew such a massive step backwards was a non-starter. But at least there had been an offer, which gave me a lift, especially as it had come from someone I admired. My one promise to myself was that I was not going to stay at Derby and play in the reserves.

The phone rang five minutes later, and it was Brian once again.

"If you come down to Brighton I'll make you captain," he told me.

"You're still in the Third Division," I replied, and the phone was slammed down even harder than it had been the first time.

Brian Clough was a man who had shown total faith in my ability, enabling me to win two promotions and a First Division Championship medal. I may have been expected to say "yes" to Brian, but despite my boyish looks I was not a kid anymore. Fighting my corner had become part of my developing character, and my character was certainly going to be tested when I eventually did make the move away from the Baseball Ground that August. On paper it looked like a dream come true, but in reality it proved to be a seven-month nightmare.

CHAPTER NINE

DISUNITED

The "dream move" was to Leeds United, and their new manager was Brian Clough. His stay on the south coast had been a short one and when the chance to take over from the departing Don Revie came along, he took it. Revie had become the new England manager and the lure of being in charge of the current Football League champions, at a club he had so often been scornful of, proved too much for Brian to resist.

Leeds had some fantastic players in their ranks and had been a force in the English game for some years. Revie had moulded the team and squad which Clough inherited and which he had personally condemned as being over-physical, intimidators of referees and disgraceful with their professional but irritating time-wasting antics. Despite all of this, he decided to accept the offer to become the new manager of the club in a move that shocked people in the game. Revie would have been a hard act to follow for anyone, but for someone like Clough, whose managerial style and football philosophy were so different, it looked a mismatch.

Brian had been at Leeds just over three weeks when he offered Derby £125,000 for both John O'Hare and I. The chance to team up with him again at a club which had won the League Championship the previous season was too good an opportunity for the two of us to turn down. Certainly, from my point of view the chance to start afresh was something which appealed to me. I was well aware that Leeds had the famous midfield duo of Billy Bremner and Johnny Giles pulling the strings on the field, but Brian had pointed out that neither of them were getting any younger, and I had enough belief in my own ability to be prepared to go to Elland Road and fight for a place in the team. I knew that with Clough in charge I would get a fair chance to show what I could do and it was up to me to impress. What I didn't know at the time I put pen to paper on a contract which gave me a small increase on the money I had been earning at Derby, was that I was about to walk into an atmosphere that at times you could have cut with a knife. I wasn't aware of what Brian had said and done with the players before I got there, but it soon became clear that he was not exactly flavour of the month with any of them, or indeed with anyone associated with the club.

When Clough and Taylor left Derby County it produced an amazing response of disappointment, warmth and nostalgic endearment. His appointment at Elland Road produced the exact opposite. The supporters hated him, the players whom he had so often castigated in the press wouldn't accept him, while even the office staff's response to his appointment fell just short of open hostility. Revie had left a vastly experienced side of established professionals, with Johnny Giles, Billy Bremner, Norman Hunter, Peter Lorimer, Paul Madeley and Trevor Cherry forming the influential militant core of Clough's reception committee.

My only experience of the Leeds players had come from playing against them, and there was the usual banter and jokes as I went around the dressing room on my first full day at the club, shaking hands and introducing myself. Billy Bremner winked and said "hello" as I walked in, and when I got to Norman Hunter he held out his hand and then held on to mine as he shook it.

"The last time you came to Elland Road you dumped me on the halfway line with a tackle. Not many people do that!" he said, laughing at the same time.

Little cracks like that break the ice and help to create a decent atmosphere in the dressing room, but I very quickly realised that some of Brian's first utterances to his new charges had been less than complimentary. He certainly hadn't endeared himself to, or impressed, the bunch of hard-bitten and experienced professionals he had inherited. There was a distinct anti-Clough feel about the place, so having two of his former players coming into the club was hardly likely to go down too well.

Occasionally players take months to settle in at a new club, some take weeks, others just days. It only took me one day to realise I was in the mire.

I didn't know it at the time, but apparently after just a couple of days at the club Brian, after watching his new players train, had had a meeting with them in which he let them know in no uncertain terms what he thought of them.

He upset the whole group by having a jibe at Eddie Gray, telling him that if he had been a racehorse he'd have been put down years ago. It was a reference to the fact that Gray had struggled with injury, but it was certainly not the sort of comment which was going to make Clough a popular figure with the players. Just to add insult to injury, he then went on to tell them that, despite all the cups and titles they had won, they could throw all their medals in the bin because they hadn't won them fairly. Nothing is guaranteed to upset a professional footballer more than for someone to call them a cheat.

Brian had gone into Leeds with his own agenda and gone about the job in his own unique way. Having flown in from a family holiday in Majorca to agree his contract and become the new manager, Clough had promptly flown back to the island again to finish off his trip, leaving the Leeds players to continue their pre-season training without him, something else that didn't exactly go down a storm. Before signing John and I, he had paid a record fee of £250,000 for striker Duncan McKenzie from Nottingham Forest, but Leeds's preparation for the new season had not gone well. They had lost out in the annual season curtain-raiser when Liverpool beat them 6-5 on penalties in the Charity Shield match at Wembley, after the game had ended 1-1. It wasn't the result of the match that caused all the headlines, but it was the behaviour of Bremner and Liverpool's Kevin Keegan, who were both sent off by referee Bob Matthewson for throwing punches at each other.

It was nine days after that incident that Brian came in for me and John, and on the day I signed Clough told me in his usual blunt fashion that I wasn't going to get into the side straight away.

"We've got Bremner and Giles," he said. "And they're two great players."

I understood exactly where he was coming from, and I certainly couldn't argue with his assessment of my new colleagues or my new position in the pecking order, but it didn't take long for all of this to change in dramatic fashion. Bremner's bust-up with Kevin Keegan had the sort of consequences neither man could have expected. Not only were they each fined £500, which was a huge sum back then, but they each received a ban until the end of September, which in effect meant that Billy would be missing from Leeds United's first team for 11 games. Having been told by Clough eight days earlier that I would have to wait for a chance to play, I was soon thrown in at the deep end.

Billy was able to play the first game of the season which saw us lose 3-0 at Stoke and then Mick Bates came in for him against Queens Park Rangers in the next match, which ended in a 1-0 home defeat. Our next match was also going to be at Elland Road, just three days after the defeat to QPR, and Brian decided to give debuts to both John O'Hare and me. He was almost apologetic when it came to telling me about his decision to put me in the side.

"I've got Terry Yorath and Mick Bates, but you're better," he said. "It's not the right time, but you'll have to go in."

We won the game 1-0 with a goal from Allan Clarke but, despite having made my debut, I could hardly claim that I was beginning to feel a part of the set-up. The other players weren't openly hostile and we all got on with training just as you would at any other club, but there was "the posse" of experienced Leeds players who I could tell were never going to accept Clough, and it was never going to be easy for John and I because we had been so closely associated with Brian.

"Don't run in front of the ball," Johnny Giles said to me before the match started, which was the support role he and Billy played. As the game progressed I was feeling my way, then I ran into a clear space, screaming at Johnny for the ball. The pass he gave me was 60-40 in favour of my marker, which ended up with me being hurt by a crunching tackle. Johnny held his hands up in apology as I looked at him in disbelief. This was a player with two great feet, who was capable of pinpoint 30- or 40-yard passes.

Soon after, it happened again and once more I was cleaned out by an opponent's tackle. Great player that he was, Johnny lost an avid admirer that day. I had always found him a difficult opponent to play against. On that occasion, I found him even more difficult to play with.

Clough's methods were so different to those that the Leeds players had become used to under Don Revie. Brian liked his usual short, sharp sessions in training and didn't go in for things like dossiers on the opposition. I was actually asked by some of them once if Cloughie ever really talked about the opposition when he was at Derby.

"Not really," I told them as they shook their heads in disbelief. "He's more concerned with what his team can do. He knows that if he has good players and those players perform as they should do, his team will win matches."

I don't think I convinced anyone, and it was obvious that Brian's appointment as manager was just too much of a culture shock for them – that and the fact that there was a growing feeling that he just wasn't good enough. I obviously knew otherwise, but despite all the ability I knew Clough had as a manager, I also realised he was in a totally different environment to anything else he had experienced as a manager. This was not Clough going into a club that was down on its luck, where he could build a team and pick the sort of players who would buy into his ways of running things. This was Clough walking into a club who were the reigning league champions, who had previously been managed by a man who had enjoyed great success and who had a squad stuffed full of experienced internationals. It was also Clough trying to operate alone because, while he had decided to leave Brighton for Leeds, Peter Taylor had opted to stay on the south coast and take over from Brian as the club's new manager.

Not having Peter there alongside him must have seemed strange for Brian, even if he would never have admitted it at the time. They were a partnership, with each man knowing what his role was and instinctively getting on with making things work. Clough never really had a sounding-board when he was at Leeds; he never had the person he could confide in or who might have told him he was doing things wrong, or should perhaps consider doing things differently. But despite Clough's undoubted self-belief, he also quickly realised the necessity to pacify the hostile reception he had received from the majority of hardened Leeds supporters. They too had read or seen his abrasive comments concerning their heroes, and it hadn't gone down well.

When we first arrived at Leeds all three of us – Brian, John and I – stayed at the Dragonara Hotel, close to Elland Road. Following one of our early training days, Brian told us not to make any arrangements for that night because we were going out with him after dinner. After we'd eaten, we all jumped into Brian's Mercedes and after a short drive stopped next to the Leeds United Supporters' Club.

"Come on, were going to see if we can sort them out," Brian said as John and I looked at each other in total disbelief.

As soon as we walked in we were booed by the majority of people there and one or two beer mats were thrown towards the stage as Brian grabbed the microphone. John and I were ushered to our seats in a corner of the club by a reluctant and unsmiling helper.

Stepping into a pack of wolves was exactly what Brian had expected. His first question to them was one they definitely did not expect. He announced that he had just come along to say hello and have a drink and a friendly chat with them, but the boo-boys were still at it.

"Can anyone tell me when the previous manager came in here to sit down, say hello, and have a drink and a chat with you?" he asked.

There was silence, followed by some of the audience looking bewildered at each other searching for an answer. The answer of course was that Don Revie had never gone in there, and suddenly Brian began to gain the upper hand. For the next 15 minutes Brian spoke to them, praising the team, the club, explaining how he had bought John and me as squad members, while at the same time answering rants from the crowd with plain common sense. At the end of his oration they stood up to applaud him

"I'm afraid I've got to leave now," he finally told them. "But I've got a match to win on Saturday."

I always admired and enjoyed listening to Brian's ability to talk under pressure, and this particular night was one of his greatest orations. My most awkward moment that night came when he threw me the keys of his Mercedes and told me I was driving.

"Have you ever driven an automatic?" he asked.

"No," I replied, realising as I spoke that the car was hemmed in with little room to manoeuvre.

"Well be careful," barked Clough. "If you scratch this car I'll cut your balls off!" He wasn't the only one under pressure that night.

While I can't say I look back on my time as a Leeds player with any great affection, there were some lighter moments during those early days, and one of them came from one of my fellow new boys, Duncan McKenzie.

Duncan was a bubbly character with loads of confidence. His favourite trick was to "nutmeg" someone in training, which meant playing the ball between an opponent's legs. After every training session some of the lads would ask, "How many nutmegs today Duncan?" It was water off a duck's back to Duncan, who had a couple of better tricks up his sleeve which would earn him some grudging respect.

"I can jump over a Mini or a Jaguar," he told us. "Although I might just have to touch the Jag as I land." His brash statement was quickly put to the test as a Mini belonging to one of the girls who worked in the club office was driven into an open space in the car park.

"Any bets?" chirped Duncan, but there were no takers, so without any further delay, he just walked up to the car and jumped straight over it, leaving everyone who was watching open-mouthed. He was like the release of a coiled spring as he bounced over the Mini.

"Has anyone got a Jag?" Duncan enquired, as people stared in astonishment. Nobody produced a Jag for him to jump, but his antics had whetted everyone's appetite for more.

"Is there anything else you can do Duncan?" asked Norman Hunter.

"I can throw a cricket ball the length of Elland Road," he said without missing a beat. "Has anyone got a cricket ball?"

This statement was followed by looks of incredulity. As the search began Duncan added that a golf ball would suffice, although he firmly assured everyone he could throw a cricket ball further. The players clearly saw scope for a bit of money to be made, so secretly, as the search for a cricket ball was concluded unsuccessfully, the apprentices were dispatched to the pitch to see which of them could throw a golf ball the furthest. Meanwhile, an excited audience in the car park were still discussing the entertainment we'd witnessed.

Word came back that the strongest apprentice had only reached the edge of the opposite penalty area, throwing from the goal-line. After hearing this, one of the senior pros asked Duncan if he wanted a bet this time.

"How much then?" asked McKenzie.

"How about a hundred quid then?" shouted someone, boosted by the report he'd got about the apprentices' attempts. There was a momentary hush in the crowded car park.

"Fine," shrugged Duncan.

We all walked round to the pitch. At the Elland Road end of the ground a new stand was under construction. The bare concrete foundations of the stand were like giant steps and dominated the scenery, while at the opposite end stood Duncan with the eager spectators behind him whispering and rubbing their hands in anticipation of winning their bet.

Duncan then casually sauntered towards the goal-line before he launched the golf ball with a lightning whip of his right arm. The ball soared over our heads and cleared the entire length of the pitch by 40 yards, bouncing once on the highest concrete step of the construction's foundations and disappearing from sight into Elland Road. We just stared after it in disbelief as Duncan continued to insist he could throw a cricket ball even further.

Duncan possessed the type of character that brushed aside any negative influences. I'll never forget our first payday at Leeds. The club must have been one of the last to pay their players in cash, so on payday the secretary would come down to the dressing room to hand out the small, oblong, brown-paper wage packets. As a newly transferred player you would automatically receive part of your signing-on fee in that first week's wage. Duncan's transfer fee had been £250,000 so when the brown envelopes arrived all the players started shouting, "That one's mine!" as they tried to grab Duncan's massive brown envelope, which included his signing-on fee, which dwarfed all the others by comparison.

There was no outward animosity towards Duncan McKenzie, John O'Hare and myself, more an exaggeration of the mickey-taking which prevails at all football clubs. Billy Bremner was always winding us up.

"Do you get paid for wearing that?" He would wryly say, pointing to the brand label on your sweater. Your reply had to be sharp, or he might follow it up with another jibe.

"You've won the bet, you can take it off now!" he'd say with everyone laughing at your expense.

When Billy shot the question at me I answered him quickly.

"Fifteen hundred quid over two years Billy," I replied, deadpan.

"How much?" he gasped, before the laughing all around made him realise I had turned the tables.

Brian's ability to win most people over thanks to his eloquence was unquestionable, but that was not going to be the case with the established players at Leeds who were never going to give him a chance. The people who seemed to be totally disillusioned by Clough's appointment were Johnny Giles, Billy Bremner, Paul Madely, Norman Hunter, Peter Lorimer and Trevor Cherry. Allan Clarke was one of the few senior players willing to give him the benefit of the doubt. Younger players like Frank Gray, Joe Jordan and Gordon McQueen were similar to me in that they wanted to play football without getting caught up in the politics, or the separate agendas of other players.

Things might have been different if we had been winning. But the results didn't really improve, which just added fuel to the fire that was beginning to rage. After the win against Birmingham in my first game I stayed in the side as we drew 1-1 at QPR and then lost in an away game with Manchester City. It was not looking good, and in our next game we could only manage a 1-1 draw at home to newly promoted Luton. It turned out to be my last appearance for Leeds at Elland Road, and I was crucified by the crowd. It was something that had happened to me with a section of the supporters at Derby, and it is not a pleasant experience. Being brutalised by your own fans for 90 minutes was gut-wrenchingly awful. After the game I sat in the dressing room, with my head down when Terry Yorath came over and put his arm round my shoulder.

"Come on John, it's not all bad," he said.

"Not all bad," I replied. "I've just been slaughtered for 90 friggin' minutes by the whole crowd!"

"I know that," he added. "But before you came to the club, they were always on *my* back!"

I'm absolutely sure Terry meant well – tongue in cheek or not.

It's difficult to describe my personal feelings at that time. I suppose it was a mixture of frustration and anger. When the whole crowd crucifies you and their damning verdict is unanimous, there is no way back. There would be no opportunity to recover in the Leeds first team. It was a hopeless situation.

Ann had been sitting in the stand among the crowd who had

been spouting their venom in my direction. When I met her after the match I soon realised she had been crying, and understandably she just wanted to get away from the ground as quickly as possible.

"I'm going for a drink," I told her.

"Where?" she asked.

"The main bar," I replied.

"You must be kidding," she said.

"No, I'm going in there, you can wait in the car if you like," I added.

She decided to come with me, something she immediately began to regret as soon as we walked into the place. The catcalls and hissing could be heard from all directions, and there were some cursing expletives mumbled as we walked to the bar.

"I'll have a half of Guinness, please," I said to the barman politely. He looked sheepishly towards me as the critical chorus continued, before passing me the drink.

"This one's on me," he said quietly.

I finished my drink, without rushing, then left the bar with Ann.

"Don't you ever do that to me again!" she said sternly.

I explained to her that I was not going to run off as a coward, like those supporters would have done. I wanted to face them and let them see they were not going to get the better of me. Not one of them had the guts to come up and confront me face-to-face.

It was not a great situation to be in. I had played four games for the club and had become the main target for the crowd. The team were not playing well, we were 19th in the table and a lot of the senior players were not happy with the manager. Something had to give and in the week following that Luton game it did.

Three days after the match, we were due to play in a League Cup tie at Huddersfield. I was not picked to be in the side, but several hours before the game I found myself sitting in the players' lounge at Elland Road along with the rest of the Leeds first-team squad and Brian Clough for a meeting which had been called by the chairman, Manny Cussins. Also in the room was Sam

Bolton, who was a director and former chairman of the club, who apparently had been against the appointment of Clough in the first place.

It was supposed to be a clear-the-air meeting, with the aim of talking about what was going on at the club and the poor way the team had performed. At one point it was suggested that Brian leave the room so that the discussion could go on without him. When he had gone, the general tone of the meeting from most of the senior players was that they didn't think Clough could manage. This was clearly not the case if you looked at his record and what he'd achieved, but I think what they were really saying was that he couldn't manage Leeds United.

I think he made a rod for his own back in the way he went about things in the very early days of his time at the club, before I'd even joined. It was pretty clear a lot of the players wanted him out, but it was the fact that it was all being said to the chairman and without the manager being there that was really bizarre. At one point Paul Reaney, who was an England full-back and one of the senior players at the club, turned to me:

"This isn't right you know, talking like this," he said.

"I know this isn't right," I replied. "What the hell am I doing at the meeting? He signed me!"

The thing which totally amazed me when Brian returned to further argue his corner was his almost apologetic manner, which then turned into compliant acceptance of the friction which existed between him and some of the players who were in the room. I expected him to spew vitriol on his smug detractors, but it never happened. At one stage Brian actually suggested wiping the slate clean and starting again. This was hard to believe. Instead of the erupting volcano, here was the polite, apologetic peacemaker. This was a side of Brian I hadn't really seen before and didn't understand.

When the meeting broke up there was no doubt among the players that Clough's position at the club had been severely compromised. There was open hostility towards him from some of them, and the fans weren't far behind. I wasn't part of the team that went to Huddersfield that night, but a late equaliser from Peter Lorimer saved the side's blushes and the game ended in a 1-1 draw. Two days later Brian Clough was no longer the manager of Leeds United. He had been sacked and as part of his settlement had managed to secure a six-figure sum after tax, and keep the Mercedes car the club had given him to use. It was a huge settlement in those days and probably set him up for life financially. After 44 days in charge of the club he had walked away with a fortune, but his reputation and his ego had taken a serious knock, there was no doubt about that.

As for me, after 25 days I found myself at a club whose fans clearly couldn't stand me, and with players who saw me very much as a Clough signing.

After Brian left it wasn't a pleasant environment for me to operate in. Having been through the situation at Derby where a popular manager had left, I had some appreciation of what a confusing time Clough's arrival must have created for the Leeds players, but it didn't help me at all, and it certainly left me high and dry when he left the club.

With Brian's departure you might imagine peace and stability quickly returned to the Leeds dressing room. The players kept telling me that if the media asked me who I thought might be taking over I should tell them that Johnny Giles was favourite for the job. Having been recommended by Don Revie, the general opinion was that Johnny would get the nod to take over from Brian. At least that was how things looked for a while before an almighty spoke was pushed hard and true into the wheels, when Billy Bremner applied for the job, to the surprise and utter condemnation of the other senior pros. As Billy entered the dressing room after we'd heard the news he was greeted by a volley of abuse.

"Fucking snake in the grass, you fucking traitor," was just one of the shouts, and there was also a lot of booing, all of which persuaded Billy to leave and go home.

So the solidarity in supporting Johnny for the manager's job had been breached in one swift action. Surprisingly, neither Billy nor Johnny got the job. Instead, three weeks after Brian's departure, the Bolton manager and the former England captain, Jimmy Armfield, took charge of Leeds.

The change from Brian's management style to Jimmy's was like chalk and cheese – they were total opposites. Jimmy was a nice man and very laid back about the way he managed. I had been used to the short, sharp style of Brian, both in the way he trained you and the way he talked to you. If Brian had something to say you sat up and took notice and he was always straight to the point when he talked to you. Jimmy, in total contrast, was quite softly spoken and it was something I hadn't come across before. Brian was a very dynamic character whereas Jimmy tended to be understated, and the difference in style was a stark one in my eyes.

Despite Jimmy's appointment, I still felt that my days at Elland Road were numbered. I had only played in four games for the first team under Clough, and it was perfectly clear that I wasn't going to get a real look-in under Jimmy either. I was consigned to having to train and play with the reserves. It was a pretty miserable time, and in terms of my football career the future looked decidedly uncertain. I decided that whatever happened I would train as hard as I could and work on my own game just as I always had done, but it was tough.

Syd Owen, who had been part of the coaching staff under Revie, often used to take training with the reserves, and he was not someone who endeared himself to me. During the entire time I was at Leeds he never once uttered any words of encouragement towards me, and I just didn't like his style or personality. He was forever criticising young players and wasn't someone I was ever going to warm to, although I do have one lasting memory of him which still smacks of poetic justice.

As part of the training kit back then we would wear heavy woollen tops which looked more like fisherman's jumpers. One day a football got stuck in between two sections of the wire mesh which surrounded the area we were training on. Syd jumped up and tried to retrieve the ball, but got the arm of his top caught on the wire and it slowly began rising up over his head as he hung there calling out for someone to help him. I looked up and laughed, before walking away. So did the rest of the players!

One day Jimmy Armfield invited me into his office and told me I had a future at the club, suggesting I buy a house in Leeds to show my commitment. I was already renting a house in Batley with Ann, so I wasn't exactly out of the area. I also felt that, despite Jimmy's words of encouragement, there was no real chance of me becoming a regular part of the first-team set-up. The biggest surprise to me was that he hadn't really seemed to give any thought to the fact that Brian Clough had signed me and we both knew that that did not exactly make me the most popular person at the club. Jimmy was a nice guy, but I thought his suggestion was a bit naive.

I actually sat through two team meetings where the players were talking amongst themselves as Jimmy spoke. There was no way on earth anything like that would have happened if Brian had been talking to the players. He would have had everyone's full attention, and it was the first time in my career I had ever seen it happen. To have little private conversations going on while the manager was talking seemed rude to me and was another indication that I needed to get away from Elland Road as soon as I could.

Not long after, it became clear just how much my services were valued as the club secretary, Keith Archer, informed me that Leeds had been offered £50,000 for me from Alan Ashman at Carlisle and also £75,000 from John Bond at Norwich.

"You can go to whichever club you want," he said handing me their relevant contact numbers.

I really didn't fancy Carlisle, so following a polite "no" to Alan Ashman, I spoke to John Bond and agreed terms one Friday.

"I'll ring you on Monday after I've spoken to my girlfriend," I said.

"That's fine, I'll look forward to it," said Bond.

On the Sunday morning I picked up a newspaper to discover that John Bond had signed Mick McGuire, a central midfielder from Coventry. I guessed he wouldn't be needing me after all.

"Shouldn't you phone John Bond?" Ann asked.

"What's the point?" I replied. It was just an example of the fact that in football nothing should surprise you.

In January 1975, four months after he left Leeds, Brian Clough was back on the sports pages when it was announced that he was going to be the new Nottingham Forest manager. I obviously began to wonder whether this appointment might offer me a way out of the nightmare I was having at Leeds. I'd already played for him at three other clubs, so it was logical to think that he might want to sign me again, particularly as he knew I wasn't getting a kick at Elland Road. I hadn't been in contact with him since his swift departure from Leeds, but it wasn't long before I got word via a reporter that Cloughie did indeed want to sign me. He told me Brian didn't want me to go off and sign for another club, but instead wait for him to come and get me. When things didn't happen immediately, I got a bit twitchy and so I actually went to his house one Saturday evening to ask if the move was still on.

"Yes it is," he told me as he stood at his front door. "But you'll have to be patient."

Brian was true to his word and a little more than a month after he had taken over at Forest he went back to Leeds with a bid of £60,000 for both John O'Hare and I. It was less than half the amount he had paid Derby for us when we'd left in the previous summer and a good bit of business by him.

Leeds were more than happy to let us go and all that was left was for me to agree terms. Terms? Who was I kidding? I would have crawled down the M1 on my hands and knees to work for someone who had previously shown complete faith in my ability. Nevertheless, I got a rollicking from Ann for taking a £30 drop in weekly wages. During the negotiations Clough also asked me if he could split the fee equally, benefiting John O'Hare's percentage of the transfer. I thought Clough was really cheeky to ask me, as he had also persuaded me to do the same when John and I joined Leeds from Derby. However, if you ever have the good fortune to meet John O'Hare you will realise why I agreed to lose money, because he's one of the nicest guys I ever met.

"I'll do it for John O'Hare, but I wouldn't do it for anyone else," I told Brian.

CHAPTER TEN

"I DIDN'T KNOW JOHN McGOVERN WAS SCOTTISH . . ."

New club, new challenge. The Forest team were involved in a Second Division relegation struggle when I joined them on 19th February, 1975, and it proved to be a painful experience for me as I tried to help them reach safety.

On a personal level, the battle against relegation was made even harder because of a pelvic strain I'd picked up while I was training at Leeds. The last thing I needed was an injury which was going to hinder my mobility. An X-ray revealed some torn fibres on both sides of my pelvis.

"You're coming apart on both sides right next to the groin area," the club doctor cheerily informed me. "I suggest immediate rest or it could escalate."

My form inevitably deteriorated with my normal week's training consisting of treatment from Monday to Friday, followed by a light warm-up the day before a match. Jimmy Gordon, who had once again teamed up with Brian, could see I had a real problem.

"Go and see the boss," he said. "It's pitiful watching you try and play a match."

I once again suffered some abuse from the fans, which I could deal with, having experienced similar protestations at all my previous clubs. Eventually the severity of the injury forced me to go and see Clough.

"We've got 10 games left to play and you are playing in every one of them," he said in his typical forthright manner. "I don't care how tough it gets, you are not missing one game."

My attempt to carry on through the pain barrier lasted until the penultimate game of the season at Norwich, which we eventually lost 3-0. Brian was away scouting, leaving Jimmy Gordon in charge of the team. I had struggled on as best as I could, until a 50-50 block tackle with Mick McGuire nearly tore me in two. As I got up to try and chase him, Jimmy was already warming up the substitute.

"I couldn't suffer watching you any longer," was Jimmy's comment as I limped off.

Following a 2-1 home win in our last league game of the season against West Bromwich Albion, we managed to finish 16th in the table, thus avoiding relegation and allowing everyone at the club to begin looking to the future and Brian's first full season in charge of the club.

My first impression of the Forest players was that with some additions the future was looking good. Viv Anderson, John Middleton, Martin O'Neill, Ian Bowyer and John Robertson immediately caught the eye, and there was one other reserve player at the time who stood out: Tony Woodcock. It is hard to believe it now, but Woodcock's potential only really surfaced when Peter Taylor eventually joined the club, after Brian nearly sold Tony to Lincoln City.

I rested my pelvic strain throughout the summer of 1975 in preparation for the new season. No jogging, running or exercise of any kind, all of which would have normally helped to alleviate the aches, pains and lung-bursting hardship of pre-season when it began. It was a pleasure to work with Jimmy Gordon again, someone with bags of enthusiasm for the game and life itself. He would have run the legs off us if Brian had let him. One drawback for a trainer like Jimmy was that, while he always wanted the players to do more, Clough always wanted them to do less.

"That's enough running, save it for Saturday," was Brian's usual command, with Jimmy desperately pleading for more stamina running. The first day of pre-season had me breaking out in a cold sweat, accompanied by a feeling of blind panic. The stabbing pain had immediately returned to my groin, making me almost physically sick. An instant consultation with the club's specialist followed.

"It may be scar tissue, which could break down as you continue training," I was informed.

"What if it isn't that?" I asked.

"Then I may have to refer you to someone else," he replied, which didn't exactly fill me with confidence. I'd never really had a bad injury and suddenly I was worried to death about my next day's training.

The following day the pain returned again following a heavy running session. Having somehow completed the session, I decided to run through any remaining pain. After three more days the discomfort gradually receded and then disappeared completely, leaving me enormously relieved. At the end of my first totally pain-free session I could hear myself reiterating Jimmy Gordon's favourite saying – "This is a good-to-be-alive day!"

Brian Clough's belief in keeping all training short and sharp was welcomed by all the players. Most clubs would spend between three and six weeks gearing up for a new campaign. Under Brian two weeks was sufficient. The subsequent pre-season matches honed up the final parts of your game. Quality always came before quantity.

Our 1975/76 campaign started with a 2-0 home win against Plymouth, but after 10 games we had secured only one other win. I used to travel into training with John O'Hare. He lived with his wife Val and family in Ockbrook, while Ann and I bought a house in Borrowash, which was an adjoining village between Derby and Nottingham. As we travelled we would always analyse team performances, and we both noticed a slight difference in Brian Clough's approach that season.

"I know what it is," I told John. "I think he's kind of going through the motions."

It was a strong opinion and I'm not sure if John agreed, but my gut feeling was that I was right. Having won promotion at Hartlepools in a team Clough and Taylor had built, then repeated the whole exercise at Derby I was convinced that the success at Forest wouldn't be as meteoric as expected. Brian Clough apparently going through the motions made him only as good as any other manager in the country. His manner appeared the same, team talks were spot on and discipline was good. It was only my long-standing working relationship with him that gave me the niggling feeling I had. I was, of course, to be proved wrong only when he was reunited with Peter Taylor.

Ann and I settled quickly in Borrowash, with our friendly neighbours Dick and Glenda. Dick was a massive Derby County fan who tried to impress his wife Glenda by building me up into something special. Then one morning with Ann at work, she saw me hanging out the washing on the line in our back garden. As I pinned Ann's underwear up she came over to speak to me.

"From the way Dick described you I was beginning to think you had two heads," she said. "But now I've seen you hanging out Ann's knickers I guess you must be normal after all!"

It was not unusual for me to do some housework because Ann worked full-time, although when a bout of ironing became tedious I remember wondering whether Franz Beckenbauer was any good at it.

That season, Derby County were in the European Cup and I treated myself by watching their thrilling first-leg 4-1 victory against Real Madrid at the Baseball Ground. Charlie George scored the goal of the match with a rocket of a right-foot shot from 20 yards, with such timing that even I had to applaud along with the rest of the ecstatic Baseball Ground crowd.

On the night of the return leg John O'Hare and Val invited Ann and I to a meal at a restaurant in Borrowash. Our enjoyment of the meal kept being interrupted by the loud clanging and clashing of pots in the kitchen. After the fourth noisy outbreak I politely asked the head waiter if there was a problem in the kitchen.

"Oh no," he said. "It's just that the cook is Spanish and every time Real Madrid score, he celebrates by throwing the pots and pans around!"

His kitchen must have been a mess because Madrid overcame the 4-1 scoreline at Derby to secure a 5-1 victory at the magnificent Bernabéu Stadium.

After being knocked out 2-1 in the third round of the League Cup at Manchester City, more cup disappointment followed when we lost a replay 1-0 at Peterborough in the third round of the FA Cup. We finished the season quite strongly, however, losing only two of our last 16 games.

Four matches from the end of the season we played Notts County in a tense derby at Meadow Lane, drawing 0-0. There is nothing better for supporters or players than the fierce rivalry generated by a local derby. Not to mention the physical frenzy that allowed you no time to settle on the ball before a crunching tackle arrived. At this time County were managed by Jimmy Sirrell, their own legendary figure, who had put together a really talented side. When the season finished they were fifth in the table, with us three places below in eighth. Following our now-routine break in Cala Millor, we began to look forward to the next season, not realising that it would be the start of an era which would surprise the entire football world.

As usual I spent a summer of practising, still searching for the elusive perfection of controlling a ball, but my form in the early part of the 1976/77 season was pretty average. Regardless of my dedication or supreme fitness, I was below my own expected level of performance. Sometimes as a professional you deliberately change parts of your routine or play, trying to gain the high-level consistency all players should seek. My form thankfully changed dramatically in October when one of our centre-halves, Sammy Chapman, was sent off at Fulham a minute before the break. Having filled in at centre-back on two occasions at Derby County, Brian Clough immediately asked me to move into the back four. Despite being reduced to 10 men, we held out for a credible 0-0 draw. Adapting from midfield to defence proved to be relatively simple, despite only being 5ft 8in tall. The ball and opposition are nearly always in front of you, unlike midfield when tackles can come unexpectedly from all angles. My ability to read or anticipate where the opposition would play the ball grew rapidly with every game. As I continued, the emergency role progressed into a permanent move. Unfortunately, there was a downside to the switch because my fitness slowly began to diminish, mainly due to the fact that my physical work had been reduced.

As a midfield player, I was expected to get up in support with the strikers when we had possession, then help the defence when the opposition attacked. At the heart of the defence, the decreased work rate made it a doddle physically. To compensate, extra training and the game of squash soon had me back to my peak. Players know when they feel fit, or should if they have anything about them. I laugh at some comments made by players who say things like, "the new manager had got us fitter than we were." Players don't work in the afternoons, so why not go and do extra training if you're not fit enough? If you feel you have over-trained then have an afternoon siesta to recharge your batteries. For a professional footballer to blame others for a personal lack of fitness is one of the poorest, most amateurish excuses imaginable.

My transition from a very average midfielder player at the start of the season to "Mr Consistency" as a defender gave me a massive confidence boost, which was also appreciated by my boss.

"John was always a very good midfield player but, playing at the back, he is something special," Clough was quoted as saying. "He has no pace, no strength, no great ability, but nobody reads the game better," he also said later.

In the privacy of the dressing room he would politely point out another opinion of me: "McGovern, my grandmother can head the ball better than you. Let the centre-half head the ball, while you sweep up behind him, or get out of the side!"

That was just the sort of comment I had come to expect from him, but I realised I must be doing something right when he made me captain. No great ceremony was involved, no

Mum, Grandma (a saint), cousin Eddie on the right and me at the front. The garden behind us is where I first started to kick a football around.

Brother Bert and yours truly with Grey Feather and Suzy, our pigeons.

Mum and Dad, what a great couple!

Captain of Henry Smith Grammar School rugby team, front row with the ball.

Kicking a round ball at last, wearing a rugby shirt, as a schoolboy aged about 13.

Central Park FC, the team I won my first trophy with. My friend Kenny Jessop is far left on the front row, with yours truly on the centre of the front row.

Hartlepools United's first apprentice, wearing a fashionable Paisley tie.

Standing proud with the Hartlepool Church League Division Two Cup.

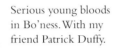

My sister June and new husband Bill (a McDonald in West Hartlepool) at their wedding.

Training on the sand at Seaton Carew, with Clough just in view.

Serious young bloods in Bo'ness. With my friend Patrick Duffy.

Iron bar, oil cans filled with cement – the sum total of Hartlepools' weights equipment.

Playing in the first team at Hartlepools United.

A signed photo I gave to Ann in the early days of our relationship.

Helping Ann's favourite player, Les Green, change his shorts.

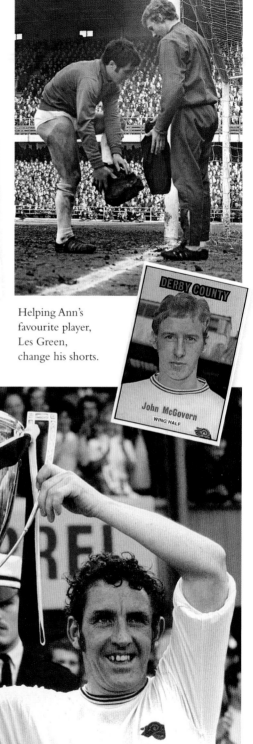

Dave Mackay holding the Watney Cup – a god amongst men.

Getting that winning feeling against Sheffield United.

Birmingham Evening Mail, March 12, 1973.

ALAN BALL

(talking about

John McGovern)

'I never get a kick against this bloke...'

● *TORMENTOR . . . John McGovern, Derby's hardworking midfield player, adopts a "come and get it" attitude with Leeds' skipper Billy Bremner in the recent Baseball Ground battle. Also in the picture are Derby No. 9 Roger Davies and in the background David Nish.*

McGovern the mighty

WHENEVER the communications media turns its attention on the Derby County side, it is usually Roy McFarland, Colin Todd, Roger Davies or Kevin Hector who is the subject — but another player has this season emerged as a major influence on the team.

John McGovern, just 22, but almost seven seasons of League soccer behind him, has now achieved a maturity and consistency to add to his undoubted skill and phenomenal work-rate.

He has become a more competitive and assertive player this season, and manager Brian Clough feels that full international honours are a certainty.

Clough explains: "When we first saw John he was 15 years old and you could have blown him over — but you couldn't miss his skill.

"We stuck him straight in our side at Hartlepool and we went back for him when we moved to Derby but there was always something missing from his play — until the last year or so.

"John had all the skill in the world, he worked like a slave for you every week, he was a model professional — but he tended to be carried along by events, rather than dictating them himself."

He added: "That has all changed now. Maturity has given him the confidence to use his skill to the full; he now decides what he's going to do and sets about it.

"I should say, in fact, that he is now emerging as one of the best midfield players in the country. He'll never be the type to run around shouting at everybody and knocking people over — but he won't be pushed around himself either."

McGovern's form, has won him back a place in the Scottish Under-23 squad, and he is very keen to go on to full colours.

● Grievance

McGovern remains something of a Scottish patriot, despite the fact that he was only a child when he moved from his birthplace to live in the North East — and, despite the fact that he felt a sense of grievance about his first taste of international soccer.

Tommy Docherty played him as an orthodox right-winger, a role he had not played since his schooldays, and after calling him off at half-time dropped him from his next team.

Derby's assistant manager, Peter Taylor, commented: "It was never on for John to be asked to play as an orthodox winger. He has got the skill but not the pace for the job.

"In midfield though, he's a different matter altogether. Just ask the blokes who face him every

by NEIL HALLAM

McGovern is ALAN BALL, who has yet to come out best in his tussles against him.

McGovern's ability to get himself between the player and the place to where he wants to send the ball has frustrated Ball every time, and the England man this season admitted: "I never get a kick against this bloke."

● Worried

Ball added: "He's not as strong and quick as some but there isn't another man in the game like him for harrying you, cutting off the angles, getting in the way . . . and he sprays it about a bit when he gets it as well."

This tenacity has made him a vital player for Derby, the man who delays and diverts the opposition's attack, and this was why Clough and Taylor were extremely worried when McGovern had to go to hospital with a suspected fractured skull after their First Division collision with Leeds two weeks ago.

The injury turned out to be just mild concussion and an ear injury.

Taylor said afterwards: "We could not have been more relieved. If we had been without John for the rest of the season the

DERBY COUNTY

JOHN McGOVERN

GETTY IMAGES

Top: A newspaper cutting from my days at Derby.

Competing against the best – Arsenal's Alan Ball.

Definitely in love –
the look says it all.

JOHN McGOVERN

Battling against Gerry
Francis of QPR.

After the event –
league champions!

At Leeds but still trying,
against Asa Hartford.

My short spell at Leeds
was very tough.

Signing for Forest (and Brian Clough yet again) with John O'Hare. This outfit was the height of fashion in those days!

With the Nottingham Forest chairman Fred Reacher after winning the Anglo-Scottish Cup (hope you like the haircut!).

As close as it gets
with The Master.

As always, with my eye
on the ball at Forest.

Seeing how real men earn a living – a visit to the pit with the Forest team.

League Champions as captain – this is as good as it gets!

Celebrating the League Cup win despite missing out on the final.

The players' wives (that's Ann with a hat on, fifth from right) on their way to the 1979 European Cup final in Munich. What a gorgeous bunch!

Serious as ever – thinking about my dad whilst holding the biggest trophy in Europe.

We've got the whole world in our hands. With the best team around, after the European Cup Final.

If you can beat this guy, you've definitely made it! Alongside Hamburg's Kevin Keegan in the 1980 European Cup Final.

Second time around it is still as sweet – winning the European Cup in Madrid.

We behaved, as these young supporters appreciated, like true champions.

Relaxing at home with definitely the better half.

Meeting a god. But Pele's humility astounded me.

Carrying Ann for a charity mile event.

With Brian Clough in Tenerife, with me feeding Alek. Two men who love kids and the family life.

Into management at Bolton Wanderers. What have we let ourselves in for?

Me and my good friend Brian Johnson from AC/DC.

Celebrating getting to the final of the Auto Windscreens Shield with Rotherham. Of course, we won at Wembley and nobody deserved it more than my joint manager Archie Gemmill.

Back in management with Woking.

Kelly, my labrador, admiring the canal, which he used to swim in next to my houseboat which I lived in while at Woking.

The BBC Radio Nottingham pundit. Well schooled by Colin Fray and Robin Chipperfield.

My son Alek and his fiancée, Lauren, at her graduation ceremony.

The McGovern clan.

My son Alek in full flow with his band, Scrim.

The Forest collection – my hard-earned medals.

discussion in the manager's office to clarify my position, or a team meeting to announce the fact. As you might expect, he did so in typically unconventional fashion, tossing the ball to me in the dressing room before a match.

"You take them out," he said breezily.

I was just glad I caught the ball.

Lead by example was what I had learned from playing with Dave Mackay, so my approach to being captain was exactly that. Cricket captains have a plethora of decisions to make, whereas football captains correctly calling heads or tails can get the job done. As the saying goes, I must have been good at the job, because I remained club captain for the rest of my playing career at Nottingham Forest.

I also got a great endorsement from full-back Frank Clark, who told me I should be captain. Frank had joined the club at the start of that season on a free transfer from Newcastle, who had surprisingly let him go after 13 years with the Geordies. He went on to have a brilliant first season with us and at the age of 32 showed all of his experience as well as superb fitness. Clough also brought in winger Terry Curran from Doncaster, and he proved to be another very good capture.

Frank and Terry were the most significant signings that season and Clough made another one at the start of the 1976/77 campaign, only this time it wasn't a player. Instead he was re-united with Peter Taylor. To describe Peter as an assistant is demeaning, as his contribution to a unique partnership was substantial. Brian Clough would always be top man, yet his change of mood was clearly visible when his friend returned to his side. The ferocity of the team talks, the discipline and the harsh truths volleyed verbally into a player's surprised face were all suddenly enhanced. The preceding season had been one of inconsistency as players got used to Brian's methods. With Peter Taylor now on board I knew things would be different.

"It's just a matter of when," I told the rest of the players.

"When what?" one or two asked.

"When we get promoted," I declared.

"Don't you mean if we get promoted?" they said.

"Not if, just when," I confidently replied.

Despite the vibrant feeling the Clough and Taylor partnership produced, our results were less than inspiring as the season began with only four wins in our first dozen games.

Our mid-season form took a substantial dip, which genuinely threatened our chances of promotion. As usual, the management had tried various tactical and positional changes in order to find that winning formula. They had also recruited a couple of new players in the autumn. One was striker Peter Withe from Birmingham, while our new centre-half was the massive Larry Lloyd who Peter Taylor found playing in Coventry's reserves. Once again, the value of having Peter Taylor around was evident, because Clough no doubt told him which position he wanted to fill and Taylor went out and got them.

Peter Withe was 25 and was being kept out of the Birmingham side by Trevor Francis and Kenny Burns but ended up as top scorer for us that season with 17 goals. Larry, at 28, and with vast experience of playing with the great Liverpool side, could not get into the Coventry first team. Larry made his debut in a 1-0 defeat at Hull in October, but before the match he had a question for Clough:

"How do you want me to play boss?" he asked.

"Larry, I paid good money for you, and if you don't know how to play centre-half I've made a big mistake," Clough told him. "Go out and play like a centre-half!"

I played alongside Larry at the back for a while, but then in March I was switched back to a central midfield role. This coincided with three consecutive home matches against Southampton, Blackpool and Leyton Orient. Despite the extra training, which I had maintained during my central defensive stint, the Southampton game really found me out physically. "I couldn't breathe in the last 20 minutes," I told the *Nottingham Evening Post* following a hard-fought 2-1 win. But making sure you did your job and ran for the team was all part of the way Clough wanted us to perform, and he would impress the need for everyone to put a shift in during the course of a match, particularly if we were defending, and the effort sometimes hurt.

"Don't just get back, sprint back," he would say. "Once you're in a defensive position then you can get a breather. If you think you are dying from lack of breath, die out there on the pitch, there are lots of people on the bench to come and carry you off!"

The Southampton victory certainly boosted the spirits in the camp, followed by four consecutive wins, pushing us towards the magic top-three promotion spots. By the time we approached our last match, a home game against Millwall, a victory was essential. Wolves and Chelsea occupied the two top positions, with ourselves, Bolton and Blackpool fighting for third place. You might call it a slight rub of the green, as an own-goal from Millwall's John Moore thankfully secured us the vital 1-0 win. Blackpool failed to win, although Bolton had Wolves to play at Burden Park the following Saturday.

Our season was over and the annual pilgrimage to Cala Millor already booked, with us flying out the same day Bolton were playing Wolves. The pilot had been under strict instructions to find out the score, and it gave him the distinct pleasure of announcing a 1-0 Wolves win, courtesy of a Kenny Hibbitt goal, which effectively meant we had secured our promotion to Division One. Once again I was back amongst the giants.

How high can you get when you are promoted, while on a plane which is still in flight? Let's just say our taste for champagne took a leap forward, with most of the other passengers joining in the celebrations. The merrymaking continued as soon as we arrived at our hotel, and the following day the other hotel guests politely asked why we had come down so early for breakfast. With drinks still in our hands, they probably should have realised that we were still at the bar celebrating from the night before.

So the promotion season proved to be a nail-biter right to the finish. We had early exits in the League and FA Cups, but we did make the season a double-winning occasion by taking a trophy called the Anglo-Scottish Cup. The tournament started in August and concluded when we beat Leyton Orient in a two-game final in December. A 1-1 away draw was followed by a convincing 4-0 home win, enabling me to lift my first piece of silverware as captain of the club. On a personal note, it had been a truly satisfying nine months. Playing as sweeper, lifting a cup, and then rediscovering how to play midfield, before winning promotion. They say that winning gives you confidence and is also a habit. I believe that season gave me immense inner confidence and belief, coping with a change in position while still maintaining the consistent form that all professionals seek.

Anyone portraying even the slightest hint of complacency wouldn't survive in a Clough and Taylor team. The pair's continual teaching, preaching, cajoling and coaching, regarding the good habits professionals need to abide by, was constant. Now that we were back in the big time, the real test of character was about to unfold.

Our first match in Division One was away against Everton, which produced a fluent, powerful, cohesive display, ending in a 3-1 win. We played so well at times that even as a defensive midfield player I tried a couple of efforts on goal in the second half. Hitting them one or two yards off target from 20 yards might be described as half-decent efforts, but the manager loudly informed me afterwards that they were "hopeless". He included the reminder that I was there to pass the ball to someone who was capable of hitting the target. I expected to be informed that Brian's grandmother could shoot better than I could, but it must have been her day off.

The rollicking, albeit on the back of a 3-1 win, was another example of the management emphasising what you were in the side to do, not what you might want to do. As Brian continued his verbal onslaught, I was saved by a loud rap on the dressing room door, and I expected the visitor to be lambasted as severely as myself. You could have knocked me down with a feather as Clough's anger immediately transformed into warm politeness when he recognised the figure in the doorway.

"Come in, come in," said Brian smiling, as the players gazed in wonder at the achievement of this visitor in infiltrating an area Brian would deem as sacred. Understandably, this was different because the visitor was none other than the Liverpool legend Bill Shankly. Following a warm exchange of handshakes with Brian and Peter, Shankly congratulated us on our performance.

Brian then invited him to do his post-match team talk, sitting down as Shankly took the floor. Without hesitation Shankly began, with his usual gritty, no-nonsense delivery, similar in no small way to Clough in his confident approach.

"The First Division season is like running a marathon," he said. "It's not a sprint, so although you had a result today the only time you really need to be in front is in May."

His sermon was sharp and concise, listened to intently by all the players. The mutual respect shown by these great managers was wonderful to witness. Built by Shankly, Liverpool was the yardstick by which everyone was measured, and his successor, Bob Paisley, was capably continuing their English football domination.

We followed this 1-0 opening fixture with a 1-0 home win against Bristol City then a convincing 3-0 win against local rivals Derby County. In the League Cup we thrashed West Ham 5-0 but came back down to earth when we were beaten 3-0 by Arsenal in front of a 40,000 crowd at Highbury, with the home side inspired by a brilliant display from Pat Jennings in goal. The confidence running throughout the club quickly overcame this defeat, and in the weeks that followed, with further additions to our small squad, Nottingham Forest began to develop into one of the most feared sides in the country.

Kenny Burns signed as a centre-forward before the season started, but in a move that was either a gamble or a stroke of genius, Brian and Peter switched him into central defence. Kenny revelled in his new role, where his striker's ability of control and composure complemented his robust physical approach to defending. Lining up alongside our other centre-half, Larry Lloyd, the players quickly and affectionately christened them the "Kray twins".

Archie Gemmill, my former midfield partner at Derby County,

was also added to the squad, arriving after an impressive away win at Leicester.

Brian called me into his office the day before our next match against Norwich.

"Skipper, you were superb at Leicester," was his opening line. "But I'm dropping you for the Norwich game – what have you got to say for yourself?"

"I'll get back in," was my immediate reply.

"That's all I wanted to hear from you, now get out of my bloody office!" he added.

Dealing with being dropped when you are out of form is a lot simpler to understand than being dropped following a 3-0 away win when you know you played well. But as an experienced professional I knew that if my attitude remained focused I would get back in, and I did.

Perhaps lady luck was smiling on me as Archie picked up an injury during his Norwich debut, enabling me to jump straight back in against Ipswich, who we demolished 4-0. This time I was back in to stay.

The signings of Kenny Burns and Archie Gemmill certainly gave the team an extra dimension. Another crucial signing was Peter Shilton, who replaced the unfortunate John Middleton. After being between the sticks for our promotion the previous year, John would have been gutted at the signing of Shilton, yet this was another example of the management's ruthless intention to improve the side whenever possible. Shilton, in my opinion, was the best goalkeeper in the country, and he never stopped working at his game. He was a superb professional, and this was reflected in his dedication to training as he pushed himself daily through punishing routines.

Later in December when Larry Lloyd picked up a foot injury, Clough and Taylor could have asked me to play alongside Kenny Burns or Colin Barrett our full-back. Instead, without hesitation, they signed up David Needham from QPR, adding another experienced quality player to the squad. Signings always produce a stimulating effect in the dressing room, if there are the right sorts of characters there in the first place. These four signings immeasurably enhanced the squad.

Successful teams are always packed with ability, the number-one trait that enables you to become winners. They also need to have discipline, something which Brian and Peter supplied in bucket-loads.

Our early-season league form continued, with our confidence boosted by a League Cup run, despite Peter Shilton, Archie Gemmill and David Needham all being cup-tied. Young 18-year-old goalkeeper Chris Woods had the unenviable task of filling in for Peter Shilton, performing with such consistency that he helped Forest make their first Wembley appearance since Jack Burkitt led them out in the 1959 FA Cup Final.

Despite the number of games we were playing, the management still fitted in a trip to Tel Aviv in November along with five other testimonial matches throughout the season. Clough and Taylor, as normal, insisted that the strongest Forest team always played, to the delight of whoever's testimonial it was. Any excuses to miss playing were instantly dismissed by Brian.

"It reads Nottingham Forest on the match programme, so Nottingham Forest will play, not Nottingham Forest reserves," he would say. "People have come to see you so you are all playing."

A demonstration of Brian's constant professional approach was perfectly illustrated at Sheffield United in October. The testimonial game was on behalf of John Harris, with Clough surprisingly absent before kick-off. A tepid 45 minutes ended with a 1-1 scoreline as we casually strolled off to be greeted by the fiery volcano in the dressing room.

"What the fucking hell do you call that?" Clough raged. "We're top of Division One and you think you can stroll about in front of a paying audience and perform like that? Any more of that and we'll be bottom of the league, you're an absolute disgrace!" and with that he walked out.

The final score read Sheffield United 1 Nottingham Forest 6. Such outbursts eliminated even the slightest sign of complacency. Clough also always made sure our feet were planted firmly on the ground.

We once had a midweek game, and the usual routine would be for the team to have the next day off, but not on this occasion.

"You're going down the pit tomorrow to say hello to some of the people who came to see you at work tonight," he informed us.

Sure enough, the next day we visited two coal faces at Calverton Colliery, complete with hard hats, knee and elbow pads as we crawled along the claustrophobic passages. I understood totally why miners would head to the pub for a pint and a fag at the end of a back-breaking shift. Even two or three days later I would still discover remnants of dust in my ears. Wasn't I lucky to be a footballer?

Despite being on top of the table in October, we then lost two games in November, 1-0 at Chelsea and then by the same score at Leeds. Having gone through what could only be described as a nightmare at Leeds, you can appreciate how keen I was to play there. My last appearance at Elland Road in front of a venomous reception had ended in despair, something I could not wait to correct. The game itself was an absolute cracker, with passing, attacks and creative play thrilling the crowd for 90 minutes. The controversial winning Leeds goal, which came while Peter Shilton was still getting to his feet following a vicious clash with Leeds centre-forward Ray Hankin, was rough justice for our efforts. My own personal consolation came from the manager.

"You never put one ball astray today," he told me as I came off at the end. For once I actually agreed 100 per cent with his comment. What we both didn't realise was this would be the last league match we would lose for a very long time.

If any one match in the season showed what Forest were all about, it was when we played at Old Trafford in December. The stadium was filled to capacity and the crowd witnessed an almost perfect display from us. The final scoreline read Manchester United 0 Nottingham Forest 4. You could not pick a Forest Man of the Match because there were 11 of them. The flowing, creative, accurate inter-passing totally destroyed United in front of their home crowd. I can always remember the slightly embarrassed look on their manager Dave Sexton's face as he followed me to give a post-match television interview, high up on one of the gantries.

As we left Old Trafford I had a conversation with a newspaper cameraman, who explained he was going to come to the City Ground to get a photograph of Kenny Burns, Archie Gemmill, John Robertson and me in kilts alongside Brian Clough. Apparently he had asked Ally McLeod, the Scottish team manager, which Forest players would be in his squad for the 1978 World Cup and he had replied, "all of them." The photographer thought the Scottish kilts concept would produce a suitable picture. I was a little surprised as I had never been in a Scotland squad before, but nevertheless I was delighted when the pictures were taken to coincide with the Scottish squad announcement. The day the squad was actually announced I received a call from the photographer who was dumbfounded that I'd been excluded from it.

"I'll ring you back," he said, assuring me he'd find out what had gone on. "I've wasted a whole day hiring kilts and taking pictures that are now useless," he added.

Two days later he rang to tell me that when he questioned Ally McLeod about my exclusion, he'd got a short and honest reply from the Scottish boss.

"I didn't know John McGovern was Scottish!" he told him.

I was naturally bitterly disappointed that I hadn't made the squad, or even been considered for such a strange reason, especially given that I had made two Scotland Under-23 appearances, and I also knew that if I hadn't made it this time, the opportunity wasn't going to come around again. I had been playing well, but at the same time I knew there was a lot of competition in midfield, because Scotland had some very good players in that area, such as the likes of Graeme Souness, Billy Bremner, Archie Gemmill, Asa Hartford and Bruce Rioch. But I wasn't about to start thinking about what might have been and, although I knew that there was no chance of me getting a full cap, I didn't let it affect me. I would have loved to have played for my country in a full international, but it wasn't to be. Looking back, I think I still managed to have a pretty good career, although a cap would have been the icing on the cake.

Revenge, they say, is a sweet thing, so after disposing of West Ham, Notts County, Aston Villa and Bury we found ourselves up against Leeds United in the two-legged League Cup semi-final, with a Wembley place at stake. I couldn't wait to do battle at Elland Road. Because of my torrid time there as a player, the local Leeds reporter rang me to ask whether I was looking forward to playing in what had been a snake pit for me.

"I suppose you will put two fingers up to the crowd if you win," he said.

"I won't do that because I'm a gentleman," I replied. "Although I might take a bow to the main stand if we get a result!"

Before kick-off Larry Lloyd was pronounced unfit, so as I was about to take the team out, Brian Clough shouted to me.

"Skipper, you've played at the back before so you can keep Kenneth company tonight."

Apart from a couple of bollockings from Kenny Burns, when I was caught out of position, things went well and we deservedly won the first leg 3-1, but I had a problem exacting revenge by bowing to my antagonists in the main stand, because they all left early and went home. After a long wait, the dream of a final at Wembley was almost within reach.

The return leg at the City Ground saw Leeds draw first blood through Frank Gray. Although Peter Withe equalised, Arthur Graham again put Leeds ahead on the night. Most teams would perhaps have wilted or panicked under such pressure. Leeds then threw everything but the kitchen sink at us to retain their 2-1 advantage at half time. The game itself was played with no real thought of defending, because we weren't going to change our offensive style. The second half saw us really motor on as goals by Ian Bowyer, Martin O'Neill and Tony Woodcock demolished Leeds in a superb display of power and precision. It was one of those games where the whole team played really well, and the collective effort was always going to be too much for the opposition to cope with. Everyone did their bit and there was a lot of satisfaction in the dressing room afterwards, not just at the result, but at the way we had achieved it. The inevitable celebrations at reaching the final never got out of hand, thanks to a warning from the manager.

"The time when footballers celebrate anything is in May, when the last match has finished and you reflect on how well you have done," he told us.

The words of wisdom were well noted by the players, who nevertheless went out to enjoy the victory in style. We were also still involved in the FA Cup with a difficult away tie at West Bromwich in the sixth round. Archie Gemmill and I had been injured in the week before the game. I was suffering from a groin strain, while Archie was struggling with a badly swollen ankle. We were unable to train all week, so when Friday arrived we were still in the treatment room. With Archie lying under our only heat lamp, Clough burst in. Our physiotherapist Tony Verity sheepishly tried to explain the extent of our injuries.

"Get your kit on now you two, you're training with the first team," Clough bellowed before Tony could get a word out.

Out on the training field, Archie and I were struggling quite badly, so before the session finished Clough beckoned us over.

"What's wrong with you Archie?" he enquired, knowing full well what it was.

"It's my ankle boss, it's badly swollen and I'm only about 50 per cent fit."

"But you're twice as quick as the opposition," Clough said. "So you're playing tomorrow, now get out of my sight!"

"McGovern," he bellowed again. "What the fuck's wrong with you?" Once again, he would have known perfectly well what the problem was.

"When I went into that tackle last Saturday against Trevor Brooking I overstretched," I explained. "They took me to hospital, X-rayed my groin and I've torn a few fibres on both sides. I just can't run boss."

"You never bloody could run," he said. "You're playing tomorrow as well, now get out of my sight!"

Needless to say, Archie and I did turn out for the 90 minutes against West Brom, who beat us 2-0, with a stunning Cyril Regis goal into the top corner of the net finishing us off. I knew Clough well enough to know that sympathy was something reserved for amateurs, but my main worry was that we were playing Liverpool at Wembley in a week's time. Thankfully, as my body seemed to be quick to heal, I made the starting XI and eagerly looked forward to walking out onto the hallowed turf for the first time.

If you are a nervous player, which thankfully I wasn't, the prolonged wait in the tunnel at the old Wembley certainly didn't help. You then emerged making your way towards the halfway line as the noise from 100,000 people erupted in your eardrums. Finally, after the introduction of dignitaries to the teams, you can focus on the task at hand. Forest against Liverpool games were gigantic clashes. Not classic matches of free-flowing football, they were more like chess games, where patience was needed to prise open an advantage.

Liverpool, of course, were firm favourites, aided in no small measure by the fact that Peter Shilton, Archie Gemmill and David Needham were all cup-tied. Although we were leading the First Division, Liverpool as European champions were far more experienced when it came to the big occasions. But our confidence and belief were vital aces that we held.

Our novice goalkeeper Chris Woods performed like a veteran, despite the match being only his sixth appearance in the first team. Liverpool probably had more possession in the first half, without really splitting open our defensive shell. My groin injury started to ache as half time approached, then, sadly, worsened which forced me off midway through the second half. Liverpool again dominated possession, while their frustrations grew at their inability to score before the final whistle came. Despite 30 minutes of extra-time, the score remained 0-0.

The replay took place at Old Trafford four days later, where I joined Peter Shilton, Archie Gemmill, David Needham and the injured Colin Barrett in the stands. Another titanic struggle evolved, until quite controversially John O'Hare, my replacement, was brought down by Phil Thompson literally on the line of the penalty area. John's momentum carried him inside the box and, despite Liverpool's lengthy protests, the penalty which referee Pat Partridge gave was dispatched with his customary efficiency by John Robertson, as Colin Barrett and I danced with glee in the stand. With more than a tinge of disappointment at having missed the game, my pride in being part of this special team made my chest swell up as big as Dave Mackay's. The Forest fans raised the roof, sharing the special moment when Kenny Burns was presented with the cup.

With our first major trophy in the bag, the relentless pursuit of the League Championship continued as Brian and Peter continued to lash us with verbal stimuli like slave drivers. No complacency or sympathy for injured players was tolerated on any level. Having spoken to players from Liverpool about Bill Shankly, and Manchester United about Sir Matt Busby, their take on injured players bears a striking similarity to Brian Clough's.

"If you are injured you are of no use to the team, you are of no use to me, or the club and you are certainly no use to your-self," Clough would remind you periodically.

A few weeks later, on 22nd April, we secured the Division One title with a 0-0 draw at Coventry. As an injured player I sat alongside the substitutes that day and turned to Brian at the final whistle to offer my congratulations.

"Thanks," was all he said as we made our way to the dressing room.

A few bottles of champagne arrived in the dressing room to toast our achievement, but the celebrations were strangely muted because we had four remaining fixtures to fulfil.

I was still injured for the midweek away match against Ipswich but thankfully recovered to receive the First Division Championship trophy before the start of our final home match against Birmingham. Having missed out on receiving the League Cup it was a massive sigh of relief to hold the trophy that gave Forest a "Double" following promotion only the season before.

Birmingham were in no mood to let us play exhibition football, and the game ended 0-0. After this, we played a quickly arranged testimonial match for Clough and Taylor as a thank you to the pair for their contribution to the club, which was a very matter-of-fact affair, with no pomp or speeches, before finishing the league season with a 2-2 draw at West Brom and the usual gritty, titanic struggle in our last game, a 0-0 draw with Liverpool at Anfield.

The League Cup and the League Championship wins made our pilgrimage to Cala Millor all the better. My wages were £130 a week and our positional bonus, having remained at the top of the league after nine games, boosted that by an extra £50 a week. We also received £1,125 for winning the League Cup, yet surprisingly there were no bonuses included in the players' contracts for winning the First Division Championship. Presumably, even the super-confident management never foresaw the improvement and maturity of their group of players coming to fruition as spectacularly and as quickly. To compensate for this miscalculation, we were offered £2,000 each to get through the first round of the European Cup. On reflection this was a shrewd offer, mainly from the club's point of view, as we had to win a two-legged first-round tie against another country's champions before we received a penny. If we did, the club would be assured of the receipts from at least two sell-out home gates, besides any prize money or television fees. We accepted, of course – with nothing in our contracts, what else could we do?

Any team's Wembley appearance is always preceded by media interviews, which multiply significantly when you are also vying for the championship. The revenue from all these interviews, newspaper articles and occasional personal appearances was pooled by the squad, enabling us to become proud Toyota drivers. So despite the omission of a League Championship bonus in the contracts, our efforts at least provided us with new motors to run around in.

CHAPTER ELEVEN

"I HOPE THAT NO ONE IS STUPID ENOUGH TO WRITE US OFF . . ."

Looking forward to the European Cup draw brought added excitement to the forthcoming campaign. Pre-season training was kept as short as possible, something appreciated by the players. Regardless of how fit or unfit you let yourself become during the summer, pre-season training could never be fully enjoyed. I was fortunate, because I trained all-year round, so it never really took its toll on me, but some of the other players would complain bitterly as professional runners or boxers were brought in to lead us on the gruelling early runs. Actually playing pre-season games was welcomed by everyone, as it was a nice break from the tough training sessions.

At the end of July we started our build-up to the season against Red Star Belgrade in Serbia. We then played Dinamo Zagreb and Osijek of Croatia before zooming off to Greece, where we drew 1-1 with AEK Athens. Then we took on the FA Cup holders, Ipswich, in the Charity Shield at Wembley, before Clough told us we were flying off to play in a four-team tournament in Spain the day after.

"By the way," he added, "if you don't beat Ipswich, you're not getting any spending money."

We turned on a powerful display to win 5-0 and guarantee some petty cash for the trip.

Winning at Wembley had thrilled everyone involved with the club, although there was one player who was less satisfied with a decision from the manager. Martin O'Neill had not only played superbly, but was also on a hat-trick when Clough strangely decided to substitute him. I could only presume that the manager thought he was overplaying when in possession, instead of keeping it simple.

Martin never forgot this demeaning action and many years later at a Nottingham television awards ceremony when O'Neill was himself a successful manager, Brian Clough was asked to present him with an award.

"I am delighted to present this management award to the one and only Martin O'Neill," said Brian as he stepped back to allow Martin to speak.

"Any manager who could take me off at Wembley when I was on a hat-trick is either a genius or a fool," insisted O'Neill, but before Martin had finished enjoying the audience's ovation Brian came forward and grabbed the microphone.

"You never were that good a player!" replied Clough to laughter around the room.

It proved that even when you no longer worked for him it was impossible to get the last word in. It was often the same when we were training and Brian wanted to make a point. He did it with the sort of wit you might expect, but at the same time you were left in no doubt at all about what he wanted, and what he expected of his players.

He was once asked by one of the midfield players at Forest whether we should pass the ball down the channels. Clough's reply was quick and as sharp as ever.

"The Channel is a stretch of water between England and France," he said. "Pass it to feet, or I will throw you in the Channel!"

He was also keen to make sure we stuck to playing football in the right way and didn't try anything on the pitch that was flashy or, in his eyes, not called for. He certainly didn't like tricks like stepovers or backheeling the ball.

"Clowns in the circus perform tricks, where people laugh at them," he informed us. "You don't want people laughing at you, so learn to control and pass the ball – that's hard enough."

Following two more pre-season games in Spain we kicked off our league programme with four consecutive draws, including three 0-0 scorelines. Our inability to finish teams off was going to frustrate us throughout the season, but we knew we were a good side and as the season progressed our reputations grew alongside those of Brian and Peter. A lot of the media wrote us off as one-season wonders, but the months ahead were to prove them very wrong.

When the European Cup first-round draw paired us against the holders, Liverpool, the media were already writing them into their headlines for the second round. Our promised bonus from the club for reaching the second round was certainly looking quite difficult to earn, but one person who was convinced we would beat them was Brian Clough.

"Oh no, not them again – that's exactly what is being said in their dressing room," he told us. "They will be absolutely petrified of you!"

Surprisingly, we had also sold Peter Withe, who alongside Tony Woodcock had been our top goalscorer for the last two seasons. With a very young Steve Elliot picked to replace Withe, and struggling to transfer his good reserve form to the first team, most people were wondering what we were going to do against the might of Liverpool.

The answer came in the form of a surprise package named Garry Birtles, who played in the first leg at the City Ground. He was a young local striker who had been signed two years earlier for £2,000 from Long Eaton United. As usual Peter Taylor had sourced him and then persuaded Clough to have a look. "The Bovril was better than he was," Clough had remarked, which seemed harsh to say the least. It might also have been a deliberate smokescreen to fend off other interested clubs.

It was like a *Roy of the Rovers* tale for Garry. Before the Liverpool match he had played in the reserves in midfield, and had played only a couple of first-team games, the last one being in the 2-1 home win against Arsenal four days before we were due to play Liverpool in the first leg.

Garry was superb as both he and Tony Woodcock caused the Liverpool defence all sorts of problems with their quick, positive running. Tony laid on the opening goal in the first half, allowing Garry a simple sidefoot into the unguarded net. To say the City Ground erupted with noise would be a massive understatement. Despite this setback, one or two of the Liverpool team, such as Emlyn Hughes and Phil Thompson, still had time to throw some jibes at us.

"One's not enough to come to Anfield with," they would say throughout the second half.

Then, with 10 minutes remaining Garry Birtles crossed a long ball for Tony Woodcock to head back towards full-back Colin Barrett, whose right-foot volley flew into the back of the net. Even the inexperienced Garry Birtles savoured the opportunity to ask Thompson a question.

"Is two enough to come to Anfield with?" he said.

Despite holding a two-goal advantage, a national newspaper poll named only three managers from First Division teams who fancied us to get through in the second leg. The game at Anfield duly endorsed our credentials as a team full of quality, character and the sort of true grit needed to be successful. The match ended 0-0, with the media begrudgingly admitting that perhaps Nottingham Forest's previous season was not a flash in the pan. With power, pace and now Garry "Roy of the Rovers" Birtles, how could we fail?

Having experienced their early days at Hartlepools, and then Derby County, I was now appreciating how good a management team Brian and Peter were. They made some surprising decisions, such as choosing me in the Hartlepools team as a 16-year-old, signing Dave Mackay for Derby County at over 30 years of age, playing Kenny Burns at centre-half and selling Peter Withe to gamble on an unknown Garry Birtles. But it was these sort of decisions that helped their unique partnership produce results faster than any other management team the game has ever seen. From a player's point of view, you knew exactly what was expected of you, on and off the field. You played with quality players who would certainly enhance your own game, and you were never asked to perform things you were not capable of doing. With the abundant quality Nottingham Forest possessed at all levels, it would have been mystifying had we not won any trophies. It was easy to work for Brian and Peter.

Having knocked the European champions out of the competition, we genuinely believed we could go on and win it. The reality of our position was that we were only through to the second round. Confidence is a factor that can overcome adversity, providing you don't lose your focus. The Forest team were full of it. Our winning ways took us through four rounds of the League Cup, another European adventure, when we crushed AEK Athens 7-2 on aggregate, before we lost our unbeaten league run with a 2-0 defeat at Anfield on 9th December, 1978.

We had gone 42 top-flight league games without losing, and it seemed like a record no one would overtake at that time. I am glad in many ways that it was Arsenal who finally managed to beat it with 49 in 2004, as they played a similar brand of football, with lots of one-touch passes accompanying the willingness to run and join in whenever required. If there was to be a comparison between past and present, I would say that we were more direct, certainly more physical and, yes, we would have beaten them!

In January 1979 we only played one league match, losing 2-1 at Arsenal, only our fifth league defeat since the beginning of the previous season. To make up for that we beat Aston Villa 2-0 in the FA Cup third round and reached our second consecutive League Cup Final, beating Watford 3-1 over the two-legged semi-final.

We also beat York City 3-1 in the FA Cup fourth round at the City Ground in two inches of snow. I remember the game pretty well for two specific reasons. First, I was waiting patiently in the dressing room before kick-off, for Brian to remind me of the goal I'd given away against Arsenal during my Derby days, just as he had done before every cup game since, but the barbed comment never came. I walked out of the dressing room and began striding down the tunnel. Just as I was about to set foot on the pitch, a hand gripped my right shoulder, and as I spun around I came face to face with the manager.

"You know what I'm going to say to you don't you?" he said.

"Yes boss, I cost you a cup final once," I said.

"And don't you ever forget it!" he growled.

The other reason I remember the match was because of the sweet 20-yard right-foot volley I scored with. I remember all my goals, mainly because I didn't score that many. Forest fans would add the lack of goals to their list of criticisms of my play. However, after the promotion season I developed a real understanding of playing centre-midfield, knowing the position inside out, while my tackling had definitely improved following the stint as a centre-half.

The understanding of the "holding role", as it's called in the modern game, was not the singular reason I didn't score many goals. Even during matches we were dominating, and where I might have felt inclined to advance, there was always a reminder from the bench.

"Where the hell are you going?" was the usual warning rattling in my ears when I vacated the central position. I still never saw the necessity of such rigid discipline until the manager, in his succinct manner, proved a point. During a home match that we were totally dominating, I sat down at half time expecting perhaps a word or two of praise.

"Where the hell do I ask you to play?" Clough shouted, with his face dangerously close to mine.

"Midfield, boss," I said slightly taken aback.

"I'll ask you again," said Clough. "Where do I ask you to play?"

My brain thankfully reacted quickly.

"The holding role in midfield, boss," I replied.

"In the first half I saw you near the opposition's corner flag, where we lost the ball, and with your pace it took you two weeks to get back," he informed me. "If I see you near the opposition's corner flag in the second half you're coming off. I don't care what you want to do, it's what you do for the team that counts."

This example gives you an idea of how well organised and disciplined the side was becoming. Experience means you know when to go, where to go and how to go, regardless of being three goals up or three goals down.

As the season progressed we were always chasing Liverpool in the league, mainly because of the number of matches we'd drawn instead of winning. We also had the added disappointment of losing 1-0 against Arsenal in the FA Cup fifth round at the City Ground at the end of February. Two days before that game a new addition had made his first-team debut for the club when he came on as a second-half substitute in the 2-0 home win against Bristol City. His name was Trevor Francis, and he had been signed two weeks earlier in English football's first £1 million deal, which saw him move from Birmingham City.

In March we comfortably beat Grasshoppers Zurich of Switzerland 5-2 on aggregate to qualify for the semi-finals of the European Cup, where we were drawn against Cologne of Germany.

Sandwiched between the Grasshoppers games there was a small matter of retaining the League Cup at Wembley.

The evening before the final, when I would be leading out the Forest team against Southampton, after dinner at our hotel Clough and his right-hand man Peter Taylor had gathered the players together for a short team talk. However, Clough had spotted one absentee, Archie Gemmill, a player so dedicated he always went to bed earlier than any other professional footballer I have ever met.

"Go and get him," Brian Clough told one of the coaching staff.

Eventually Archie appeared, clearly none too pleased at being summoned from his bed, and sat down looking as annoyed as could be. Before he started speaking, Clough walked up and down in front of the players, looking to see if our concentration and mood was positive. One glance at Archie must have told Brian that his little Scottish midfielder was annoyed. Clough approached him.

"Would you like a drink, Archie?" he asked.

"I want to go to bed, boss," Archie replied firmly.

Clough hesitated, then spotted a waiter on the far side of the room.

"Hey pal, I'd like a dozen bottles of your best champagne," he shouted at the waiter before turning back to the rest of us.

"And you lot are going to drink it because it's expensive," he told us.

The champagne duly arrived, so with a squad of about 15 players, plus one or two coaching staff together with Brian and Peter, we quickly finished the champagne. Clough again looked round at the players, finally settling his gaze on Archie, who was looking even more miserable than he had been before.

"Did you like the champagne, Archie?" Clough asked.

"I want to go to bed, boss," Archie said once more.

"Waiter, pal," Clough shouted immediately. "I would like another dozen bottles of that champagne."

The bottles duly arrived and, although it took longer the second time around, we managed to finish them. By this time some of the players, me included, were getting slightly fidgety, or perhaps just slightly merry.

"Did you like the champagne this time, Archie?" Clough enquired.

Archie rose from his seat, and immediately there were a few disgruntled comments from the rest of the players.

"For Christ's sake, Archie, don't say you want to go to bed, we're half pissed as it is," someone said.

"That champagne was great Boss, can I have another glass?" Archie said looking straight at Clough.

"We've got a cup final to play tomorrow," screamed Brian. "Get to bed now you little shit!"

Some players suffer from pre-match nerves, but when my head touched the pillow that night I was out like a light.

Our preparation the next morning was unchanged from the previous year. Breakfast was optional, then we all had to be downstairs at 11 o'clock to go for a stroll. After lunch, we took a short bus ride to Wembley. The sights and sounds of the crowd as the bus eased its way through the fans were always something I loved. I used to just sit quietly, looking out of a window as I tried to drink it all in. The coach made its way to the dressing-room area at one end of the stadium and then the huge doors opened up allowing the bus to drive into the tunnel and actually park next to our dressing room. Playing in a cup final at Wembley was not only special, but different as well.

During the pre-match warm-up, more than a few players complained about the quality of the footballs. They were new Football League balls, with red-coloured panels complementing the normal white ones. Someone had had the truly uninspired brainstorm of introducing this untried innovation for the final.

Back in the dressing room, acting on the players' criticism, Brian, dressed in a suit and tie, inspected one of the balls. Trevor Francis, who was cup-tied, was standing quietly in the corner looking really smart in his club blazer.

"Our Nigel would like one of these," said Brian as he held the very muddy ball. "Get that cleaned for him would you Trev?" he added as he threw the ball at Trevor Francis. Trevor caught it, his blazer splattered with mud as he did so. I am sure Trevor was annoyed, but he dutifully disappeared into the washroom with the ball.

The main difference between playing at the old Wembley compared to normal league grounds was the extended walk from the end of the pitch to the centre of the field; that's often when nerves strike a player, but it never happened with me. It can be a bit disconcerting for a player, because once you are out there on the pitch you realise just how big the place is, and how far away the fans are, but at the same time there seemed to be an almost constant wall of noise coming from the two sets of supporters. I just felt impatient and eager to start playing.

I tried unsuccessfully to spot my better half, Ann, in the stands, then, following a courteous introduction of the team to the dignitaries of the day, one of whom was Lord Westwood, we got down to business.

Snow surrounded the pitch after some snowstorms during the week. The pitch looked fine on the surface but was in a terrible state because they'd just had the Horse of the Year show on it and the surface had never really recovered. Instead of looking and feeling like a bowling green, it resembled the pitch at the Baseball Ground when I played for Derby. It was muddy and cloying, detrimental to our quick-passing game, and the pitch slowly deteriorated as the game progressed.

Our first-half display was poor, and after 16 minutes Southampton took the lead through David Peach. As we walked back to the centre circle to kick off I felt a punch in my back, and I whirled round to see a grinning Alan Ball, the Southampton captain.

"What do you want Bally?" I snarled.

"This is Wembley, son," he said, grinning like a Cheshire cat. "Try and enjoy it while you're here."

The dressing room at half time was not a pleasant place to be. The manager compared us to creatures who lived below rocks in the bottom of ponds. "How dare you underperform with your wives, girlfriends, relations and supporters in the stands," he added before we re-emerged into the arena.

Our performance improved markedly in the second period, with Garry Birtles scoring twice and Tony Woodcock grabbing our third before Nick Holmes scored a consolation second for Southampton. After Garry had put us 2-1 up, I passed Alan Ball as I ran back to the centre circle. I really wanted to whack him, but decided to pinch his bum instead. He turned on me fuming.

"What do you want?" he spat.

"Well this is Wembley, Alan, why don't you enjoy yourself while you're here?"

Revenge is sweet, although, with Ball on a revenge mission of his own, I kept eyes in the back of my head until the final whistle blew. So, duff balls or not, I lifted the League Cup at Wembley.

"What's it like?" supporters ask. It's simply an explosion of adrenaline mixed with an immense pride, joy and excitement.

Then we carefully descended the many steps to the pitch for the traditional lap of honour as we savoured that glorious feeling of success.

The following day I was casually reading some of the press comments, which cited an inspirational half-time team talk by the manager as the reason for our triumph. There was, of course, another possible explanation: perhaps it had taken us all until half time to work off the effects of the champagne from the night before!

Following the comfortable passage against Grasshoppers, our opening leg of the semi-final of the European Cup would prove to be one of the most fluctuating matches of a glorious season. Our confidence was sky-high as we took to the pitch at the City Ground against Cologne. We had won four and drawn one of our previous five league matches, but nobody realised that this was going to be one of the classic ties in European Cup history that would have the Forest fans crowing for years to come.

Our normal tactics were to try and run the opposition off their feet, hustling at every opportunity, giving them no time on the ball. For once, in the first half, our total commitment going forward caught us out. On the developing mud bath, we suffered from some superb counter-attacking, which gave a 2-0 advantage to our opponents through Roger Van Gool and Dieter Muller. We pushed forward relentlessly until Garry Birtles finally headed in after 27 minutes. Shots were raining in at both ends, with no apparent willingness by either side to defend, and this only intensified the excitement, producing a pulsating, nerve-tingling atmosphere. Defensive tactics were cast aside, as both sides served up a football fiesta, and at half time Cologne led 2-1.

The second half continued in the same vein, as the pitch began to resemble a ploughed field. Another Forest assault on the Germans saw Ian Bowyer strike a superb equaliser from 15 yards, then the rarity of a John Robertson header incredibly put us 3-2 in front. Something even rarer occurred when Peter Shilton let Japanese substitute Okudera fire a 20-yarder under his dive to earn the visitors a more than favourable 3-3 draw. A national newspaper headline of "Forest Sunk By Jap Sub" hinted that our European campaign might be over.

Having played with a heavy cold I could barely raise a gallop the next two days and missed out on our 2-1 win at Derby County on the Saturday. Following draws against Leeds and Manchester United at home, we won 2-0 at Birmingham, before flying to Germany for our second-leg tie against now red-hot favourites Cologne.

One of Brian and Peter's great attributes was their ability to mentally relax the squad before big games. They never built up the reputation of our opposition, concentrating solely on reminding their players how good they were. I vividly remember Brian being interviewed immediately following our 3-3 draw against Cologne in the first leg. Looking straight into the lens on the camera he said, "I hope that no one is stupid enough to write us off." The media, in general, had written us off, though. So had the Germans who printed a European Cup Final brochure featuring Cologne! Forward planning by the Germans was understandable because, with three away goals that might eventually count double, they didn't even need to win the game.

Before we took to the field in Cologne there were the usual "How are you?" enquiries from Brian and Peter to a few of the players, with "Fine, boss" as the standard reply.

"I'm delighted," Brian said, "Because this lot are in for the shock of their lives."

There was a subtle difference between the two games with Cologne. The first had been frantic, hectic, end-to-end football with no inhibitions. The second game became more of a tactical affair.

In the first half the Germans, as expected, made the early running, missing a great chance when Muller shot wide when ideally placed. In the second half of this very tense encounter we won a corner on the left side of our attack. John Robertson floated a near-post corner to Garry Birtles, whose flicked header reached Ian Bowyer on the six-yard line. Ian didn't miss from there, and for the remaining 25 minutes the red wall would not be broken.

Arms lifted in unison as the final whistle signalled our win and a place in the European Cup Final. I turned as someone in a suit ran past me. I could not believe anyone had reached the pitch that quickly, but it was our commercial manager John Carter, running around like a wild thing. I ran off looking for the nearest red shirt to hug, as the jumping, fist-pumping, arms aloft salutes celebrated the moment. The underdogs had done it. The has-beens, the nearlies, the unfashionable team of misfits, had reached the final of the European Cup against the odds.

In the buoyant dressing room the manager conducted his usual post-mortem with compliments offered to various players. Knowing I had played well, I was tentatively hoping for a favourable comment from Clough. But he didn't say anything to me, which disappointed me slightly, knowing how well I had performed.

Before I got in the bath, though, I caught him looking at me as I cleaned my boots on a sock. A polite nod of his head as he looked at me said it all. That look made me feel like a million dollars. No words were required, as I knew Cloughie meant well done. Such recognition was echoed by German midfield legend, Günter Netzer, the following day when he was quoted by the German national press.

"Who is this McGovern? I have never heard of him, yet he ran the game in the second half," he said.

We lost only one of our remaining seven league matches, 1-0 to Wolves at Molineux, making it the second consecutive season in which we lost only three league matches. Having drawn so many games, however, we finished runners-up to Liverpool, who had again won the Division One title. With our last league game being played at West Bromwich on 18th May, we still had 10 days to fill before travelling to the Olympic Stadium in Munich for the final of the European Cup.

Leading up to that final, our training decreased with shorter sessions but still with that explosive intensity, keeping our concentration firmly in place. Our biggest problem was the fitness of Archie Gemmill and Martin O'Neill. They had both pleaded their cases, trying to convince Brian that they were 100 per cent fit. Trevor Francis, who had not played in any of the previous European matches because he was ineligible due to the timing of his signing, was another contender for the final line-up.

Our opponents in the final were going to be Swedish side Malmö coached by an Englishman Bobby Houghton. Idle hands make the devil's work, so before we flew out to Munich we played Mansfield Town on the 23rd May in the County Cup Final. This game allowed Archie a run out following injury which meant that, along with Martin O'Neill, he had proved his fitness, if selected for the final.

In Munich, with the players gathered round him, ears at the ready, Brian announced the team. Archie and Martin were not playing. I would find it hard to describe the feelings of Archie and Martin, who were both massive contributors in all the previous rounds leading to the final tie, but I know that they must have been devastated. My own feeling was one of relief once I found out that I was definitely in the side, and someone else who was going to play was my roommate, Trevor Francis, who would make his European Cup debut. Despite being a recognised striker, Clough and Taylor picked him to play in a wide-right position. Malmö had injury problems as well, with their two recognised strikers unable to play.

With our chests puffed out with pride, we walked out for the kick-off. It's strange to recall the magnificent Olympic Stadium in Munich was only just over half-full, an impossible statistic in modern-day football. Regardless of this, we were confident and eager to put on a show for our legions of fans who had faith-fully followed us throughout our European campaign.

Compared to our epic semi-final battle with Cologne, the game against Malmö was certainly no classic. We took control of the match immediately, dominating in most areas, with an early effort from Garry Birtles going close. Malmö's nearest effort was a tame lob, which Peter Shilton had no trouble catching, following an unusual Kenny Burns slip. Just before half time Ian Bowyer swept a ball out to John Robertson on the left. Confronted by two defenders, a quick feint threw them both off balance. A precision left-foot cross had the keeper struggling, as the ball found Trevor Francis at the far post. His header was unchallenged, such was the quality of the cross, but coming in from his wide position Trevor still had to keep his eye on the ball, connecting perfectly to score.

The goal portrayed the Forest style perfectly: win the ball in midfield, give it quickly to the genius on the left wing, then feed on his delivery to complete the end product.

We should have added to the single-goal tally, John Robertson going closest when he struck the post after Trevor Francis tried to repay the compliment which had brought his goal.

When the final whistle sounded we ran around aimlessly like giddy schoolboys let out of school early, before lining up to climb the steps towards the coveted trophy. After a little hesitancy from the dignitary presenting the cup, I double-checked to make sure the UEFA badge was front-side before lifting the trophy. Inside I was bursting with pride, and I then had to walk carefully down so that we could go on our lap of honour, with Larry Lloyd waiting to relieve me of the burden of carrying the huge cup. Larry was always my shadow when it came to helping me carry such a weight, but even if the cup had been made out of solid lead, I would still have managed it in one hand that night. In reality the European Cup is surprisingly light. And that first time I lifted it in front of those delirious Forest fans I felt strong enough to take on Muhammad Ali with one hand tied behind my back.

When we returned to Nottingham for an open-top bus parade through the city centre, almost 200,000 people came out to cheer us on. At last we were awarded some recognition from the media, as our record had obliterated any last doubters following the consistent quality we had produced over the last two seasons.

My wages at that time were £200 per week, although the £5,000 bonus we received for the European Cup win made me feel rich. Had we lost the final our appearance bonus would have been zero. As the management always reminded us, bonuses are paid for success, not failure.

Having played almost 70 games that season, I considered myself worthy of a rise, and I duly signed a new contract giving me £240 a week, rising to £300 two years later. Having won promotion at Hartlepools on £18 a week, then at Derby on £25 a week, the First Division Championship at Derby on £60, promotion at Forest on £100 a week and the First Division Championship at Forest on £130 a week the year before, I considered my new contract well earned. My love and obsession with playing football had given me respect from all corners, and in many ways that meant more than money. Sure it was important, and it was nice to get paid for what I did, but it was never my number-one priority.

Perhaps naively, I never really argued with Brian and Peter over the terms of a contract. Basically, I always earned enough to live comfortably and perhaps the management were right when they told me, "You should be paying us to play at this club!" I also understood that Clough and Taylor had their limits regarding how much they would give you and perhaps considered their offers to be fair. In a nutshell, the money didn't bother me, as I was living in utopia, doing exactly what I wanted to do. Being young, fit, healthy and happy is an unbeatable combination.

CHAPTER TWELVE

REPEAT PERFORMANCE

"I've had to pay £500,000 to replace you," I was politely informed by the manager a few weeks after captaining Nottingham Forest to our historic European Cup success. He was referring to one of his big signings of summer 1979, Manchester City midfielder, Asa Hartford. The comment wasn't really necessary, because the signing had already put me on my toes.

Frank Gray, a left-back from Leeds United also joined the club. Frank Clark had retired and Colin Barrett, our other full-back, was struggling against his long-term knee injury, so Frank's signing was a real necessity.

With five pre-season games still to play, I knew the first-team picture would be clearer once our league programme started. Then suddenly Archie Gemmill left to sign for Birmingham City, leaving the midfield selection between Asa Hartford, Martin O'Neill, Ian Bowyer and myself for three places. When we played a game in Spain I lined up alongside Martin and Asa, with Ian Bowyer the unlucky one. While Asa was a very gifted player, his style didn't really seem to suit the team, and, with the benefit of hindsight, a casual conversation after the match indicated that the management were thinking the same thing.

Brian asked me to accompany him on the short walk back to our hotel.

"I want you to sign a new contract," he said.

"I've just signed one, boss, before the tour," I replied, wondering why it could have possibly slipped his mind.

"I have to give you wages comparable to the new signings we've brought to the club," Brian continued, "so when we get back to Nottingham you can sign it then."

I knew I had played well, but I was slightly dumbfounded by the manager's statement. When he asked me to walk with him I half expected a discussion on how I had found playing with Asa, or at least a telling-off for doing something wrong. You can imagine my surprise when we got back to Nottingham to find my wages hiked to £400 per week, a huge increase on the £240 I'd signed for just two weeks before. At this time players' wages or details of contracts were not public knowledge and it never concerned me how much other players were earning. It was nice to get more money, but my satisfaction came from being able to stay in what I considered to be a very special team.

When our league programme started we won our first three fixtures, with 1-0 victories over Ipswich and Stoke, before a resounding 4-1 win at home against Coventry with a midfield made up of O'Neill, Hartford and me. I was playing as well as I could and even managed to score two against Coventry. Surprisingly, after this particular game Asa was sold to Everton. As quickly as he'd arrived, he'd left. Perhaps because the management's thoughts on replacing me had changed – who knows?

In 1979/80, our league form was inconsistent. Although we did lead the table on several occasions early on and into the autumn, a bad November and December saw us slip down the league and by the turn of the year we were in eighth position. In contrast, we were able to keep our supporters happy with our performances in defence of the European and League Cups.

In the European Cup we took care of Sweden's Osters Vaxjo, beating them 2-0 at home and drawing 1-1 at their ground. In the League Cup we demolished Blackburn 7-1 on aggregate over two legs, before going to Middlesbrough and beating them 3-1 in a straight knockout tie in the third round.

We then beat Arges Pitesti of Romania 2-0 in the second round first leg of the European Cup at the City Ground and followed that with a 2-1 win away from home. We also brushed aside Bristol City 3-0 in a League Cup replay after a 1-1 draw away from home.

Clough and Taylor were always pulling surprises on everyone, so when we carelessly lost our proud, long unbeaten home run to lowly Brighton, a lot of people might have thought we would strengthen the squad. Instead, we sold Tony Woodcock to Cologne, to be replaced soon after by Stan Bowles. Tony Woodcock in his prime being replaced by Stan was a strange managerial decision. As players you accept that comings and goings are part of everyday life, but you still carry your own opinions, and I put this exchange firmly in the debit column. Archie Gemmill and Tony Woodcock both going were transfers that bemused players and the public alike, although I knew there would be no problem with Stan, despite his colourful image, under the disciplined management at Forest.

What went in Stan's favour was his ability to settle in, which from a social point of view took him 10 seconds. I really appreciated his bubbly personality, although I refused to join in with his betting habit, which would extend to which raindrop would reach the bottom of the coach window on a rainy away trip. As a striker Stan was certainly not the bravest, at times, so when he went down injured following an aerial collision at Coventry in his third game screaming loudly, hands covering his face, I immediately shouted for the trainer. As I reached him, lying prone, hands still covering his face, he was screaming in apparent agony.

"Stan, Stan!" I pleaded. "Are you okay or is it a bad one?"

Slowly his hands parted, unveiling his face, with his eyes staring at me inquisitively.

"Oh it's you Jock," he said smiling. "I'm only having a breather."

We also signed Charlie George from Southampton on a month-long loan as we struggled to maintain consistency, a factor we had lost in comparison to our last two seasons.

Our league form continued to be indifferent at the start of

the new decade, but once again our cup form proved to be a different matter. At the end of January we beat arch-rivals Liverpool 1-0 in the League Cup semi-final first leg and, although we then lost 2-0 to them at home in the FA Cup fourth round, we went on to secure a slim 1-0 victory at the City Ground over Barcelona in the first leg of the European Super Cup. I was left out, or "rested" as the manager put it, for the Barcelona game then relieved to be chosen for the return leg at the magnificent Nou Camp Stadium.

Our national media devalued the Super Cup as a meaningless exercise. The 90,000-odd people that turned up emphasised a slightly more serious appreciation. The prestige of a possible Spanish victory over the European champions guaranteed the near-full house. The atmosphere was electric, with their fans driving on the home team, who levelled the aggregate scores through a penalty. However, the true grit that had become our trademark saw us regain the lead when Kenny Burns firmly headed in from a corner. The only unusual occurrence in the course of our fluent display was John Robertson's penalty miss, proving that he was human after all. Despite that, we won 2-1 on aggregate thanks to another inspired performance.

The post-match celebrations in the dressing room were well underway when Clough shouted over to me.

"Skipper," he said, which always quietened the room. "You played well tonight. In fact, you were our fourth-best player!"

As we left the stadium, walking towards our coach, we were applauded continuously by a phalanx of smiling Barcelona supporters. This appreciation provided further proof of Nottingham Forest's growing reputation throughout Europe.

The League Cup semi-final second leg followed, with us again holding onto a slender 1-0 lead to take to Anfield. I attended a Forest supporters meeting prior to the game, with the consensus of opinion among even some of our die-hards that 1-0 might not be enough.

"Well we've just done exactly that in Barcelona," I told them, "so why not at Anfield?"

The performance at Anfield was once again both determined

and organised. John Robertson put us 1-0 ahead, but Liverpool replied in the dying seconds with a goal from the man they called "Supersub", David Fairclough.

Games against Liverpool were tense struggles, wars of attrition rather than flowing, skilful classics you might expect from two great sides, but the score remained the same, allowing us to make our third consecutive League Cup Final appearance at Wembley.

In March we took on Dynamo Berlin in the European Cup and played four league matches plus the League Cup Final against Wolves. Our inconsistency proved problematic when we lost 1-0 to the East Germans in the first leg at the City Ground, but our third consecutive Wembley appearance as favourites should have guaranteed enough of a performance to overcome Wolves. A hugely disappointing display saw us gift a tap-in winner for Andy Gray, following a kamikaze collision between centre-half Dave Needham and goalkeeper Peter Shilton. Neither side had looked likely to score, so it was inevitable a mistake would provide a winner, which unfortunately came for the opposition that day.

There was no ranting and raving from Brian after the game; I think he just saw it as a one-off. It wasn't as though we were in some kind of slump in form. We'd lost a football match, end of the story. Obviously everyone was disappointed and it would have been great to have got a hat-trick of victories in the final of the competition, but we all knew we had to look forward and not dwell on what had happened. We also knew that there was another huge game coming up.

With the European Cup return leg against Berlin only a few days away, the big question was whether we could recover mentally and physically to win in Berlin. Wembley is a wonderful venue when you win. Losing a final there can leave you drained and despondent, a feeling exacerbated by watching the winning team celebrate.

Ironically, I had organised a party at my house to follow the final. This was the first time I had ever arranged what was supposed to be a post-match celebration. It's not that I could be accused of counting chickens, this was a get-together to rekindle our relationship with some close friends. I was the last to arrive at our house and Ann had already warned our guests of my potentially black mood, so when I walked in the place was pretty quiet. After a few words of sympathy followed by an uneasy silence I'd had enough.

"Somebody better get the Quo on, this is supposed to be a party, let's get it rocking!" I shouted. I then picked up a glass of wine, turned up the music, grabbed my air guitar, and dismissed any depression as I proceeded to boogie the night away. Perhaps I was mellowing with age, in stark contrast to my angry young man stage of life earlier in my career when I would lock myself in the bedroom for hours following every defeat.

With the shock of losing at Wembley behind us, the mountainous task of overcoming a 1-0 deficit away from home loomed in Berlin. Our first training session in Germany took place in Arctic weather and was watched by some of our country's finest journalists. I was questioned by one of the reporters who was slightly bemused by both the laughter and frivolity on show.

"You've just lost a League Cup Final on Saturday, yet here you are on Tuesday and the atmosphere sounds like you had won," he said.

I explained to him that being one goal behind was probably placing more pressure on Dynamo Berlin than us. Besides, I assured him, we could never play as badly as we had at Wembley three days before. He said that he understood my sentiments, but at the same time foresaw major problems in us making further progress in the competition. Once again Forest had been written off by the media. It was understandable, of course, as few teams overcame deficits to win an away second leg. This, however, was no ordinary team.

The freezing cold conditions didn't stop us wearing short-sleeve shirts and making a confident start. It would prove to be another of those special nights where we won against the odds. As a player you can sense when the opposition's heads go down, and feel their dismay when you go a goal up. We went 1-0 up after 15 minutes through an opportunist Trevor Francis toe-poke, which instigated that look of despair on the opposition's faces. Then before half time Trevor spun brilliantly on the corner of the six-yard box to smash in a second, a goal of the highest quality, which stunned the opposition. Dynamo visibly wilted after conceding a third goal from the penalty spot just before the half-time whistle when John Robertson slotted home. It was impossible to reproduce another half of such power and quality, but we still ran out 3-1 winners after Terletzki netted for them on the coldest night I ever played a game of football. Our reward was a semi-final against the Dutch masters, Ajax.

Despite the cup success in Europe, our league form continued to be distinctly average. Wins against Southampton and Manchester United at home were offset by defeats at Brighton and Aston Villa. The two away losses really ended our chances of catching Liverpool in the chase for the title, and just days after the Villa game we had to focus our attention on the visit of Ajax.

The match produced a typical effort from us. Swift attacks, crisp, accurate passes, with support to whoever was on the ball in all areas of the field. Trevor Francis, who had been outstanding in Berlin, smashed in our opener after 30 minutes. His volley from five yards following a John Robertson corner again showed his striker's instinct for being in the right place at the right time. Trevor's persistence also set up a second goal, as he hooked the ball from a wide position into the six-yard box past the Ajax goalkeeper, who was waving to complain that it had gone out of play. The call never came, despite continued protests from them, which then turned to dismay when one of their defenders handled in panic as he desperately attempted to clear the ball. Needless to say, John Robertson fired home from the spot. With a 2-0 advantage we knew it was going to require something special from Ajax in the return leg to overcome us.

With 10 days to go before our next league match, most teams would have organised a break from playing. For Forest it was a trip to the United Arab Emirates and Bahrain plus a game against Lincoln for Bert Loxeley's testimonial. In such a busy season, with a small squad, these trips, of which there were many, could have been described as unwise, or unnecessary.

Despite this, the harmony and spirit among the players always produced enough laughs, practical jokes or dungeon humour to shorten the duration of the trip. There was also the promise of some decent spending money for the players, although this entice-ment turned out to be conspicuous by its absence in reality.

Having made the short trip to Amsterdam for the return leg it was decided to take a pre-match walk along the canals, followed by a stroll into the red light district, with Clough and Taylor leading the way. Not being a regular visitor to such areas, it was interesting to see the "ladies of the night" actually on display in such brightly lit shop windows. There were also some strange-looking bouncers or security people, usually just sitting on a chair or stool, smoking, eating or drinking as they waited for passing enquiries. As we passed a voluminous dark-haired woman who was munching noisily on a massive loaf, one of the lads as a prank sneaked up behind her chair and shouted, "Boo!" She didn't see the funny side of this schoolboy piece of humour, however, swiftly rising from her seat roaring like a dragon. Immediately this "brave" football team bolted like scared rabbits as she lurched forward like a demented banshee in hot pursuit of us. Fortunately, because she was carrying so much weight and had the added handicap of her sandwich, the chase only lasted a few yards, when she suddenly stopped, giving us an extended two-fingered gesture accompanied by a torrent of abuse.

Just to round off our adventure, as a joke, Peter Taylor tried to barter for a team discount after discussing terms with one of the door-front agents, who had asked him if we really were Nottingham Forest. This was Peter at his best, making us all laugh, including the manager. It formed part of a close together-ness we all shared and enjoyed.

We left the red light district behind us and approached the Ajax fixture with confidence. Ajax predictably took a leaf out of our book, with an all-out attacking policy. Their initial onslaught had us resolutely defending with our customary unified determination. Their main threat creatively was midfield maestro Soren Lerby, an exceptionally talented player. They also had a vastly experienced defender, Ruud Krol, helping to drive them on from his position at the back. Our most worrying moments were from free kicks on the edge of our penalty area, giving Peter Shilton a chance to shine with two super saves. One in particular that sneaked through our defensive wall was world class. We survived the first 45 minutes, before Ajax finally scored from a corner, headed in by Lerby. Despite the Dutch side's continued pressure throughout the second half, we soaked up everything they could throw at us. In the end the score remained the same but regardless of the defeat, which was our first loss away from home in the competition, we were able to celebrate reaching the final of the European Cup for the second successive year. With Liverpool being chased by Manchester United for the league title, we knew our European campaign was the only real option of winning a major trophy.

With the final against Hamburg to look forward to, we picked up some major problems. First Trevor Francis ruptured his Achilles tendon during a 4-0 win against Crystal Palace, then Stan Bowles fell out with the management saying he no longer wanted to play out on the right, ending his chances of playing in the final.

To remove the players from the normal pre-match media circus the management decided a week in Majorca with no real training or curfews would put us in a relaxed mood. This tactical approach would have been condemned as suicidal by other managers and coaches, but it was one of the reasons the Clough/Taylor regime was unique. Gambling and taking risks where others feared to tread, backed by a totally bullet-proof approach, allied to their confident swashbuckling style, made them what they were and produced success. Our opponents' preparation was already laid out. The German football season ended a week before the European Cup Final, so Hamburg would certainly have the edge on us in terms of match fitness.

The magnificent Bernabéu Stadium, home of the mighty Real Madrid, was a superb venue for a European Cup Final. Strangely, though, on the morning of the match the six-yard areas of the pitch were relaid with block turf, resembling the size of house bricks, something I had never seen before in my career.

As the match started, our line-up included 17-year-old Garry

Mills, replacing Trevor Francis up front. We only had four instead of the normal five substitutes on the bench, because Stan Bowles was absent. Despite us having won the trophy the previous year, Hamburg were favourites to win this time out. Their main attacking threat was Kevin Keegan, whose outstanding career was still in its prime.

The first 15 minutes of the game saw Hamburg dominate possession, although Keegan's darting runs were abruptly curtailed by Mr Burns and Mr Lloyd. Kenny was yellow carded after a particularly bruising challenge on Keegan. He also paid Kevin a tongue-in-cheek compliment.

"You bounce really well Kev – nice perm by the way!" he told him in reference to Keegan's afro-style mop of curls which were in fashion at the time. Kenny's idea of a wind up.

Yet another hefty challenge saw Kevin drift into midfield, so I pointed out to him that he was a striker and should be playing up front.

"I don't think Kenny is in a good mood!" quipped Kev. He was right because Kenny (and Larry) would both certainly have rather played against a big bruiser than a jinking, darting, small man with lots of energy like Kevin, whose effort and determination proved to be a real threat throughout the match.

"I'll tell you why Kenny's not in a good mood," I replied. "Cloughie says that after the game, win or lose, we can't have a drink with our wives. They are staying in a different hotel to us and Kenny promised his wife that he would have a drink with her. Even we won't go near him!"

After 20 minutes we produced a telling blow, following a well-constructed move which started on our right flank with Martin O'Neill. The move carried forward into the Hamburg half through Frank Gray and Garry Mills. The ball eventually ended up with John Robertson, who as normal was confronted by two defenders blocking his touchline advance. Without hesitation he jinked inside them, and played a one-two with Garry Birtles before hitting a firm right-footed shot from the edge of the penalty area. The ball swerved right, beating the goalkeeper's desperate dive, to clip the inside of the post on its way to the net. Robbo stood, hands in the air, taking the crowd's multi-decibel eruption in salute as we piled on top of him in appreciation.

With only 20 minutes of the match played, the Germans still had enough time to make amends. To say that Hamburg threw everything at us would be an understatement, as wave after wave of white shirts surged forward towards our goal. We had probably the best goalkeeper in the world at the time, plus a ruthless shield of tireless workers, who were unwilling to concede anything in front of him. We tackled, blocked, hustled and harried until we dropped. We eventually did drop, but only after the final whistle.

For everyone associated with the club, this was another dream realised, and that big shining cup was just waiting to go back to Nottingham. At the final whistle I got a rush of pure adrenaline and I desperately needed to share the moment with my team-mates. Groups of two or three players just merged together, wallowing in the irreplaceable, sublime joy of victory. There was no order to our celebrations until someone reminded me that there was a trophy to collect. Unusually, it was presented on the side of the pitch, with very little ceremony, but that didn't really matter. We had won the European Cup for the second year running. Against all the odds, little old Nottingham Forest had matched and bettered the achievements of some of the giants in European football. Following the required press photos there were more celebrations, as we danced towards our ecstatic supporters to show them the huge cup. The players and fans were united in sharing the ultimate glory of another magical European adventure. I personally thought this win overshadowed that of the previous year, as it is always difficult to retain a trophy, especially with the quality that Hamburg possessed.

The dressing room was a happy place after the match, but there were no wild celebrations. I'd been tapped on the shoulder by Brian pretty soon after leaving the pitch.

"Get yourself showered and dressed," he told me. "You're doing a TV interview with me."

It was pretty unusual for any of the players to do an interview after a match, because Cloughie tended to do all the talking for us, but I was happy to do it and then went back to the changing room to join the rest of the lads. There were pictures being taken of the team with the cup and I stood out like a sore thumb, because I was the only one with a jacket and tie on.

The team had stayed outside Madrid at a hotel in the mountains, while the rest of the Forest party, which included wives and girlfriends, stayed at a hotel in the city. Brian lost no time in telling the team that we were heading back to the mountains for a few drinks to celebrate the victory. He didn't want anyone going into the city and visiting our friends and family, but after some drinks when Brian and Peter were no longer around, a few of the lads jumped in a taxi to carry on the celebrations in Madrid. They were out all night and only returned the next morning just in time for breakfast.

"Surprised to see you lot up so early," said Peter Taylor with a knowing glint in his eye as they shuffled through the hotel lobby.

The thing I remember most about getting back to England was the amount of fans who turned out to see us arrive with the cup, and we continued the celebrations the next day with an open-topped bus procession through Nottingham, with fans turning out in force once again.

For the third consecutive season Forest had won a major trophy, giving the club and the city of Nottingham a legacy of achievement to be proud of. A massive bonus, which added to the club's respect throughout the world of football, was the conduct of our supporters during the European campaigns. We won like champions, while they had conducted themselves like champions.

To maintain the level of performance we had shown since winning promotion in 1978 was always going to be difficult, yet the inconsistency we had acquired in our league form by 1980 exposed the difficulty of retaining near-perfection. Players get older, sometimes their attitude changes following unbridled success. New players are always part of a club's development, but it is improved quality which is essential in any competitive team sport. We had probably reached a peak with the win against Hamburg. None of us probably knew it at the time, but that fact was shown to be true in the months ahead. We had won a European Cup, the European Super Cup, finished fifth in the league and reached the final of the League Cup. That level of achievement was always going to be hard to maintain or improve on, and the cracks slowly but surely started to appear following that magical night in Madrid.

CHAPTER THIRTEEN

BEGINNING OF THE END

During the 1980/81 season the near-invincible reputation of Forest was diminished. Young players such as Colin Walsh, Bryn Gunn, Stuart Gray and Gary Mills emerged, but surprisingly Garry Birtles was sold to Manchester United and Martin O'Neill to Norwich. Larry Lloyd decided to go into management at Wigan. John O'Hare retired and Ian Bowyer joined Frank Clark at Sunderland. The major signings made by the club were Ian Wallace from Coventry, Raimondo Ponte from Grasshoppers Zurich, Peter Ward from Brighton and Norwegian centre-half Einar Aas. Things were changing at the City Ground.

The sale of Garry Birtles was another of those out-of-the-blue moves that genuinely shocked the Forest supporters; it was similar to Tony Woodcock's switch to Germany, and the season would prove to be one in which the magic failed to materialise as changes, for once, did not produce consistent results.

Before the season started I visited New York where, at a summer training camp, I met the world's greatest footballer, Pelé. The meeting was arranged partly through my co-traveller Roger Whittaker and someone else who is still a close friend, Burt Haimes. Pelé kindly interrupted his coaching session to speak with me about football. I was amazed by his humility and enthusiasm for the game. He even apologised for his lack of English. My Portuguese was non-existent, so how could I complain? As I left him I asked why he had come to America from Brazil.

"I lost my money through some bad investments," was his reply. So I left the world's greatest footballer comforted by the knowledge that he can get caught out just like the rest of us.

Forest's pre-season tour to North and South America in July of 1980 was to produce some discontent between the players and management, which would simmer for a large part of the coming season. Our planned 10-day tour, taking in five matches at Vancouver, Tampa Bay, Columbia, Peru, then Toronto, yielded the "Trans World Travels Taylor" nickname for Peter Taylor, who had apparently organised the gruelling schedule.

Starting in Vancouver, then eventually coming back to Toronto in Canada, seemed bizarre. In July the heat was going to kill us, if playing 6,000 feet above sea level in Columbia didn't choke us through lack of oxygen, or the 90 degrees plus 90 per cent humidity in Florida didn't dehydrate us.

It was a well-known fact that playing in such prestigious matches should provide some extra spending money above the regulation $10 a day we were given. This was mentioned to the management by me as captain, but it wasn't too well received. Their answer was that any extra money for the players would be earned as the season progressed, depending on how we were performing.

The tour started with a 1-1 draw with Vancouver White Caps featuring a rare McGovern goal, courtesy of a lob over a surprised Bruce Grobbelaar. Trying to comprehend which boundary lines were which was tricky, as the grid lines from their American Football were still evident on the artificial surface.

The following game in Florida brought some comedy, as well as some serious sweating. The Tampa Bay Rowdies' star player was Roy Wegerle, nicknamed "The Cowboy", who played on the wing. With the American's love of the cowboy genre, plus the razzmatazz, every time Wegerle received the ball, a bugle sounded the charge on the public address system. We were so taken by this that we accidentally (on purpose) gave Wegerle possession just to hear the cavalry charge over the loud speakers.

After an hour of the game, in 90-degree heat we were running on memory, and the match finished 0-0. Following this, we had a trip to Columbia to look forward to.

We played against the Columbian National team, who unsurprisingly were quite sharp, unlike ourselves who had had one day to recover from the heat and travel before playing at 6,000ft above sea level. Whatever oxygen was around never really found its way to the men in red, as we were trounced 5-0. The mood in the camp was only lifted by an announcement from "Trans World Travels Taylor" that, due to an airport-workers strike in Lima, the Peru game was cancelled. The cheers were audible for miles.

The extra days' rest proved beneficial as we finished the tour with a 3-1 win in Toronto.

It was an absolutely crazy schedule. Generally footballers tend to just get on with things and although the lads weren't happy, and there were a few grumbles throughout the trip, there was never any chance of a revolt. We put up with all the travel and gritted our teeth, but it was certainly not the best way to prepare for the start of a new season. And that wasn't the end of it. After returning to England, we still managed to visit Ireland, Denmark, West Germany and Switzerland before our opening league game at Tottenham Hotspur!

During our pre-season tour there had been some serious discussions between the management and players about bonuses for the coming season. Players' individual contracts were self-negotiated while the squad contracts were all covered by the same incentives, so that the whole squad would get the same amount for win bonuses etc. Once agreed, the incentives had to be registered at the Football Association headquarters in London on noon of the first day of the season.

By the eve of the Tottenham match no agreement had been reached, with Brian and Peter informing us in no uncertain terms that our demands were not acceptable. Their offer of a slight increase from the previous season's bonuses was all we could expect, take it or leave it.

After dinner I phoned a few of the players to get their

opinions, suggesting that the increase offered by the management was better than nothing. If we didn't sign the new ones we would be in exactly the same position the next year. I saw no mileage in being stubborn to the point of losing money. Also, in my humble opinion, I didn't think the issue should have been argued so close to the start of the season.

The meeting the next morning ended with Clough plonking the incentives on a table at the side of the room.

"If you want to sign them, there they are, if not you'll be on the same as last season."

The room fell decidedly silent before a few rumbles of dissent could be heard.

"You had better make your minds up quickly," added the manager. "Ken Smales [the club secretary] has to get them over to the FA pronto."

I walked up to the table grabbed one of the sheets and signed it. Yes I had broken ranks, which annoyed some of the players, but you have to be your own man and stand for your own judgement.

I was the only player to sign, which meant that I got the new bonus that had been offered. It might not have been exactly what we all wanted, but as far as I was concerned, the money was going to be better so why wouldn't you want to sign up for it? The only other dissatisfied party was Ken Smales, who literally ran out of the room to catch a taxi to the FA headquarters at Lancaster Gate.

The game at White Hart Lane finished in a 2-0 defeat, with more gripes about the incentives issue punctuating the homeward coach journey. Despite this early setback, we remained unbeaten in the league, and also had League Cup victories over Peterborough and Leicester, until 27th September when we lost 1-0 at Arsenal.

There were one or two more critical comments thrown at me personally regarding my decision to sign up for the improved incentives. But after the first league table of the season was published, which didn't happen until after the first three games had been played, and the bonus scheme kicked in, the complaints soon evaporated. Nobody had forced my team-mates not to sign and we all had to live with our own choices. It didn't cause any long-term friction between us. Throughout my life and career I have always tried to avoid protracted arguments, especially those involving money which, in my opinion, really is the root of all evil.

Following our European Cup successes, money issues were discussed more frequently, with suggestions that some of the friendly matches or testimonial appearances that we made should be rewarded financially. Other teams got paid to play in matches home or abroad and we didn't, which rightfully aggravated our players.

We started our defence of the European Cup with a 1-0 loss in Bulgaria to CSKA Sofia. The return leg at the City Ground was expected to see us drive forward in our inimitable swashbuckling, free-flowing style of attacking football. But when the final whistle sounded following a 1-0 defeat, the "Kings of Europe" had been reduced to ordinary citizens. There were no excuses from management or the players. We all knew there was no point in post-mortems about what had gone wrong. We hadn't played that badly and losing to a single goal in each game reflected that, but at the same time we weren't good enough to beat them and sometimes you just have to accept that. Throughout my time playing for Brian Clough there was never a time when he let his teams get carried away with what they had done. Win, lose or draw it was always important that you were realistic about what had happened, and that meant there were never excuses made if we didn't get the result we wanted. We had come close to getting a result against CSKA on both occasions, but we hadn't managed it. We weren't good enough to do what we had set out to do, end of story. Going into the competition we believed we could win it for a third time, but it wasn't to be. When we lost, we did what we always did when we had a setback and started to look forward to the next game.

As the season unfolded, the breathtaking disciplined displays that had thrilled football supporters at home and abroad would only surface sporadically. The team personnel started changing, with Ian Wallace and Raymond Ponte vying alongside youngsters Colin Walsh, Stuart Gray, Bryn Gunn and 18-year-old European Cup finalist Gary Mills for first-team recognition. Trevor Francis, whose Achilles injury had forced him to miss the European Cup Final the season before, only became fit at the end of December.

Our ignominious exit from the League Cup via a 4-1 thrashing at Norwich on 28th October – not the best 31st birthday present for me – underlined that we were a team in decline. The next month saw us win one, draw two and lose three successive league matches. One of the losses was 3-0 at home to Tottenham, and it was particularly memorable from a personal point of view as I had been dropped in favour of Raimondo Ponte. Sitting on the substitutes bench next to Brian was always an education and he would occasionally put you on the spot. During the second half he turned to me.

"Do you know what's wrong with that Raimondo Ponte?" he asked. In the process of formulating a diplomatic answer regarding someone I had been replaced by, I hesitated, before I opened my mouth. Before I could say anything Brian told me.

"I bloody signed him, that's what's wrong with him."

This frank admission saved me from answering his question and made me think. Peter Taylor signed all the players, or normally did, yet here was Brian openly admitting that he had signed Raimondo. For me the statement was quite significant. It was an admission of a change in the way things had always been done in the past. One reason for the success of Clough and Taylor was the fact that both stuck to what they were best at. Brian was a great manager and Peter was the best judge of a player I have ever known. If Cloughie wanted a striker, Taylor would go out and get just the sort of player who would fit into the team they were managing, but suddenly here was Brian saying he was the man signing a player.

After the match Ann and I had been invited to join Archie and Betty Gemmill for dinner at their house. When we got there we were surprised to see that Archie's other guests were none other than Brian and Barbara Clough. Brian was understandably feeling low after a 3-0 home defeat and spoke very little until asked to comment about the match. After a frank description of ineptitude of his team he was interrupted by Barbara.

"You bring it all on yourself; it's your job so learn to live with it," she reminded him.

This mild rebuke from Barbara, who was happier discussing other topics rather than football, edged Brian into a really quiet period during the dinner party, and I think it showed that behind every great man is a woman helping him to keep his feet on the ground.

When the general conversation entered a musical debate regarding the merits of The Beatles and The Rolling Stones I could have gone on all night, having fancied myself as the next possible Mick Jagger during my Sixties' playing days at Hartlepools. I loved discussing the two bands, as I owned nearly every record they had made. After different points of view had been fired from every corner, Brian interrupted us.

"Actually, for a period I thought that The Rolling Stones were better than The Beatles," he told us. I think that he just wanted to get into the conversation, as I am not sure he knew too much about the Stones' music. Being absent from the discussion and not having an opinion was not really Brian's style, so he had chipped in with the comment, even though I'm sure neither band were particularly his cup of tea. He was, of course, a massive Frank Sinatra fan.

Towards the end of November we beat Valencia in the first leg of the Super Cup, which gave us hope of retaining the trophy we had won when beating Barcelona the season before. A first-leg 2-1 win gave us a slender lead. What a difference a year makes, however, as a 1-0 defeat in the return leg in December saw us receiving the silver runners-up medals instead of gold. Fernando Moreno, the great Uruguayan striker, scored in Valencia, where their supporters celebrated by pelting our team coach with oranges as we left the stadium.

Having lost out on European Cup and European Super Cup glory, we still had a mammoth journey to Tokyo to endure in order to play the World Club Championship match against Nacional of Uruguay in February, in what was to be Larry

Lloyd's last game for Forest. I was injured at the time, which usually meant being excluded from the trip. On this occasion, however, I was informed by Brian that the reason for my inclusion was to dish out the lads' money, which was an accumulation from all the so-called friendly matches worldwide we had played. Needless to say, the players were unanimously delighted, having been promised the payout for months on end. I was bitterly disappointed at being injured, but honoured to be travelling halfway around the world for such a prestigious game.

The real touch of genius in eliminating jet lag was Peter Taylor's idea of keeping us on British time. This involved taking sleeping pills after the first leg of our journey from Heathrow to Alaska. When we arrived in Japan, we were not allowed to go to sleep, as we played things by his rules. The tactic seemed bizarre at the time, yet achieved the desired effect.

Watching from the sidelines is completely frustrating when you are injured. Seeing your team-mates out-play the opposition for long spells but lose 1-0 has you wanting to climb up the wall. With a brand new car being offered for the Man of the Match, which we were all going to share, I watched as another bonus disappeared when goalscorer Waldemar Victorino was voted for by match sponsors Toyota. There was a general feeling of frustration and disappointment when we lost out on a trophy and the share of a car.

"Never mind lads," I told the players. "At least we'll get our money, at long last."

But when I went to see Brian about collecting the money I was in for a shock, as Brian told me there would be no money.

"The agent hasn't turned up," he said.

"I am not going to tell them that alone," I said. "I need an explanation."

"Don't worry," said Peter Taylor. "The agent is coming over to England shortly, and I personally guarantee the lads will get their share."

I went back to inform the players, who rightly were very angry, feeling let down on a promise once again.

Eventually the agent did arrive in England. One Friday morning after training, I was told by the manager to gather the players in the Trophy Room. This was standard practice before all home games.

"Come and let me know when the lads are ready," Brian told me.

Having informed them of the agent's arrival, the players were there in record time, with none of the usual stragglers holding up proceedings. I knocked on the manager's door, which was unlocked, and as it slowly swung open with a noisy creak I casually scanned the office. Brian and Peter stared back, from behind the large wooden desk.

"What the hell do you want?" shouted Peter, as he threw himself forward onto the desk, arms outstretched trying in vain to cover bundles of money covering the surface.

"Come back in five minutes," Brian said.

Peter was still bent forward almost double, arms spread eagled, in a comic pose.

"Go on, get out!" he shouted.

I was still laughing at Peter's animated performance as I entered the Trophy Room.

When I returned to the manager's office, a cardboard box was thrust into my hands. Finally, our worldwide travels had seen us justly rewarded. The final share-out was two or three hundred pounds each, which thankfully dispelled the grumblings of discontent in the camp.

We showed no ill effects from our long round trip to Tokyo as we beat Bristol City 2-1 to reach the FA Cup sixth round. Our last chance of a trophy disappeared, however, in March, with our elimination from the competition following a replay against Ipswich. I was still carrying an injury, returning to the side in April for a 0-0 draw against Liverpool. Einar Aas, who was Larry Lloyd's replacement, played his second game for the club against the Reds. A Norwegian from Bayern Munich who spoke good English, and as honest as the day is long, Einar was a really nice character who fitted in immediately with all the players. Similar to other newcomers, though, he still found our lack of discussion concerning the opposition unusual.

One of the manager's off-the-cuff training exercises also caught him totally by surprise. A typical jog along the banks of the Trent was brought to a halt adjacent to a wasteland covered in knee-high nettles and brambles. As regulars, most of the players quickly pulled up their socks above their knees, anticipating the barked order that followed.

"On the shout, I want you through those weeds to the far side and back, last man is on press-ups," said Clough.

Before Einar could adjust his socks, the manager shouted, "Go!"

Off we went like amateur hurdlers as we vaulted over the thickest patch of nettles and thorns. As we reached the far side, Einar shouted to me.

"John, what does this have to do with football?"

I winked at him.

"Einar, don't be last," I told him as I skipped round a nettle patch. Einar finally finished the run, shaking his head in disbelief, his legs scratched and stung.

Unorthodox training with the manager in charge meant constantly being on your toes. Being last in an exercise meant only 10 press-ups as punishment, but it was pride in never getting caught that was the motivation for the players.

Nottingham Forest ended the 1980/81 season in seventh place, which in the opinion of most supporters wasn't bad. The prestigious feats of winning the League Championship, European Cup, or any major trophy would sadly be postponed for a few years. The European champions' squad was being reshaped in quite dramatic fashion.

During the 1981/82 campaign another two stalwarts and European Cup heroes, Kenny Burns and Frank Gray, left the club, while Ian Bowyer made a surprising return to Forest and Jurgen Roeber, Chris Fairclough, Willie Young, Calvin Plummer, Peter Davenport and Steve Kendal all made their Forest debuts. We also signed Justin Fashanu from Norwich for £1 million. Justin only lasted one year at the club. To be honest he never really settled in. His lack of control at times let him down, making him something of a misfit, in a side schooled in keeping the ball.

I had an injury-hit season, suffering the frustration of missing too many games. Before it was over, while Brian was away on a short holiday with his family, which was not unusual, Peter Taylor called me into his office to tell me I was on the transfer list. "We've had a good run," Peter informed me. "But all good things come to an end."

He also told me Ian Wallace and Justin Fashanu would be on the list. When I walked slowly out of his office I was a little bemused. I considered the only change in my attitude or commitment to the cause had been one or two niggling injuries. I had never really had a poor run of form, but Peter never gave me a detailed explanation of why I was being transfer listed.

When Brian returned from holiday he called me into his office.

"Who told you that you were going on the transfer list?" he asked. "That's my decision, I'm the manager of this club. You are going absolutely nowhere!"

The next day I was summoned to see a somewhat agitated Peter Taylor.

"Look, I told you that you were going and you're going, it's over, finished. As soon as someone comes in for you I will let you know, but it's finished," he said.

This message was delivered at lightning speed as Peter paced up and down behind his desk. I had the distinct feeling of déjà vu the next day when Brian asked to see me after training.

"I knew that Justin Fashanu and Ian Wallace were going on the transfer list, but *Taylor* never mentioned you," he told me, with the name "Taylor" spoken loudly. I waited for some kind of clarification.

"I decide who stays or leaves this club," Brian said casually. "Get off then."

This going/not going routine was getting annoying. Obviously, the management team themselves were at cross purposes. There is no surprise in an argument between partners who are constantly embroiled in the pressures of football management. All partners, husbands, wives, girls and boyfriends have arguments, but the way Brian had said, "Taylor," and not "Pete", "my mate" or "Peter", suggested something far deeper than a simple football issue.

Another incident on the training ground gave me a massive hint regarding my immediate future at the club. Trainer Ronnie Fenton had set up a shooting session for the strikers. They would receive passes from midfield players' turn, then fire shots on goal. Ronnie named the first-team strikers, and then added the midfield suppliers to feed the balls through to them.

"I'm a midfield player," I said to Ronnie, thinking he might have left me out by accident. The reply was blunt. "You can fetch the balls from behind the goal if the strikers miss the target," he told me.

Club captain one minute, ball boy the next.

I could have, possibly should have, spoken out at the belittlement in front of the other players. But I kept my own counsel, knowing that there was something unusual behind Ronnie's deliberate slight.

I sat in Brian's office after some further confirmation that he alone would decide my future. He made a statement that finally put to rest any doubts in my own mind as to my next move.

"I have had 10 enquiries regarding the names on our transfer list," he began. "Considering Wallace cost over a million and a quarter and Fashanu cost a million you'll be pleased to hear all the enquiries are about you, but I see no reason why you shouldn't play at least 20 games for me next season."

It was a distinct change from me going nowhere to the suggestion of playing 20 games. There were 42 league games alone to consider.

He informed me that one enquiry about me was from Bolton Wanderers, who were looking for a player-manager. Then he asked if I wanted to speak to them.

"The experience will do you good," he added. Before I could reply he also threw something else into the conversation. "Two players have been given £25,000 each when they left this club. I will get you something as close as possible, for the loyalty you have shown this club," he assured me. The whole thing was getting bizarre. Having never received any previous signing fees, I was now being offered what I considered a fortune to leave the club. I finally, sadly, conceded that the split or disagreement between Brian and Peter had been temporarily healed, with Peter forcing the issue of me leaving the club.

I travelled to Bolton where I had a brief interview with the chairman Terry Edge and secretary Des McBain. A couple of days later Brian called me into his office to inform me that Bolton wanted me for the job as player-manager. Following another brief meeting with the Bolton chairman, to agree terms, I went to see Brian regarding his promise of my loyalty payment.

"You're getting nothing," he shouted at me. "I am not paying you to leave this club!"

I had always been slightly cautious during discussions with Brian, especially when it came to money matters. On this occasion, however, I reminded him of his promise to pay me for my length of service. He made an excuse, then cut short our discussion, saying he needed to talk to the chairman. After tying up the loose ends to join Bolton, I went back to Brian to ask him once again to keep his promise. He agreed to meet me in the Jubilee Club at the Forest Ground. I thought the social club rather than his office was a strange place to meet, but nevertheless I agreed.

"What can I do for you?" was his opening line as he glanced casually around the lounge, seemingly disinterested.

"I've come to ask you once again for the money you promised me," I told him.

"Why should I give you anything?" he said, still not looking at me.

"Because you promised," I replied, "and I have never asked you for anything I didn't deserve in the 14 years I have worked for you." For once he looked nervous.

"I'll have to clear it with the chairman, wait here," he said as he left his seat. After walking through the door, he returned 30 seconds later having supposedly contacted the chairman, and then leant across the table and whispered.

"The chairman says you can have £5,000," he informed me before turning to walk away.

At the end of 14 years there wasn't even a handshake from Brian or Peter. No sentiment, just our normal business arrangement. They paid me my wages, I did my stuff on the field, end of story. For all the Hartlepools, Derby County and Forest fans who have continually said to me, "Brian Clough and Peter Taylor loved you," or "You were Cloughie's blue-eyed boy," please replace the word "loved" with "respected". It ran both ways, for them and me.

I owe Brian and Peter gratitude for the fact that I possess a cupboard full of medals. In return I gave 100 per cent loyalty and commitment every time I played for them. Who could have more satisfaction than me looking back from our initial meeting when I was a 15-year-old schoolboy? I was someone they would eventually trust to captain the fantastic group of players who won everything at Forest. They taught me how to play the game, the beautiful passing game, which I will never forget. They instilled in me high standards and good habits. They enriched my life in many ways. They helped me enormously through the tough challenges that the world of football produces. They were not perfect, no one is I suppose, but they were, without exception, outstanding in their handling of players, especially the skinny kid they met in Hartlepool.

The Forest team that I had the honour to captain, and which won the First Division, two League Cups and also two European Cups, not to mention going a record 42 games undefeated, was truly brilliant. It is something I believe will never be achieved again, in such a short space of time.

CHAPTER FOURTEEN

BEING THE BOSS

The first thing you learn as a manager is there are not enough hours in the day. The first things you learn about being a player-manager is that there are even fewer. Bolton Wanderers were struggling in the Second Division when I took over, which in hindsight, should have prompted a myriad of questions from myself to the chairman. Pertinent questions regarding finances, transfer funds, wage limits and the scouting network to name but a few. It transpired that they had no money, no scouting system and their training ground was in the process of being sold to a building company. My approach was the same as always: get on with the job.

I inherited a coaching staff of two, Charlie Wright, reserve-team coach and Walter Joyce, first- and youth-team coach. The physiotherapist was a really pleasant man called Peter Nightingale. Normally you should employ your own people, but Terry Edge persuaded me, for strictly financial reasons, to accept the resident team. To be honest, because the move from Forest had been quite sudden, there was no one I could have brought with me at such short notice anyway. With Walter and Charlie's help I organised a normal pre-season training schedule, including a lot of stamina work. I surprised a few of the players with my endurance during a lengthy cross-country run.

"I thought you couldn't run," Mike Doyle the ex-Manchester City player gasped after finishing well behind me.

"I'm slower than I look," I replied, as a couple of the younger players sniggered to themselves.

The squad I had inherited was quite experienced, and it included Peter Reid in midfield, Paul Jones at centre-half, defender Mike Doyle, ex-Leicester full-back Steve Whitworth, goalkeeper Seamus McDonagh, winger Jeff Chandler, ex-Man City striker Tony Henry and centre-back Gerry McElhenney. These were the mainstays of the team plus younger players, such as striker Chris Thompson, left-back Mike Bennett, forward Wayne Foster, midfielder David Hogan and young centre-half Neil Berry.

Once pre-season finished I looked forward to my league debut for the club, away to Burnley. I had not played in all the pre-season games as I had spent time examining whatever playing quality I'd inherited. There is a great cliché in football about a side looking good on paper, and the Wanderers squad for the 1982/83 season did look good on paper, but unfortunately, to complete the cliché, you don't play on paper.

After a creditable 0-0 draw in our opening fixture at Burnley, we followed it with a 3-3 away draw to Carlisle in the Milk Cup. Our third fixture at Burnden Park saw us really turn on the style, as we humbled Newcastle 3-1 despite the threat of an effervescent Kevin Keegan playing against us. With misguided optimism flying around the club, everyone plummeted back to earth as we lost our next five league matches. Having struggled to avoid relegation in the two seasons before I joined the club, the writing was well and truly on the wall.

In early December I received a very early morning call from the Bolton chairman Terry Edge. It was at 12.30am to be precise and he sounded anxious.

"Can you come round to my house straight away?" he asked. "It's urgent."

I looked at my watch and wondered what the hell he wanted at that time in the morning. I arrived at his house in Worsley at around 1.15am and soon found out that he wanted me to sell someone before Saturday. The urgency derived from the fact that the club was broke, losing £10,000 a week. If we didn't provide some money before Saturday, Bolton Wanderers would no longer exist. I told him that few managers, if indeed any, would appreciate being woken at around that time on a Friday morning.

"It could be our last chance," he pleaded, "Can you sell anybody?"

There were several bleary-eyed directors at the same meeting trying to come up with a solution. I left an hour or so later, knowing I was training in a few hours, with everyone frantically suggesting all sorts of survival plans. With relief from all concerned, Bolton Wanderers somehow managed to survive this crisis, partly due to a lottery scheme called "Lifeline", which Edge launched. My good friend Brian Johnson, the lead singer of AC/DC, agreed to have his photograph taken alongside myself to help advertise the scheme. Not bad for a born-and-bred Newcastle United fan like Brian. I did manage to repay his generosity later in the season by giving him my 1980 European Cup-winning Forest shirt. It was scant appreciation from me to Brian, as I am the biggest AC/DC fan in the world, and I consider myself fortunate in being able to say hello to the band now and again.

We had known each other since 1980, about six months after Brian joined the band as lead singer. I had gone along to Radio Leicester to do an interview ahead of a Forest game. The guy who interviewed me had to cut the thing short because he had to go off and do an interview with AC/DC. When I heard that I couldn't believe it, because I was a big fan of the band and had bought tickets to go and see them the next week in Leicester. A few days later I got a call from the same guy at the radio station.

"I told AC/DC that you were a big fan," he said, "and they want to see you before the gig."

It was really good of them to ask me but I was a bit reluctant at first, because I didn't want to impose on them. I was firmly persuaded by two mates I was going with, Chris and Peter, that it would be a great idea to see the boys before they went on stage.

In the end I agreed and we just seemed to click. I've remained good friends with Brian and Malcolm Young ever since. I don't see a lot of them due to the nature of their business, but we have always kept in touch on the phone and it was because of one of these calls that Brian ended up helping me out at Bolton. To Malcolm, Brian, Angus, Phil and Cliff, many thanks for the hours of pleasure you have given me at your concerts, plus the aching joints that follow the air guitar boogie sessions.

So the Terry Edge-inspired Lifeline helped to save Bolton Wanderers Football Club from oblivion. Sales of players also helped to keep the club afloat. Peter Reid went to Everton for £60,000 in December, which was, despite the desperation of Bolton's financial situation, a paltry fee, considering he was potentially one of the best midfielders in the country at that time. The transfer fee fully exposed the club's financial plight. It was only 18 months earlier that Bolton had been offered £600,000 from both Everton and Wolves, although his persistent injuries contributed to the knockdown fee. One signing we managed to make was to take striker Neil Whatmore on loan from Birmingham.

When your better players leave the club you have to maintain a positive attitude. This does introduce pressure, but you must learn to live with it. I knew we had to sell in order to survive, and the chairman kept me informed of any potential sales. Except one.

I was enjoying a rare afternoon off at the pictures in Manchester, the week after our 3-2 home win over QPR in March. As I left the cinema, I was suddenly accosted by an extremely irate Wanderers fan who screamed at me.

"Why did you sell Tony Henry, the best striker we've got?" he asked.

I told him politely that I hadn't sold Tony Henry, before he stormed off, a torrent of abuse accompanying his departure.

When I arrived back at my house, I received a phone call from a very apologetic Terry Edge who explained the reasons why Tony had been sold to Oldham for £20,000. For the first time since I had joined the club I lost my head, spewing out a tirade of condemnation. Then I started firing off reasons as to why we were struggling, citing the loss of Tony Henry as yet another act of sabotage on my position as manager. Eventually I calmed down while Terry explained that if Henry had not been sold, I would not have a job to go to. He apologised unreservedly, promising it would never happen again, adding that he had tried every avenue to contact me without success.

Without our top goalscorer, my job became almost impossible, simply because we didn't have the facility to adequately replace him. We scored one goal in our next six games and the season ended disastrously with a 4-1 loss at Charlton on the last day, relegating Bolton Wanderers to Division Three.

"Is there a different feeling between winning European Cups and getting relegated?" asked one smart-alec journalist at the post-match press conference. I let him off with a nasty stare, before suffering the morgue-like atmosphere that accompanied our coach journey back to Bolton.

Looking back on my first season in management, I have to admit that through naivety I did make some mistakes. Despite having to make sweeping changes, I should have tried to bring in reliable workers when possible. My knowledge of players was limited, as previously my concentration was simply on playing and enjoying the game. As manager, unless you have a good friend you can trust, it takes time to complete all the homework required to guarantee you sign a good player. Thankfully, Walter Joyce had been tremendously loyal in offering me his extensive knowledge of possible signings.

In most cases his judgement was absolutely spot-on. I should have sought Walter's advice when I first joined the club, because at the start of that relegation season we signed Ian Moores. He was a tall, fair-haired striker from Tottenham, but his record of 29 appearances and five goals spoke for itself.

Walter, thankfully, recommended the signing of left-back Ray Deakin, who made his debut in October 1982 and enjoyed three good seasons at the club. Not bad for a free transfer from Port Vale. I signed Stuart Gray on loan from Nottingham Forest along with a full-back called Brian Borrows from Everton. When Walter took me to see Borrows play for Everton reserves, he was shocked when I said we were leaving after only 15 minutes of the game.

"Why so soon?" he asked,

"I've seen enough," I replied.

"No good then," he added.

"You're joking," I replied. "I'll talk to Howard Kendall in the morning."

The next day I phoned Howard and pleaded poverty, which happened to be the truth. He listened patiently, before reluctantly agreeing to a fee of £5,000. Walter and I met Borrows in a motorway service station on the M62 a couple of days later. He quickly agreed terms, apart from his reasonable demand for a very small signing-on fee. It took great control from my point of view to keep a straight face and tell him that his manager had agreed to pay him any signing-on bonus out of the transfer fee.

"You'll never get away with that one," said Walter as we drove back, "Howard will go berserk when Borrows asks him."

Needless to say Howard did go berserk.

"How can I pay Burrows a signing-on fee when you are only paying five grand for him and he's played in my first team?" he yelled down the phone. Once again, I pleaded with Howard, telling him a church mouse had more to spend than I had.

"You cheeky bastard," he shouted, as he slammed down the phone. These exact words were repeated by Walter Joyce, when I joyfully told him Borrows was signed. He was a tremendous professional who was eventually sold to Coventry for £80,000 in June 1985.

Stuart Gray was a most-welcome loan signing, courtesy of Brian Clough. I never imagined Brian would let me sign Stuart, as the last time I had spoken to Cloughie he threatened to hit me! This threat emanated from a newspaper article I had agreed to do with a Sunday tabloid. As usual, the journalist had twisted out of all proportion my comments regarding Brian. When I phoned him to apologise, he issued the threat of punching me on the nose the next time he saw me.

He also asked me how much I got for the article! When I told him, he quickly replied: "Put it in the bank."

I assumed he still respected my honesty, while pragmatically giving me the benefit of the doubt on this occasion.

When Nottingham Forest reserves came to play at Burnden Park, I was sitting with my chairman, Terry Edge, when Brian appeared in the visiting directors' box. At half time as we came together to leave the stand, Brian, in his usual flamboyant style, kissed me loudly on the cheek. I am not sure how Terry viewed this, but he sat two seats away from me during the second half of the game! Terry was a typical macho man, who didn't enjoy the sight of grown men kissing each other, not even on the cheek.

Relegation was hard to take. At the end-of-season board meeting, there were only minor grumbles regarding my contribution. The majority of directors were citing the monumental difficulties I had experienced as they surprisingly gave me a new two-year contract and the dreaded vote of confidence. I gave a sensible report, then asked about the possibility of signing players permanently, lads like Neil Whatmore, who had been productive in his loan spell from Birmingham. I was hoping for something positive from my employers, after a season where the continual threat of closure had hung over the club.

"As you are aware, the club has been going through some severe financial problems," was the line they trotted out. It was not the one I wanted to hear, and I was also told it was necessary to impose certain wage restrictions.

"We have been working hard with the bank and in order for the club to survive. Next season we cannot pay any player more than £150 per week," I was told.

I froze momentarily before replying very slowly.

"You must be joking."

I looked from director to director, with half of them unable to look me in the eye.

"All my first-team squad are on over 150 quid," I informed them.

"We realise that, but we have no option," was the terse response.

"No point in asking about signings then," I quipped. "But what the hell do you expect me to achieve with nothing?"

"Just survival at present," said one director quietly. I took a deep breath, before trying to lift the desperately depressing mood of the meeting.

"Well we've got some good kids and what would you say to us finishing halfway up the league?" I boasted, surprising even myself with this immediate optimistic reply.

"That would be a bloody miracle," George Warburton, who was one of the directors, said.

"You did hear what we said about the wages?" another voice jumped in.

"I did and I will take a £50 drop in wages to help the cause," I said, and was told there was no need for the sort of gesture I had suggested.

"It's not a gesture, and I have got another couple of ideas on how to raise a bit of money, which I would like to spend on players." When I finished there was no reaction.

As we approached the start of the new season I actually did spend £2,000 of the club's money on a striker called Tony Caldwell from local side Horwich RMI. One of the directors, Gordon Hargreaves, had mentioned him to me, so the scouting duo of Walter Joyce and yours truly had dutifully been to watch him on three occasions. For a prolific goalscorer, he chose all three games not to score, but his crashing tackle on an opposing centre-half clinched the signing. At 25 years old and with no league experience, you could say this was a gamble. For £2,000, it was a very big gamble for Bolton Wanderers given the parlous financial situation at the time.

As a player with Derby County and Nottingham Forest, the dedicated drudgery of pre-season training was always invigorated with a change of scenery, which was usually abroad. While not quite managing to produce such exotic splendour, I decided to take our new young squad to Ireland for a pre-season tour. So with a large helping hand from my Irish connection – his name was Gerry – I booked the hotels, organised the match payments and even hired the bus. I had asked the club's permission and was bluntly told it would be okay as long as it didn't cost us anything. Having thrived as a player on similar trips, I knew this bonding experience would develop the squad both as players and as men.

So following the gruelling, punishing regime of pre-season training, off we went to Ireland. We even squeezed in Gordon Sharrocks, the local Bolton reporter, as our guest. I had invited the directors of our club who, having considered the million-to-one possibility of being targeted by the IRA, politely declined. They couldn't have appreciated the wonderful Irish hospitality which I'd experienced at Nottingham Forest that welcomed all football teams to their lovely country.

Apart from Tony Caldwell, my other new signings were Peter Valentine, a free transfer from Huddersfield, Eric Snookes, a free from Rochdale and five home-grown 18-year-olds. They were Steve Thompson midfield, Neil Redfearn midfield, Simon Rudge striker, Stevie Saunders striker, and Walter Joyce's son, Warren, a midfielder, plus Simon Farnworth, another homegrown player, who was a goalkeeper.

One of the established senior players who had survived the cull from the previous season was Jeff Chandler, a winger who could produce something out of the ordinary. His ability to beat opponents, provide opportunities for his team-mates and score goals himself made him an essential component. I was relieved to keep him. Jeff's only failing was his fear of being kicked, which on occasion involved his less-than-total commitment in tackling situations. I remember one board meeting when a director asked me, "Why does Jeff Chandler jump out of tackles?"

"Because I tell him to," I replied. "I've got other players in the side to tackle, but they can't produce anything near the quality contribution that Jeff Chandler gives the team." End of discussion.

So with a totally new-look squad we embarked on a four-match tour of Northern and the Republic of Ireland. We beat Sligo Rovers and Finn Harps, both 2-1, then proceeded to beat Carrick Rangers, before finishing with a 0-0 draw with Glentoran. As expected, the benefit of keeping the players together had been a tremendous bonding success. The finances at times were precarious, which was unfortunately my sole responsibility. I remember standing on the pitch before the Sligo game, when one of their officials came up and politely informed me that they couldn't pay me the agreed match fee, as they hadn't sold many tickets.

"I need that money to cover our hotel and travel," I explained sharply.

"I'm sorry," he said, staring at his shoes.

"Okay, we're not playing," I replied.

"There are already people coming into the ground," he replied in desperation.

"I don't give a shit," I told him. "I've agreed a fee, which barely covers our travel and hotel which, by the way, I am totally responsible for. If you don't provide me with a signed letter guaranteeing we will be paid, we are not playing here tonight!"

With his face getting redder and redder he despairingly asked me to be patient with him as he hurried away. He returned very quickly to summon me before one of his directors, who happened to be an Irish FA member. A signed letter was swiftly produced guaranteeing our match fee. Well done, boss!

So Bolton's team of young, hungry, inexperienced boys began the tour with a 2-1 win. Tony Caldwell, our star signing, made his debut, which was more memorable for a glaring miss than anything else. He had been put clear in the opposition's half with nobody within 30 yards. As he approached the goalkeeper he tried to evade him one way then the other. The keeper, however, never dived, just shuffled one way then the other, staying between Caldwell and the goal. As a last resort, Tony tried a full speed jinking motion to try and go round him, falling over the ball in the process, as the absentee defenders returned to duty.

After the match, Gordon Sharrocks cheekily asked me how I thought Tony Caldwell had performed.

"If he maintains the standard of his debut, I'll be out of work very shortly!"

I did, however, explain to Gordon that, having come from amateur Horwich RMI to full-time professional football at Bolton Wanderers, you must make allowances regarding his debut in a new team. I know managers talk a lot of bullshit at times, but I had one of those strong hunches that Tony would eventually make the grade.

He got his chance sooner than expected, when we lined up for our first league game at home to Wimbledon to start the season. The starting line-up contained just one player from the season before – Jeff Chandler. The rest were kids, free transfers. Borrows and Caldwell were the only players I had paid money for.

We won 2-0 courtesy of goals from young Simon Rudge and Tony Caldwell. I knew as a manager that having so many young-sters in your side would always produce a high level of energy. With five 18-year-olds as regulars over a gruelling nine-month season the major question would be whether they could last the pace. Despite an excellent start, the answer inevitably was no.

We more or less peaked in January when Tony Caldwell scored a brilliant goal, enabling us to beat George Graham's Millwall 2-0 at Burnden Park. I had also signed Graham Bell, an expe-rienced midfield player, from Carlisle on a free in January as we tried to maintain a good standard.

The five 18-year-olds who, for a few months, had performed miracles, slowly but surely fell away. Mentally and physically they were drained, having given their all. Despite having prob-ably the youngest side in the league, plus a mixture of cheap buys or free transfers, Bolton finished a credible 10th in the league. As a manager I was proud of the honesty of my team and told them that one of the directors had informed me at the start of the season that a top-half finish in the league would be nothing short of a miracle.

We were no world-beaters, simply a living, breathing, vibrant example of what honesty and endeavour can achieve. A major factor that season was their hunger and desire to enjoy playing the game. When you've got five previous youth-team members playing for peanuts and loving every minute of it, it is refreshing to see. Following their endeavours, I gave them all new contracts, plus a slight increase, without them needing to ask. When they all signed up I was delighted. The reaction of the board of directors was astonishing. They actually gave me a dressing-down for giving them rises. This reaction following such stringent budgeting was difficult to accept.

As the 1984/85 season approached I found myself dealing with a new chairman, Neil Riley. Terry Edge was a genuinely likeable character, a self-made successful business type, with a glint in his eye to match his personality. I never managed to fully enjoy discussions with the new chairman, while at the same time never actually falling out with him, but I was aware that I was not his choice for the job.

Before the pre-season training began, I had a mild confront-ation with one of the players, George Oghani. I signed George from Hyde United in October 1983 for £3,000 with a further £2,000 if he made 15 appearances. His grumble was that I would not play him as it would eventually cost the club the extra £2,000.

"Some of the players also told me, you never go back to a player you don't fancy," he said enquiringly.

"George," I told him. "If you set your stall out during pre-season training, with the right attitude, I personally will pay the extra £2,000 to Hyde United."

He took me at my word as he ran almost everyone into the ground during the pre-season build up. He then went on to 21 goals from 47 starts in league and cup. I didn't end up paying the extra £2,000 to Hyde United myself, but did end up out of pocket that season thanks to George's lack of wardrobe. He turned up for our first home fixture without the regulation collar and tie. When I questioned his lack of discipline on this he told me why it had happened.

"I don't have a suit, boss," said George. When I realised he was telling the truth I promised to buy him one when he scored his first hat-trick for the first team. It took him until October in the 4-0 hammering of Preston. When George scored his third, Brian Borrows and a few of the other players mimicked the straightening of a tie towards me in the dugout. The big surprise for me was getting a receipt from George for more than £100. I had never paid that much for a suit for myself!

A couple more players made their debuts during the season. Jimmy Phillips was a young left-back with a great cultured delivery when he passed the ball. He did have one major failing, and that was the fact that he was exceptionally nice. Apologising to an opponent after tripping him was an indication of his genteel character. As the manager, it was my responsibility to educate the players, so during a one-on-one coaching session I told him he would get absolutely nowhere in football unless he started kicking the opposition. I have never played against a full-back who didn't physically try to intimidate his opponent. Being a young, keen learner, Jimmy listened to his coach. His first tackle in the next match sent his opponent flying around six feet in the air, as he nearly cut him in half.

The following day I had a knock at the door of my house. A very irate Mrs Phillips, Jimmy's mum, berated me as strongly as a nice lady could. She bitterly resented my instructions to her son regarding his tackling ability. Strangely, I never received a call from her when a few years later Jimmy signed for Graeme Souness at Glasgow Rangers for £500,000.

A young centre-half called Mark Came also made a somewhat disastrous debut, following his signing from Winsford for a fee of around £500. Walter Joyce had again been the scout and, as usual, had dragged me out on a freezing wet night to see Mark play. We stayed even less time than we had when watching Brian Borrows, around 10 minutes.

"The game's just started," Walter said to me.

"Those two tackles he made in the 10 minutes we've watched him make him ideal centre-half material for me Walter," I quipped as we speedily headed for the exit.

I decided to give Mark his debut in a Milk Cup tie away against Notts County, who were a very good side at the time. At half time the score was 6-0 to Notts, with a shell-shocked Mark sat with his head down in the dressing room.

"Get your head up Mark," I shouted over at him. "Never, ever put your head down in the dressing room again."

The final scoreline of 6-1 was still embarrassing, but one of those football days that can have you shaking your head in disbelief because everything has gone against you. After all the hard work you have done in preparation for the match, everything goes horribly wrong. Thankfully, Mark survived the experience to have a fine career at Bolton, becoming captain after I left the club.

My relationship with the new chairman, Neil Riley, deteriorated. He proudly mentioned his connections at Liverpool and said that if we needed a centre-half he could persuade them to loan out Phil Thompson. I phoned Bob Paisley out of courtesy, asking him if I could have Jim Beglin on loan.

"Sorry John, but he is first in line if I have any injuries," he said. "But you're a good judge, because he can play."

I tentatively asked him about Phil Thompson.

"His legs have gone and I couldn't recommend him to you," replied Paisley, and my chairman was none too happy that the loan deal never materialised, but Bob was a great judge of a player and there was no way I was going to take Thompson if there was any doubt about him being able to do a job for me.

Since the second league match of the season, Riley had become increasingly nervous. I had to calm him down following a confrontation with me in the tunnel at the Baseball Ground immediately after our 3-2 loss to Derby. The match itself had been a brilliant game of football, but the loss, coupled with our 1-0 league opener defeat to Bristol Rovers, had him shaking with anger. My previous chairman, Terry Edge, was always positive and gave constructive advice, suitable suggestions on problems, appreciating that I had bugger-all financially to work with.

My sixth sense told me that my time was up, even before I was officially sacked on 7th January, 1985. Half of the directors couldn't even look me in the face at the final meeting, brave men that they were.

Getting the sack is never a pleasant experience, but at the same time there is nothing you can do about it. I was not Riley's appointment and I think he wanted his own man in the job. It was no good sitting around and brooding about it – in football management, being sacked goes with the territory.

I had a free weekend very soon after being dismissed, where

Ann and I had booked a couple of days at Gleneagles, the famous golf hotel in Scotland. As we registered I printed "redundant" as my present occupation, which raised a startled eyebrow from the receptionist.

In some ways it helped to get away. I had time to consider, ponder, and then formulate the next move. Getting the sack did not fill me with despair, only disappointment. I had certainly learned the hard way, making no more honest mistakes than anyone would have done in their first managerial role. Since arriving at Bolton I had launched a kit sponsorship scheme, taken a drop in wages, run a marathon, organised a dance for the supporters and self-financed a pre-season tour of Ireland, all in an effort to help the club financially. I could not have tried harder, which I thought would stand me in good stead for capturing my next job.

Mind you, Ann did jovially question my managerial ability when Bolton won their next four league matches. I received an apologetic phone call from Jeff Chandler, citing the luck of the devil as the main reason for their winning results, though. Sure enough, they then lost five and drew one of their next six league matches, restoring Ann's dwindling faith in my ability!

CHAPTER FIFTEEN

ISLAND IN THE SUN

T he first person who called me after I was sacked was called Tony Bentley, who ran a Ford car dealership in Salford. All he said to me was that he would always find a job for an honest man. This phone call worked wonders in lifting my spirits, helping to erase the stigma of self-doubt that inevitably accompanied my dismissal. I'd met Tony some time before and we quickly became close friends. We became even closer when he actually did give me a job, but not in the motor industry.

Tony helped run local football club Horwich RMI, and he initially recruited me to help train the players, before eventually persuading me to play, then, following some heavy persuasion, to manage the team. He was a successful businessman, with a wickedly dry sense of humour. He, his wife Angela and three sons lived close to us in Bolton, at a place called Smithills. We would spend many a night in his cellar-cum-snooker room resolving the world's problems. The reason I accepted Tony's invitation to become involved at Horwich was because I'd had no replies from four football league clubs I'd applied to regarding their managerial vacancies. Four applications and not even a polite reply accelerated my decision to work for Tony, but only on the strict understanding that I was paid nothing. He did, however, allow me the extended loan of a demonstration Ford car, to run about in. I also became friendly with Tony's good friend, Dave Russell, his wife Jean and son Mark, who played for us at Horwich. As I didn't have prior knowledge of players or standards in non-league, Dave was priceless when it came to the signings we made. Ann and I remain close friends with these lovely people.

This was literally my last playing stint, and it proved to be a memorable one because we won a competition called The Dairy Crest Floodlit League Cup. The final was played at Deepdale, Preston North End's ground, where we won 1-0, and I was absolutely thrilled to have won another medal playing the game that I love so much.

One day out of the blue I got a surprise call from Terry Edge the former Bolton chairman. He told me he was going to live in Tenerife, buy a bar/restaurant and wanted he wanted me to manage it for him. I knew he had sold his successful security business and, because I had enjoyed a stable working relationship with him at Bolton, I agreed to go with him on a reconnaissance trip, simply to assess the possibilities. I had no immediate future job in football, so what could I lose?

Our week in Tenerife was spent viewing various properties and bars, looking at locations as well as the housing situation, in case the move came to fruition. During the week I had the opportunity to play squash against an established estate agent on the island named Lawrence Howard. When he found out about my possible plans to come and live in Tenerife, he immediately offered me a job selling property. I told him I'd think about it and let him know. Having visualised and considered the less-than-appealing prospect of working behind a bar, I was pleased to have another job option offered to me.

When I got back to Bolton I told Ann that we were going to live in Tenerife. My big selling points consisted of the beautiful sunny weather, the chance to learn Spanish, plus the guarantee of a job. We had also been trying for over five years to start a family without success. I encouraged her by saying the change of scenery might help in that respect. Because I have always committed myself 100 percent to any job I told her we would move lock, stock and barrel and wouldn't come back within three years, in order to give it a real chance of working.

So the Spanish adventure in Playa de Las Americas was about to unfold.

The first difficulty we experienced following our move to Tenerife was finding out how long it takes to get jobs done. The well-worn cliché of mañana, mañana – tomorrow, tomorrow – is well used and absolutely true. One Tuesday morning we were waiting for our belongings to arrive from England, so that we would have a bed to sleep in, but the removals lorry didn't turn up until the Friday afternoon.

I was stomping around like a tightened piano wire for the first year, full of pent-up anger and frustration. Eventually the penny dropped, and I began to realise that it was the way things happened there. After all, I was the foreigner, so I needed to relax and enjoy the slower pace of life. Once I did that, the enjoyment of living in a sunshine paradise was truly wonderful.

Our first home was a small bungalow on a new complex called Garden City. It had a small garden at one side, making it an ideal home from home. I had an initial meeting with Lawrence and he took me with him on a tour of the sites and locations he was selling on, introducing me to the various site agents. I was a quick learner, and shortly afterwards he trusted me to take a client out on my own, during a busy period at the office. Because of my inexperience, Lawrence advised me to leave any financial discussions until we returned to the office, following the tour. Talking to people has never held any fear for me, and I settled in quickly selling my first property to my first customer and earning my first commission. We were paid commission only, and I had to cover all my other expenses. Despite delays from developers in fulfilling their payments, the system worked quite well.

I settled into life as an estate agent, with the added bonus that most of the residents and ex-pats enjoyed a game of squash during the siesta time. Taking time off between 1pm and 4pm is a very agreeable system and, with the relentless heat of the Spanish sun, the siesta is a welcome necessity.

With nearly everyone speaking English, there was no difficulty settling in, but you certainly earned the locals' respect if you tried to converse in their native tongue. Ann and I took a few lessons before work got in the way of the classes.

Living in the Tenerife sun does give you the opportunity to sunbathe every day if you wish, but I found that sunbathing lost its appeal very quickly. We were living in a climate where the shade often seemed more appealing and just walking about gave you a suntan.

During our first year of Tenerife life we enjoyed some fantastic news: Ann was pregnant. As residents of Tenerife, we were financially covered by a private medical scheme, a stipulation of living there. This encouraged us to have a Tenerife baby and 10th January was the given date for our new arrival.

On 31st December we were enjoying a New Year's party, when a sudden thunderclap of fireworks made us both jump. Ann swears to this day that the shock started things off, and on New Year's Day she felt very uncomfortable. In the early hours of the following morning, her waters broke. With no relatives or close friends to call, I had to get her to the clinic, quickly. We knew nothing about childbirth, so it was a fraught and panic-stricken couple that arrived in the dead of night at the hospital. I ran straight up to the front door which was locked, then started hammering on the glass with both fists. I hammered away for what seemed like an eternity and before spotting a sign saying that in emergency we should use the back door, so I ran round the back. Unbeknown to me, however, the night porter had gone to the front door as I now pounded away at the back!

We eventually got inside, allowing Ann to receive the attention she needed. Her doctor, Pedro Luis Corbiella, lived in Santa Cruz, the capital, which was 30 miles away from our home. With both expectant parents firing off question after question in rapid succession, the bemused attendant managed to calm us down by ringing the doctor. He was composure personified as he explained that our baby would be born at 9.30am when he arrived at the hospital. He had previously informed us that the baby would be delivered by caesarean section, so the pains of labour were not going to be an issue. He duly arrived, and on 2nd January, 1987, at the time he had given us out popped our son, eight days early. He didn't have a name because for some reason we were convinced it would be a girl. I suggested Ethan after John Wayne's character in *The Searchers*, which Ann thought was a bit hell, fire and brimstone. She preferred Dominic, which just didn't suit him. Eventually we decided on Alek John Luis, the Luis part coming from the name of Ann's doctor, who along with all the staff were brilliant. The John part was because Terry Edge, our fellow adventurer, thought it a good idea for him to have my name in there somewhere. The name Alek just flew into my head, and it had a certain Scottish flavour to it, although I was once told by some Lebanese property developers who I was working with that it is in fact an Arabic name.

A week later we steadily walked out of the hospital, into a clear blue sky, with temperatures around 70 degrees. I call them the eighth wonder of the world, babies that is, and they have a profound way of changing your life forever. Winning League Championships or European Cups just paled into insignificance by comparison to holding our son in my arms.

The biggest life change I noticed as a father was the lack of sleep. Unfortunately for us both, Alek used to scream the house down, approximately every three hours. Looking back, you wonder how you coped, especially when it lasted for three years. One saving grace was the year-round sunshine, which compensated in many ways.

With our new arrival came the constant stream of visitors, from both sets of parents to best friends and Uncle Tom Cobbly and all. We did enjoy one luxury that few had on our complex, and that was a telephone. Trying to install a telephone in those days was a long, drawn-out and testing experience. Once installed, people would ring you sometimes in desperation, trying to contact a friend or relative they had heard was staying on our complex. Sometimes all they wanted was to pass on a message.

One time, Ann picked up the phone, then shouted over to me.

"It's someone called Robert Plant, do you want to talk to him?" she asked.

"*The* Robert Plant?" I enquired.

"He just asked if you were *the* John McGovern," she told me, and with that a massive Led Zeppelin fan enjoyed a 10-minute conversation with one of his rock heroes. The reason for his call was that Robert had missed someone at the airport and following extensive enquiries had heard they were holidaying on our complex. He asked if I could locate them, then possibly let them talk on my phone at a suitable time. I didn't let him down, and received a reward of his latest cassettes to prove it.

During our conversation he asked my opinion on his latest work. I told him that while it was good, nearly every rock fan in the world wanted to see him front Led Zeppelin again, which eventually happened with the Plant and Page tour.

Life was never dull while living on a holiday island. I received another call from Alan Hill who had become the assistant manager of Nottingham Forest after Brian and Peter's partnership split up.

"Brian wants you to find us a quiet hotel in Las Americas with a tennis court. He is bringing the lads out for a break," he told me. Following some lengthy enquires, I found a suitable venue and phoned Alan back.

"Brian wants to know how much commission you are making on the booking?" he asked.

"Tell him to fuck off," I shouted angrily and slammed the phone down.

An apology soon followed, plus the insistence that if there was anything I needed to please ask. So I did, and it proved to be quite embarrassing for the Forest party. When I went to welcome them at their hotel, there were some red faces amongst the players, who were all carrying large boxes of disposable nappies! The nappies were an extortionate price in Tenerife, so I was presented with five very large boxes, with two squash rackets as a welcome bonus.

While the Forest team were enjoying their mid-season break, it was refreshing to catch-up with football conversation. Ian Bowyer, my former Forest midfield companion, who remains a friend to this day, was in the party, and it was great to talk to him again. I also enjoyed a long conversation with Brian without the intrusion of football. He quizzed me about life in the sun, Ann, and especially Alek, who we took along for him to see. I realised that I had never really enjoyed a social conversation with him before. It had always been a manager-player situation. He even came round to our house after we had been out for a meal and enjoyed watching a John Wayne film with us.

He did leave with one major complaint regarding the McGovern hospitality. Ann had asked if anyone would like coffee. Brian said he would, softly adding the words, "with a brandy". I was enjoying a Carlos 1 Spanish brandy, but Ann hadn't heard Brian's whisper. When Brian left following the movie, he mentioned to Alan Hill that he'd had five coffees without one brandy!

"I'll be awake all bloody night," he moaned.

As parents we were as doting as any, but the constant appearance of visitors and lack of sleep was slowly draining us of energy, Alek's three-hour wake-up calls giving me particular difficulties because I am such a light sleeper. Following a lengthy succession of bad nights, I contracted a head cold, which developed into a chest cold of some magnitude. I briefly went into work but then had to excuse myself, before heading for the clinic. I explained to the doctor that I needed some antibiotics for my cold. He insisted on X-raying my chest, then pointed out the black clouds inside my rib cage on the X-ray, which were diagnosed as pneumonia. He would not let me go home, confining me to bed immediately, despite my protests.

I spent a week in hospital and could not remember the first three days. After unsuccessfully trying to discharge myself, I walked out at the end of the week into the usual glorious Tenerife sunshine. About 10 days later I was the recipient of a severe rebuke from the doctor who had diagnosed me. He caught me playing squash, after warning me that any involvement with the game within three months was likely to produce a relapse, but the thrill of chasing a ball, thankfully, had never left me.

Fit and healthy, it was back to work again, and I was learning all the time. I also met and sold properties to some interesting people. I even managed to teach Lawrence, my boss, a lesson.

Our office closed at around 7.00pm, and if anyone strolled in at closing time they were generally window shoppers or non-buyers. One particular closing time I was asked by a casual enquirer about one of our best-selling complexes. A company called Gigansol had only built in Los Gigantes, another resort 40 minutes away up the coast from Las Americas. The artist's model our potential client had been studying was at present under construction, with no show apartment available to view. He asked me if I could show him the Gigantes complex, but mentioned he was flying home the next afternoon. My boss moved quietly behind him to signal to me over his shoulder, to get rid of him.

Perhaps it was my naivety or honesty, but I agreed to take him there early the next morning. Lawrence said I was wasting my time, but as with any customer I gave this guy my attention and respect. We drove up to Los Gigantes the following morning to view the lovely work of Gigansol, which certainly impressed my client. When we got back to the office he left a cheque deposit for five properties. Lawrence was dumbfounded.

"What the hell do I know about selling property?" he said with a smile.

Despite this guy walking into our office only five minutes before closing time in a T-shirt, shorts, and socks with sandals, he was a customer and as such needed to be treated with the same respect you would give to any customer, whether they were going to buy or not. Basic manners cost nothing.

This initial success encouraged my transition as an estate agent, which meant that I didn't feel homesick. Ann, Alek and I had a great time living in the sun of Tenerife, where meeting old friends and making new ones was a continual process. Jack and Sue from Bradford, two of our closest friends, were very welcome visitors, while a surprise visitor was Tony Bentley from my days at Horwich. He, along with his family, plus Dave Russell and family, came to say hello, with reminiscences of football success at Horwich filling the air with laughter.

I was revelling in a football-free environment. I now had a son, a new job, which I believed I was improving at, while living in a sunshine paradise – what could possibly be better? My career as a footballer had been incredible, from promotion at Hartlepools, to League Championships at Derby and Forest, to the glory of two European Cups as captain of Nottingham Forest. My lengthy dependence on football, following the disappointment of not picking up a second job in management after Bolton, had been replaced with a firm belief that if you are prepared to work hard, you can turn your hand to anything given a fair rub of the green. If you can sell a property based on an artist's model, while standing in the middle of an empty piece of waste ground, which was previously a banana plantation, you can do anything.

I was explaining this exact scenario, in confident estate agent spiel, when my potential customer Terry Warrender and his wife Jennifer looked at me.

"Are we supposed to believe that?" he asked. Before I replied, he smiled and brought us all into fits of laughter. Little did I know that Terry and Jennifer were to become customers and later my bosses. Terry was a businessman who had forged a name for himself in the aircraft service's industry. Warrender Aircraft Service's was based in Timperley, South Manchester, and provided a laundry and cutlery packing service for a myriad of airlines, including British Airways, Cathay Pacific, Qantas and American Airlines. Once Terry and Jennifer had signed-up to buy their apartment from the plans and artist's impressions, they made regular return trips to coincide with completed building stages, when they paid their next instalments. This was common practice when purchasing a property from architect's plans. On his final visit for the completion of his property, they would have to travel to Santa Cruz, Tenerife's commercial capital, to make the final payment including taxes. When all taxes are paid the client would then collect their title deeds, called the Escritura. This confirmed the purchaser's ownership of the property.

I accompanied Terry and Jennifer to pick up their title deeds. Unfortunately, Terry had forgotten his Spanish cheque book, which would have been disastrous, had I not offered a solution. I offered to pay his taxes. He stared at me in total disbelief.

"I know you'll pay me back, I trust you," I told him. Terry

paid me back immediately when he returned to England and then on his next visit to Tenerife asked me if I would work for him in his Manchester factory.

"I know nothing about the aircraft services business," I said.

"Maybe not, but you knew nothing about being an estate agent before you came to Tenerife. Besides, you're the most honest man I know on this island," he replied. It was a lovely compliment, and I thanked Terry, before telling him that I was really pleased he and Jennifer liked the property, but declined his job offer.

I must have been really enjoying life in Tenerife as I never experienced any homesickness whatsoever. Alek was growing well, Ann was a doting mother and so all seemed hunky-dory. Then a recession hit the English property market which accelerated the decline in foreign property buys. Lawrence, my boss, asked me to take a cut in commission.

"The other boys in the office have agreed," he told me.

"Sorry Lawrence, I don't want to take a cut", I said. "Besides, in a recession shouldn't you increase, not decrease commission?" He tried to backtrack, saying I could take less of a cut than the other salesmen, to which I politely said no.

Ann was surprised to see me home so early after the meeting with Lawrence, then dumbfounded to find out I had walked out on principle.

"Here we go again!" she said.

"Don't worry," I told her, "I'll work it out."

Within weeks I had visited all the main developers in the area. I produced an introductory letter promoting myself as an independent agent, which surprisingly was accepted across the board. I then registered myself with a Spanish solicitor, before starting work as a self-employed agent, and with my fingers crossed.

I worked independently for about a year, during which time to my surprise I made a profit, despite no relief regarding expenses. One of the hurdles to overcome while living in Spain and working for yourself is that there is no tax relief on working expenses such as petrol, car expenses, stationery and phone bills.

You can claim for nothing and everything comes out of your own pocket.

Ann, Alek and I moved to a three-bedroom villa from our two-bedroom bungalow. The view from it in San Eugenio Alto overlooked the newly built Puerto Colon marina, with spectacular sea views beyond. Alek was approaching nursery age, so I had surveyed the local schools and was totally unimpressed with the standards. I was also advised by some neighbourly ex-pats that, should we return to England when Alek was a few years older, he would be miles behind in his academic standards.

At the same time I was pondering Alek's future, Terry Warrender paid a visit, again asking me to work for him. I took a deep breath, having only just moved into our villa.

"Okay Terry," I said. "I'll come and work for you providing you pay for my relocation and buy my car, so I don't have to take it back to the UK."

We shook hands on the deal, and then I went home to tell Ann.

"You've just fitted the last picture in the villa," she said.

"It will be better for Alek," I told her, and knew exactly what she was going to say next.

"Here we go again!" she said while scratching her head.

We left with many lasting memories of Tenerife: its people, its culture, plus the bonus of a lifetime, Alek. After waiting so long for a child, we finally felt the delight and feeling of "wholeness" that having a child brings.

CHAPTER SIXTEEN

WAY OUT WEST

When we got back to England we stayed with Ann's parents in Mayfield near Ashbourne, until we found a suitable house in Bowden near Altrincham in Cheshire.

I will never forget my first day at work as Warrender Aircraft Services manager. I decided that the best way to get started was to learn about every single job the company did. I began by learning to fold blankets, which involved bending, shaking and folding all day. When I woke up the next morning I literally had to fall out of bed, because my back was so stiff and painful.

"You'll have to take the day off," Ann suggested, but my pride wouldn't let me. First day at work, then I go off sick. No chance! The embarrassment would have killed me. I gritted my teeth, feeling like I'd done three weeks pre-season training. I truly struggled and was eternally grateful when the first week was over.

I then went in to overdrive, taking in all the different functions of running a factory. Terry was a great boss, with bundles of enthusiasm, impressing every worker with his fearless approach to the job. Why did I learn so quickly? Just by asking when I needed help. After a couple of months I could wash, dry, iron, fold napkins or pack cutlery with the best of them. I also completed all the road trips, to familiarise myself with the destinations for our deliveries to Heathrow, Gatwick, Birmingham, Stansted or locally at Manchester airport.

After studying some of our service engineers, I learned how to replace hoses on washing machines, or guide bands on the huge industrial irons. Eventually, following some product study I changed most of our suppliers, which pleasantly surprised the accountant, enough to put a big smile on his face regarding the reduction in our running costs. I thought Ann, with some of her friends, might like to fold napkins in their spare time, the towelling ones that are hot and scented and are mostly given out on long-haul flights. Getting this job done off-site certainly perked up the girls at the factory, the napkins being their least favourite job.

After a year, I had the temerity to asking for a pay increase. Terry pointed out that one of the section managers at British Airways, responsible for an annual £4 million budget, was paid the same as me. Without hesitation I told Terry I was better at my job, regardless of the budget differential.

"He is a clock-on, clock-off merchant," I explained. Then I gave an example of how the same manager had failed to leave notification to his second in command after we delivered extra linen for an emergency flight. It was something I would never do, as clear communication in business is essential. Besides I was on call 24 hours each day as the company key-holder, should an emergency occur in the factory. Terry went along with my explanation, saying: "The only thing I'll ever lose you to is football."

He was a Manchester City fan, which invariably led to conversations concerning football. He provided strong arguments during football discussions, while appreciating the point of view from a seasoned professional. He was also a very generous boss, who threw big Christmas work parties. Everyone always had a great time at a Warrender's Christmas do. He also employed a comedian called John Martin at another large birthday bash, and he asked me if I had considered after-dinner speaking, enthralled by some of my footie stories about Brian Clough. I told him I hadn't, and he encouraged me to try it, just for the challenge.

Over a year passed, by which time I had competently learned

to perform most jobs in the factory, even supervising an emergency clean-up operation following a flood. My other minor
claim to fame was opening a new factory unit in Bathgate,
Scotland. This included designing the whole layout of the factory.
On completion I was like a cat on a hot tin roof when Terry
came to inspect it, wondering if all the machines were in the
correct locations. This new unit was required to service contracts
for Edinburgh and Glasgow Airports, and I held my breath as
Terry walked through the entrance. He looked one way, then
the other, said a polite good morning to all the staff then turned
to me.

"Great, now where can we go for lunch?" he asked.

It was a big relief. I actually thought I had bitten off more
than I could chew when I volunteered to set out the whole
factory from an empty shell.

With the new unit completed, it was back to Manchester,
where there were always problems to solve, and it was my
responsibility to do so. At short notice an emergency had arisen,
regarding a rapid linen delivery to Inverness airport. Whoever
the unlucky delivery driver was, they would have to leave in the
middle of the night. The marathon drive attracted no potential
volunteers, so I decided to deliver the British Airways linen
myself. At the time I was driving a Ford Fiesta turbo, the company
car of my choice. It got me there comfortably, clocking 130mph
at one stretch of clear motorway, which was the fastest I had
ever driven in my life and as close to taking-off as possible.
Thankfully, at 4.30am there were no other vehicles in sight.
What a car!

Back to sanity, following the delivery to Inverness I was treated
with a polite enquiry from the catering manageress, who asked
me if I would like a cup of tea and a couple of bacon rolls. I
sat there and put my feet up, staring into the golden, breaking
early-morning sunrise, drinking scalding hot tea and eating
gorgeous hot bacon rolls, feeling like a millionaire.

Out of the blue, in 1992, I received a surprise call one day
from my old Forest team-mate Peter Shilton. He told me he had
an interview at Birmingham City for the manager's job, and

wanted to know if I would be his assistant if he was successful. I told him it was a hypothetical situation but said that if he did get the job he should give me another call. While I had never actively approached any club regarding a return to football, the confidence that my previous two jobs had given me had prepared me for any eventuality, but there was one major stumbling block and that was the superb working relationship I enjoyed with my boss Terry Warrender. Terry had been very generous, besides giving me enormous respect. Any decision would have to be considered at length, despite my love of football.

Momentarily, sanity prevailed, because Peter failed in his application for the Birmingham position.

"You must be crackers," Ann told me when I mentioned the possibility of going back into football. "Terry said you had a job for life and now you're thinking about football again. You must be daft."

There was certain trepidation when Peter rang me again not long after his initial call, this time to tell me he was the new Plymouth Argyle manager. Once more there was the offer to be his assistant.

"I'll come and discuss it with you Pete, but nothing is certain." I told him.

Our first meeting was not fruitful because Peter offered me less money than I was earning at Warrender Aircraft Services. He seemed surprised when I declined his offer. As a family man I couldn't consider losing money, despite the obvious attraction of returning to football.

Peter must have been quite persuasive with his chairman, and soon after our meeting he was back on to say that I would be on the same salary as I was at Warrender. Needless to say, he needed me there as soon as possible, which would in turn leave Warrender's requiring a new manager at short notice. Terry reluctantly accepted my resignation, repeating his prediction.

"I knew I would only lose you to football," he said. Ann was as pragmatic as ever, voicing her usual "here we go again" sigh.

There was one massive problem to overcome. We had been renting out our villa in Tenerife, which helped pay for our house in Bowden. The property market in Tenerife was still in deep recession, making any attempted sale financial suicide. The English property market was also depressed, with the McGoverns desperately requiring a base in Plymouth. We managed to solve the property conundrum by renting out our house in Bowden. We also rented a smart, terraced property in West Hoe, Plymouth. Problem solved. Or so we thought.

Re-entering the football arena following an absence of seven years was a far-from-smooth transition. Joining a struggling side like Bolton Wanderers had taught me the need for lots of positive energy. To relocate and settle requires speed, coupled with patience. Plymouth, as a football location, is something of an outpost. The wonderful landscapes and seascapes of Devon and Cornwall, however, significantly support any argument regarding a move to the West Country. For Alek, now five years old, the beaches with rock pools, where we would spend hours catching crabs and fish, were a natural, enthralling adventure playground. Ann quickly set up our lovely apartment in West Hoe, a place that had a superb park and children's playground, not to mention tennis courts just a stone's throw away. One added historic attraction of our location was the adjacent Plymouth Hoe, with stunning panoramic views of Plymouth Sound.

When inheriting a struggling side the first major step, if it is possible, is to sign fresh blood with as much quality as your chairman can afford. Peter must have done his homework as the Plymouth chairman Dan McAuley was extremely generous with his hard-earned money.

Having been exceptionally fit footballers, both Peter, who was still playing, and I could lead by example when the running started, as I had maintained my fitness by playing squash and running regularly. There's no point in a player complaining during a lung-bursting cross-country run if the management duo is leading the pack. This side of my return to football was easily overcome, while being responsible for new routines didn't gel as quickly.

I was responsible for handing in the Football League regulation team sheet to the referee an hour before kick-off. Despite a lapse before my first match against Derby County on 7th March, 1992, humble apologies saved me from being reported by the sympathetic referee. Peter, however, fined me £20 for my error! "Just as an example," he explained.

At Warrender Aircraft Services I had literally been my own boss, and given carte blanche on how to run the company. Now I was second in command, making it essential to develop a sound relationship with the manager. For the uninformed, I had better explain that as an assistant football manager, your decision-making is literally zero. Managers make all the decisions, whether it is training, travelling, days off, discipline, coaching . . . whatever. His word is final. I understood this totally, having experienced management over the two-and-a-half years of my previous tenure at Bolton Wanderers.

As an assistant, you obviously discuss all management issues with the manager, giving your opinion whenever the need arises. You will never agree on all issues but, following any debate, the manager will then make the final decision. My first minor reservation when it came to my relationship with Peter came during an early coaching session, where in my opinion his instruction to the midfield players was somewhat misleading. Following the session I pointed out that, having been a midfield player for donkey's years, my input might be beneficial. This suggestion was dismissed, which slightly disappointed me, as it seemed a small issue in the vast scale of running a football team. The main task at struggling Plymouth was to change some of the players, with new blood urgently required. But because it was March, we had less than two months to save Plymouth from relegation.

Kevin Nugent from Leyton Orient became our first major signing. His agent Alan Harris, a former Plymouth player in the Seventies and brother of Ron "Chopper" Harris, had a vastly superior opinion of Kevin's ability than yours truly. When Peter and I asked what kind of signing-on fee was required, a quote of £100,000 was calmly mentioned. At this point I burst out laughing, which neither the player, his agent, nor Peter appreciated. A brief interval ensued, with Peter informing me that he was not amused by my laughter when we badly needed to sign him.

"How many times has Nugent played for England?" I asked Peter, because to demand such a signing on fee required more substantial credentials than his present career at Orient offered.

After we reconvened, sense prevailed with a massive reduction in the player's demands. Perhaps it was my Scottish upbringing, but I regarded his first demands as totally unacceptable. My stance was influenced by never having had any money to spend at Bolton. Common sense told me to treat the club's money like my own, which was always hard-earned.

Peter had employed David Coates as his chief scout, and he set up the Nugent deal and proved influential in a number of our future signings. Peter asked me to suggest other players, particularly a left-back, which was another urgent requirement.

"He's playing at Bradford reserves this week," I informed him. This meant us both completing the lengthy trip. Steve McCall was the target, and he was playing for Sheffield Wednesday reserves. I had made numerous phone calls regarding Steve's ability, character, attitude, marital status, age, temper, habits, injury history and all other points to cover my recommendation. It was normal procedure, to try and guarantee that Plymouth would get a reasonable return for the £25,000 they eventually paid for McCall.

All signings are a gamble, whether you pay a big or small fee. It is always a question of whether they will they fit in, hit form, stay fit and settle. Persuading players to come to Plymouth, a football outpost, inevitably meant paying them over the odds. If they produced the goods, there was no argument and Steve McCall turned out to be an outstanding success, justifying the whole deal. Despite these promising early signings, though, we were still relegated following our last home match, a 3-1 defeat to Blackburn Rovers.

Two signings boosted the squad before our following league programme started. Gary Poole, a right-back, was recruited on a free transfer from Barnet, while Warren Joyce, the midfielder

I had given his debut to at Bolton, also joined from Preston. New faces would continue to appear in a season of transition. With money being spent, expectations soared. Plymouth Argyle spending large amounts of money on players was an exciting novelty for the ardent Pilgrims supporters. If you spend money in football you must guarantee results. While the changes of personnel didn't have a dynamic effect on our results, a change in the playing rules did.

From the start of the 1992/93 season, goalkeepers were no longer allowed to pick up the ball from a backpass, and this was to cause many goalkeepers, including Plymouth's, a major problem. Peter may have won 125 caps for England yet, despite his denial, he struggled to deal with this significant change. While Peter would laugh off suggestions that he could not handle the new rule, we did bring in a young goalkeeper called Ray Newland, who would make more appearances than Peter did over the season.

We continued to spend, signing Steve Castle, a midfield general from Leyton Orient for £195,000, and then we pushed the boat out signing Hartlepool winger Paul Dalton for £275,000. Centre-half Keith Hill and right-winger Craig Skinner also joined the club as we searched for the winning formula we needed. Our away form was as bad as our home form was good. By early November we were unbeaten at home, yet had won only one league match away, so it was hardly surprising that certain newspapers had the Plymouth Argyle management team as hot favourites for the sack.

In November a televised first-round FA Cup tie with non-league Dorking heightened the pressure. Peter Shilton, who had played the previous 14 games, left himself out of the side, giving novice Ray Newland an unexpected debut.

As I walked into the Dorking ground I noticed a sports reporter from a national television station.

"Have you come to see us get the sack then?" I shouted over to him.

"Yes we have," was his instant reply, his lips almost salivating at the thought.

"Bastard!" I muttered to myself as we quickly headed for the away dressing room.

We survived that day, edging to a very tense 3-2 victory. In very difficult circumstances we came through and all the press who had come to see an upset had to go home disappointed. The victory eased the pressure on us. Had we lost who knows what would have happened?

Another new signing, Richard Dryden, also made his debut on that dramatic afternoon. Despite this welcome cup win, our poor away league form returned as we lost 3-0 the following Friday at Stockport.

Our next game was a home fixture against Bournemouth, where before the match I was to experience my first and only dream about football, which turned into a reality. The dream involved a trialist who had deservedly earned a contract. His name was Paul Boardman, the son of comedian Stan Boardman. I'd met Stan at the Grand National one year, and when I joined Plymouth he had rung me up to ask me to give his son a trial, volunteering to pay all his own expenses during his trial period. He did very well and was then selected to start up front against Bournemouth. On the eve of the match, I was asleep, experiencing a very clear dream. I was looking at Paul Boardman, who scored with a right-foot shot in the top corner giving us a 2-1 win. When I woke up the next morning I told Ann, who suggested I tell someone.

"Nobody is going to believe me," I said. "In fact, I don't believe it myself, because I've never dreamed of anything with such clarity in my life."

The dream was still crystal clear and lingering somewhere in my subconscious as I got to the ground and then watched the match unfold. It was turning out to be a frustrating 1-1 stalemate, until late in the second half when Paul Boardman gathered the ball, sidestepped a challenge and rifled a right-foot rocket into the top corner of the Bournemouth goal. Our bench erupted, with everyone leaping into the air to celebrate Paul's brilliant strike. Suddenly Peter Shilton turned and saw me sitting motionless in the dugout.

"We've scored," he shouted to me.

"I know I've seen it before," I replied shaking my head in disbelief.

I never actually told anybody apart from Ann about the dream, and if I had I doubt that they would have believed me anyway.

A win momentarily relieves the pressure on the manager of a struggling side, but as Plymouth's season progressed, the pressure and expectancy ramped up. Mr McCauley, our benevolent chairman, was as eager as the fans for some tangible improvements. His fiery temper would sometimes erupt without warning, creating an uneasy working relationship between him and the two of us. When the chairman lost his temper it was advisable to steer clear. And sometimes his arguments defied all rationality.

With a home match against Huddersfield imminent, Mr McCauley, possibly for cash flow reasons, desperately needed the match on. The weather had other ideas. Despite forking continually, then attempting to cover the worst central area with tarpaulin sheets, the lack of basic drainage finally proved fatal. As one apprentice attempted to lay the tarpaulin he was thrown skywards, almost breaking his neck, as the gale-force winds whipped up the cover like an exploding air bag. After the game was inevitably called off I received a solicitor's letter from the chairman which basically said that I should have ensured that the game went ahead.

Being threatened with the sack because of poor results is not unusual in football management. But being threatened with dismissal due to the weather was certainly harder to comprehend.

I actually got my own solicitor to reply to McCauley's letter, but at the same time I knew that it was no longer a muddy pitch I had to worry about, it was the thin ice that both Peter and I seemed to be skating on.

There was no respite from the poor away form and, having lost 3-1 at Ipswich in the FA Cup, we then went to Bolton in the league and were defeated by the same score. We had a chance to regain some pride as we played Torquay in the AG Trophy on 20th January, but despite playing our strongest side we lost 2-1 as Neil Warnock's team physically battered us. Normally the manager would go into the boardroom after a match to give his opinion.

"He'll be expecting us," I told Peter.

"I'm not going in," he replied.

So yours truly went in to brave the impending tornado. As soon as I entered the Torquay boardroom Mr McCauley stormed up to me delivering both barrels at full volume.

"Call yourselves fucking managers," he screamed and then continued his ferocious assault for the next five minutes.

When he'd finished he turned and stormed off, his gin and tonic shaking in his hand. One of the Torquay directors sidled up to me and said that he had never seen anything like that in his life. I thanked him for his concern and told him, had the chairman and my own position been in reverse, I might have said the same thing. In management you have to accept the responsibility for defeat. We still needed to produce a successful team.

Having walked something of a tightrope that season, we eventually finished 14th in the league, yet remained in our jobs. Before the following season started Mr McCauley had seen us recoup over £700,000 from two sales as Andy "Jock" Morrison and Nicky Marker, our two centre-halves, joined Kenny Dalglish at Blackburn Rovers. Gary Poole had also left for Birmingham in a deal worth £350,000, not bad for a free transfer. These outgoings went a long way to balancing the books, which certainly eased the strain on our chairman.

Meanwhile, the unfortunate injury-hit Warren Joyce left for Burnley. Steve Morgan, a central defender, also joined Coventry City, leaving scope for a few changes. With new faces Dominic Naylor and Mark Patterson, both full-backs, midfielder Wayne Burnett and centre-half Andy Comyn recruited, an improved season was an absolute necessity if we were going to keep our jobs.

As assistant to Peter, who was still playing, I used to cover most of the scouting, as it was always important to watch players. From Plymouth this required countless hours of travel on my days off. Ann would sometimes protest, before accepting that it was part of the job. To use your own judgement on any recommendation, it is vital to see players with your own eyes.

Having filled most of the positions in the team, I still kept mentioning my reservations concerning Peter's continuance between the sticks. "I know you are close to making your 1,000th league appearance, which would be an incredible feat, but would you rather achieve that or stay in management?" I asked him. I couldn't make it clearer than that. He didn't receive this suggestion too well, despite my insistence that we should sign another keeper.

His inability to handle the backpass rule saw him sometimes having to kick balls away for corners. Peter eventually relented when I unearthed a very confident young keeper from Cheltenham called Alan Nicholls. I had been warned about his volatile character, yet was certain in my own mind regarding his ability, despite having only watched him twice. When questioned by the chairman about him, I gave him a worse-case scenario and explained that we would probably have to fine him a few times and maybe even suspend him for off-field misdemeanours as we broke him in.

"Then why the hell have we signed him?" enquired an anxious Mr McCauley.

"Wait until you see him keep goal."

During the season he was to play over 40 league and cup matches, eventually gaining England Under-21 recognition. He cost the club a mere £15,000. Despite his previous off-field misdemeanours, which happened before I signed him, his ability to keep goal was unquestionable.

One player we didn't sign was a Luton Town midfielder called Geoff Aunger. Peter Shilton had a good relationship with David Pleat, the Luton manager. He had agreed a fee of around £50,000 when I suggested that we should have a look at the boy first.

"I've already agreed the deal with David," he said. I insisted on checking out the player, convincing Peter that my playing career of 17 years in midfield should guarantee my judgement.

My first trip to Luton was a disaster as the reserve match was called off due to flooding, after I had arrived at the ground. My second trip proved more fruitful and I watched most of the reserve match, before being joined by David Pleat. David's assessment of Aunger didn't quite match up to his very average display during the match, but everyone has a different opinion of players. I returned to Plymouth to tell Peter that I didn't think Aunger was worth anything close to £50,000 and suggested that he wouldn't improve our squad. Peter insisted that he'd already agreed the deal, which forced me to make my position quite clear.

"If you sign him, I want it known at board level that I was against the move 100 per cent," I told him.

We didn't let the argument last, eventually dropping the move. I was an assistant, but would stand my corner if I considered I was in the right. Aunger was eventually given a free transfer by Luton.

Kicking off our league programme with a 3-2 home defeat by Stockport, followed by a 3-0 Coca-Cola Cup loss away to Birmingham, was not the best way to fulfil the eager, almost desperate expectancy of the Home Park faithful. Our third match saw midfield dynamo Steve Castle score twice, as we earned an away point at Hull. The next two home matches against Birmingham and Port Vale were both 2-0 victories, as young keeper Alan Nicholls came into the side.

Consistency eventually replaced erratic performances during the 1993/94 campaign and the threat of imminent sacking diminished. Young local talent such as Martin Barlow, Marc Edworthy and Michael Evans joined established players such as Adrian Burrows and Dwight Marshall. They all contributed and enjoyed the confidence and quality of Steve Castle and Paul Dalton, who became Home Park favourites.

I was delighted at how the season progressed, especially after persuading my ex-Forest team-mate Ian Bowyer to take over the youth team manager's position. As the season developed, Steve Castle became a powerhouse in the midfield engine room, with his superb heading ability making him a real threat from set plays. At the end of the season he had managed to score over 20 goals. A massive contribution from a midfield player, who fully deserved the supporters' accolades. He helped us to maintain a challenge for promotion throughout the campaign.

One other addition to our squad was another non-league signing called Richard Landon. He joined us in January, then despite the consistency of Nugent and Marshall managed a few games as the season finished. I am sure he will not forget his hat-trick at Hartlepool, as we wound up our league programme in style with an 8-1 victory. Despite this win our cheers turned to sighs of disappointment as Port Vale secured a 2-1 victory at Brighton in the very last game of the season, edging us out of the automatic promotion spot.

This, of course, meant the play-offs, an unfair illogical system, where following 46 league matches over 10 months of the season you then have to play against teams you finished above to prove who deserves promotion. You will gather from my description that I do not like play-offs.

We were matched against Burnley, who had finished 12 points behind us, making us the favourites over the two legs of the semi-final tie. The first match at Turf Moor was a tense, hard-fought stalemate which ended 0-0. The return match at Home Park was watched by a tremendous crowd of 17,500. It was one of those days you find difficult to explain. We started out positively, with attack following attack, but got caught by a Burnley break to lose a goal. Then we lost a second goal to a counter attack. The final score was 3-1 to Burnley, with Home Park resembling a morgue after the final whistle. There was no consolation for players, managers or supporters, just a horrible feeling of dismay and desolation which would only fade over time.

One big positive factor for me following an (almost) successful season was that I had signed a new two-year contract with the club. This was particularly important because I was experiencing serious financial difficulties.

My tenants in Tenerife had stopped paying their rent, as had my tenants in Bowden. With no rental income coming in to pay our outgoing rent on our place in Plymouth, my savings were draining to a dangerous level. At least during the close season I knew I had some time to solve the problems, if only I could get rid of my squatters, or hopefully sell the properties.

I did have one source to recover a loan from, which I thought would prove simple. Peter Shilton had borrowed £5,000 from me, which he explained was a short-term transaction. Due to his complicated financial holdings and signing-on fees, it was supposedly an interim solution. Having asked him for the money back, when my own financial situation deteriorated, he promised me it would be repaid imminently, but it didn't happen.

The reason I needed the money back, apart from my property-related problems and the fact that the debt was overdue, was that I had borrowed the money from the bank myself for this short-term loan, as I didn't have that amount of cash readily available. The loan was gaining interest.

I eventually confronted him and asked him to fulfil his promise.

"I have part of my signing-on fee due next week and I'll pay it all back to you," he promised.

Having been previously let down, I decided to check the validity of his statement. I went to see the club secretary, Michael Holliday, and asked him discretely if the manager had a signing-on amount due in his wages, stressing I didn't need to know figures as this was a personal request which I needed to keep confidential. He simply told me that there were no extra amounts being paid to the manager in his forthcoming wages, as they had been fulfilled in total.

I made one more request for repayment of my loan, which was not forthcoming. Now I had a major problem in working with Peter.

Despite this personal problem, Plymouth still had to prepare for the coming season. No matter what my differences with the manager, football must go on. We discussed signing a centre-half. I had suggested a Cambridge player called Mike Heathcote, with Peter recommending Port Vale strongman Peter Swan. As I was his assistant, he outranked me, so Peter Swan it was. Swan was a strong character, very similar to Steve Castle, which somehow was unsettling in the dressing room, and with the season about to begin it did not augur well for the weeks and months ahead.

At this time Archie Gemmill, my midfield partner from Nottingham Forest, told me he had been given the Rotherham United manager's job. He wanted me to join him as soon as possible as joint-manager. I told him bluntly that I had signed a new deal at Plymouth, which would make it difficult for me to leave.

"See what you can do," he replied, leaving me to consider a move which would offer a possible solution to the growing untenable relationship with my present boss. Then I learned that Peter had borrowed money from a friend of mine, which was the final straw for our working relationship. I confronted Peter once again, and told him that what had gone on between us over the loan meant our working relationship was over. I turned, walked to my car and drove home.

Minutes after I had sat down after arriving home at our first-floor apartment in West Hoe, there was a ring at the door. It was Peter Shilton and he rang the bell several times, but despite his attempts, I would not answer his shouts or repeated knocks on the door.

I called the chairman, asking for an immediate meeting, informing him I could no longer work with the manager. He reluctantly met me with two other directors. I explained that I had a personal problem with Peter and could not continue to work with him. Dan McCauley was understandably quite annoyed, telling me I had just signed a two-year contract and that he would sue me if I walked out. Eventually I told him I had no option, without wishing to divulge my personal reason.

"I will keep your reason in the strictest confidence, as we have to consider our course of action," he informed me.

I told him of my unpaid loan and he reluctantly agreed that my situation was understandable, allowing me to leave the club. As far as I was concerned, the matter would not leave the meeting I'd had with the chairman. From my point of view, keeping the facts in confidence would suit all parties

Unfortunately, for whatever reasons, the chairman released my comments to the press the following day. I wasn't pleased at all to have all of this made public, but once it had happened there was very little I could do. So I left Plymouth, with some unforgettable memories, not necessarily on the football scene. I had committed myself wholeheartedly in helping the improvement of the football club. And, despite the long hours involved in the job, I still enjoyed my rare time off. I also achieved a lifetime ambition, by dancing on stage with one of my guitar heroes.

Ann and I had taken Alek to the Pavilion Concert Hall in Plymouth on Thursday 19th November, 1992, to watch Chuck Berry. At the end of his set, Chuck beckoned people on stage to dance with him on his final number. Alek and I both jumped at the chance, boogieing feet away from the man himself. After his initial move, Alek moved to centre stage, dancing to the crowd with confidence beyond belief. Small wonder he's now lead singer in a rock band called Scrim.

Ann and I also took Alek to see Michael Jackson at Wembley, where following a postponement we marvelled at the performer's special magic. Again, as soon as Jackson began his show, Alek ran to the end of our aisle to boogie on his own. This provided great entertainment to a beguiled group of spectators in one of the corporate boxes behind us, who watched his every move.

While at Plymouth I certainly had my differences with chairman Dan McCauley, but I also respected him immensely as a man. I salute him for giving his management team money to help improve the team, which gave the Plymouth faithful the exciting 1993/94 play-off season to remember.

I have since met and shaken hands with Peter Shilton, who eventually paid back the debt he owed. Life is too short to hold grudges.

Back then I sadly left Plymouth behind, and it was off to Rotherham for two more informative years in the crazy world of football management.

CHAPTER SEVENTEEN

"I CAN'T HELP BEING ME, AND YOU CAN'T HELP BEING YOU"

When I agreed to work with Archie Gemmill as joint-manager, it was purely for the reason that I had five years' experience in the job. At the initial press conference we attended in September 1994, Archie was asked why he wanted me alongside him.

"Because he won't stab me in the back," was his typically curt response.

Like Plymouth, Rotherham had a very generous chairman, Mr Ken Booth. He gave Archie and me money to spend and then attempted to recover it as earnestly as possible.

One major stumbling block I had to overcome was the answer Archie gave me to my pertinent question.

"Where have Phil Henson, the previous manager, and his assistant John Breckin gone?" I said.

"They're both being kept on," he replied. I looked at Archie long and hard.

"You mean we are running the team with the previous management team still at the club? You must be bloody joking, we have got absolutely no chance!" I told him.

"Phil is the new chief executive and John Breckin will help with the coaching." Archie confirmed.

How bizarre, I thought to myself. I had no problems with either John or Phil and certainly didn't want to put them out of work, but I knew that this arrangement had never occurred before during my time in football.

Playing with someone, as I had with Archie, was one thing, but working with him in management was something totally different. Thankfully, all I saw in Archie as a player, such as dedication, determination and commitment, was reflected in his approach to management. When it comes to management and playing the good cop, bad cop routine, I'm afraid Archie could only qualify for the bad cop role. He was always seriously focused in his dedication to the job and this came over in the way he operated. I could often see the funny side of things, but Archie was infinitely more blinkered in his approach to management and there was really no room for frivolity compared to myself.

Moving from Plymouth as a family didn't take too long, despite the handicap of scouring the Rotherham/Sheffield area while Sheffield was installing its new tram system. The traffic was in absolute turmoil. We did find a property, where my previous experience as an estate agent served me well. I had looked on the chosen site, then been fobbed off by the sales lady saying the well-positioned property I wanted was reserved.

"How long has it been reserved and how much is the reserve deposit?" I enquired.

When she informed me that the prospective buyers had reserved the house with £50 without having sold their current property I was amazed. I told her bluntly that I could pay a ten percent deposit immediately. She stubbornly repeated it was reserved.

"If you don't phone your boss with my offer in the next five minutes, I will," I told her firmly, looking at my watch. A short while later we had secured the property.

As luck would have it, coincidentally we sold our villa in Tenerife, greatly easing our financial position. Within a year we also sold the Manchester property, although we lost over £30,000 on the deal, but it allowed us to clear our mortgage in Sheffield.

Despite Rotherham's humble status, the chairman had produced a tremendous training ground at Hooton Roberts, with excellent training pitches and rolling tree-filled hills surrounding the complex.

Getting to know the players as quickly as possible was essential as ever. Our initial assessment made changes inevitable. We brought in midfielder John McGlashan, striker Bobby Davidson, winger Andy Roscoe and centre-half Mark Monington, as well as another midfield player, Gareth Farrelly, and forward Nathan Peel. Despite making changes, the Millers' results showed no massive improvement over the 1994/95 season. Finishing in 17th position was certainly an average start. Not quite a relegation battle, but a season of struggle, lacking the consistency that helps you sleep comfortably. There were deep discussions with Archie as to what was required to make the next season a success.

Despite Archie's serious approach there were one or two comical moments, too. One happened during a training match at Hooten Roberts. Carey Williams, a young striker, wasn't sure where to run in order to lose his marker, or provide a target for the supporting midfield players. At half time he approached Archie, desperately pleading to him:

"Boss, where do I run?"

"You see that hill over there," I said pointing to the incline behind him. "Just run up there Carey and, when you get to the top, keep going."

Before Archie could tear a strip off me, Carey had about-turned and was halfway up the hill until we shouted him back.

The next day our chairman Mr Booth appeared at the training ground. He called me over and started ranting about how the manager had told a player to run up a hill, which wasn't the kind of behaviour he respected. I interrupted him mid-tirade to explain that whoever his informant was, his facts were wrong. It wasn't Archie, it was me, I explained, trying to convince him it had been a joke. His face remained impassive, as he shrugged his shoulders and quickly headed for the exit. I thought how small-minded it was to go to the training ground over a minor player-manager exchange of words. I also wondered who the informant might be. If he made that trip for something so trivial, what would it be like over a major issue?

Another incident caused a minor head-to-head between Archie and I during a game at Millmoor. We were defending a corner, with difficulty. The ball was bobbling haphazardly inside our penalty area, following four or five attempts to get it clear. Archie was literally screaming for someone to put his foot behind the ball and kick it anywhere. Suddenly, our centre-half had an almighty swing, attempting to smash the ball to safety. Unfortunately, standing in this path was our centre-forward who obligingly bent over so he could kick it over him. The centre half volleyed the ball straight into his backside and the ball rebounded like a rocket past our bewildered keeper before shaving a goalpost on its way out for a corner. I burst out laughing, along with everyone on the bench, followed by the 4,000 spectators.

Archie rounded on me, screaming that we nearly lost a goal and I didn't take the job seriously enough. With players and spectators now watching I said nothing, preferring to talk it over in our office after the match. Once behind closed doors, Archie further repeated his misgivings about my approach to the job. I don't remember exactly how we finished the discussion, but I did say "I can't help being me, and you can't help being you."

One thing was certain, our differences in character were never going to interrupt our strong, loyal and long-standing relationship. We were both totally focused on trying to improve the team.

During our 1995/96 season we made two major signings: Mike Jeffrey, a quality striker from Newcastle, and Paul Blades, a defender from Wolves. Archie also signed a winger named Trevor Berry from Aston Villa and Gary Bowyer, a full-back, who was Ian's son. I recommended the signing of Darren Garner, a midfielder who I knew from Plymouth, who also joined us.

We struggled for consistency, and as we reached November we slipped below halfway in the league. One shining ray of hope was a 4-1 win over Wigan in the Auto Windscreens Shield in

November. This followed a 7-0 hammering at Wrexham and a 3-2 loss at home to Bristol City. Despite 100 per cent commitment from players and hour after hour of post-mortem discussions between Archie and myself, our inconsistency continued.

By 6th January we had slumped to fifth from bottom of the table, before a 3-2 victory against Lincoln in the Auto Windscreens Shield quarter-final revived us. We then won four league games in a row, before hammering York 4-1 as our Auto Windscreens run continued. All of a sudden the pressure lifted, smiles replaced scowls and a feel-good factor infiltrated Millmoor. Sometimes you need a lucky break, and that 4-1 led to some better form for the team. Being successfully involved in the cup run got us into the habit of winning. Winning breeds confidence, which started to flow through Rotherham Football Club in torrents.

We then took on Carlisle in the northern final first leg of the Auto Windscreens at Millmoor, winning 2-0 courtesy of a Shaun Goater goal and Neil Richardson penalty. Suddenly, people started talking about Rotherham going to Wembley. Only two months earlier I was praying we would stay in our jobs – how quickly things can change.

On the 12th March, one week after the first leg, we went to Carlisle with a 2-0 lead. Our performance perfectly reflected the mood within the club. At the final whistle, Nigel Jemson, our loan striker, raised his arms aloft to celebrate his two goals, in an historic 4-0 aggregate victory that achieved the dream for players and supporters alike. Rotherham United were going to Wembley.

We drew 2-2 at home in the league with Shrewsbury just one week before we were due to meet them at Wembley on Sunday 14th April. For the football club it was a time to celebrate. Archie and I had been to Wembley as players, winners and losers, so we knew that regardless of the thrill involved it was not a nice place to lose. Archie decided that we would go down to London on Friday, train on Friday night, then go to a game on Saturday, before taking it easy for the final on Sunday.

"Can we take in a film?" I asked, recalling a habit from my playing days.

"Okay, you can make the arrangements," Archie replied.

I showed him my prepared schedule, which included a Chelsea v Leeds match, followed by a walk down the King's Road to the cinema.

"What are we going to see?" he enquired.

"A great film called *Trainspotting*," I told him with a smile.

"Oh no," he groaned, "We can't watch that – I'm in it."

I knew the movie included a clip of Archie scoring his sensational 1978 World Cup goal for Scotland against Holland.

"It will do the lads good. Besides, they will give you loads of stick." I said.

I knew Archie didn't want to go to that particular movie, but I insisted. I felt it would help the team spirit before such a big game.

The initial stages of our Wembley adventure started well, as most of the players won bets at the Chelsea v Leeds game. Then, following a brisk walk down the King's Road, we settled down at the cinema to watch *Trainspotting*. My plan worked a treat, as Archie's appearance in the movie was accompanied by a chorus of catcalls and whistles. After the movie finished our coach driver picked us up on cue to take us back to the hotel. Dinner followed, before bed, and the players were able to look forward to the biggest day in most of their lives.

Any Wembley final is memorable for supporters, players, directors, managers, relations and everyone involved. The Auto Windscreen Shield, or similar-titled competitions, provide people involved with minor teams a rare opportunity to bask in glory at the famous stadium. For Rotherham United it was one of those days. Our on-loan striker, Nigel Jemson, repeated his feat of the northern final second leg by scoring twice as we overcame Shrewsbury, 2-1.

The words, "Rotherham United have won a final at Wembley" immediately restored some much needed pride at the club. Struggling league form was instantly forgotten as the jubilant support of approximately 18,000 Millers fans went wild as the final whistle blew.

In the dressing room after the game, Archie presented the chairman with his winner's plaque, which brought a rare wide beaming smile to his face. I had a chuckle to myself at the rarity of both Archie and the chairman smiling openly together. I kept my plaque along with the Manager of the Month award, which I had won jointly with Archie in January for four wins and one draw. Special dispensation was acquired from the Football League in order to give the award to joint managers, as we were titled. Winning as a player at Wembley is an unforgettable experience. As a manager it is no less exciting, just different. Rather like seeing your children grow into maturity.

By the season's end we had finished in 16th position, with the illumination of that glittering Wembley final fading quickly. I knew that we would have to show a marked improvement in 1996/97, especially with regard to our league form. We had spent a considerable amount on transfers, which had to be reflected in results.

Shortly before we began our league programme I received a message call from Phil Henson, our chief executive, passing on an urgent message from the chairman. We had to sell Matt Clarke and Shaun Goater. Both goalkeeper Clarke and Shaun had been consistently good performers the previous year. The timing was horrific, and I knew their immediate loss would severely handicap our hopes for the coming season. As every football-wise person knows, these positions are the most difficult to fill. Archie did his best, at such short notice, by signing Steve Cherry in goal and Lee Glover in the striker's position, while I also recommended the signing of striker David "Junior" McDougald from Brighton to give us striking options.

Our season started disastrously, and after a 1-1 away draw at Walsall we lost our next six matches. We also lost striker McDougald with a back injury, along with Glover our other striker with an ankle injury. Having been forced to replace Shaun Goater, then losing the two replacements, the future was looking bleak. We then played a local derby at home against Chesterfield, who were flying high at the time. This was not a good time to lose a derby game, but we did, by the only goal of the game. The chairman called us to a meeting the following week.

"I'll start with you," he said, pointing at me.

He first asked me if I wanted to resign, to which I replied that I didn't, so he then said, "You're sacked," before asking if I had anything else to say.

For what it was worth, I told him that selling our goalkeeper and striker just before the start of the season made it difficult for us to replace them at short notice. I also told him that the commitment of the players was fine, so I had no reason to resign.

Mr Booth then turned to Archie and asked him what he wanted to do?

"I came to the club with John and will leave with him," he replied.

It seemed bizarre that the chairman asked Archie what he wanted to do. If Archie left on my behalf, it was an incredibly loyal gesture.

So that was it for us both, leaving me with a horrible empty feeling, and another reminder of how quickly football fortunes change; Wembley heroes in April, then looking for a job in September. There had been no lack of effort or commitment from either of us. No matter how hard you try, sometimes things just go against you. So I found myself once more looking for gainful employment.

CHAPTER EIGHTEEN

HOUSEBOATING IN WOKING

I immediately started job-hunting, which took me to franchise fairs and business seminars, and I also began scouring the newspapers for any suitable openings. Two lucrative jobs I looked at were packing fish in Alaska and diving for diamonds in Angola. These options might look somewhat extreme, but I had a family to look after. Ann gently reminded me that my swimming was pretty poor, my diving experience nil and I get seasick! Maybe not, then . . .

Following discussions with Domino's Pizza during a franchise exhibition at the NEC in Birmingham, I saw an advert for a football manager's job at Woking FC. I like pizza, but the idea of paying what I considered an extortionate commission to the company for setting up the franchise seemed extremely unreasonable. Despite the Surrey location, I optimistically fired off a brief CV to the new chairman of Woking.

I was out walking our dog Kelly the next day when by chance I found a four-leaf clover. "Look at this," I beamed showing Ann the clover, "maybe it's a lucky sign."

Two days later I received a request asking me for an interview for the Woking job. Sheffield to Woking is a fair jaunt, over three hours with clear traffic, but being considered for the role made me feel great. It was a job in football.

Clean-shaven and suited, off I went to the stockbroker belt of Surrey. The interview lasted literally 10 minutes, with polite exchanges concluded with a polite handshake.

"We'll let you know," I was told.

A few days later, I got a call asking me to ring the Woking chairman and was told I had the job.

Woking were in the Vauxhall Conference, having enjoyed considerable success under their previous manager, Geoff Chapple, especially in their FA Cup exploits. The biggest problem I had to overcome was the geography.

"Alek is settled in his school and we're not moving him again!" said Ann. So accommodation was going to be difficult, purely from a financial position. Even rented property in Surrey goes for a premium. With only a one-year contract, moving house was not really a realistic proposition.

I visited various properties to rent, realising I couldn't afford to lease a place for interim purposes. Then on another exploratory outing, travelling over the Basingstoke Canal at West Byfleet, I spotted a "For Sale or Let" sign adjacent to a houseboat. After further investigation, I inspected the lovely two-bedroom houseboat. It was complete with central heating, mains sewage, plumbing and electricity, with a big garden. It was £25,000 to buy and I had in total about the same amount in capital, so I went for it.

The houseboat was absolutely ideal, despite having to carry my groceries for about 40 yards up the tow path from the car park. I made Ann jealous by telling her that I shopped at Waitrose in West Byfleet. So it was a case of living on the riverbank all week, then either returning to Sheffield at the weekend, or Ann, Alek, the dog, friends and school friends of Alek joining me to enjoy life on the river.

The first question I was asked by the chairman, John Davies, was would I accept working with former player Brian Finn as my assistant? I said I would like to speak to him before deciding, which was agreed. I was working in a different league, in a new area, with a chairman that was new to the world of football. I needed someone I could trust and was delighted when Brian Finn impressed me at our first meeting. I was later quoted as saying that if you broke Brian in two he would have Woking FC running through him like a stick of rock. He proved to be a genuine guy and a pleasure to work with. His lovely wife Anne also put up with me for a few days, before I discovered the houseboat.

Before we started the 1997/98 season I brought in a fitness coach called Jez Cartwright, who was excellent, leaving the team in superb condition to start the season. Following his stint at Woking, he then deservedly moved up the leagues to Middlesbrough.

Having assessed the players during pre-season training as well as friendly fixtures, my first competitive match was a 1-1 draw against Telford. I wrote later in *The Cardinal*, Woking's seasonal magazine, that our performance frightened me to death, as it was my first real experience of non-league football, having been so used to dealing with players at a higher level, despite taking into consideration a slightly improved second half.

One pleasing factor during the opening matches was the confident displays by our young right-back, 19-year-old Kevin Betsy. He also scored a superb individual goal as we beat Northwich Victoria 1-0 at the end of August. Betsy would go on to attract many league scouts as the season progressed, scoring another six goals from his attacking full-back role.

Every manager has to make changes to his playing squad, and I quickly informed my chairman which positions needed strengthening. I had asked Phil Ledger the club secretary for copies of all the player's contracts, to assess where some wheeling and dealing might be introduced to subsidise the necessary recruits. At first I got no reaction so I asked him again. At the third time of asking when I still hadn't received them I wondered what was going on. It was common practice for the manager to possess copies of all players' contracts. Eventually Ledger complied, following my strong complaint to the chairman regarding the inexplicable delay. I also asked the chairman what signing-on fees were permissible, as I was going to require them with future signings.

"Woking FC does not give players signing-on fees," he told me, believing that the club's status as one of the best non-league teams was attraction enough. I told him politely that despite having a lovely new stand, behind one goal, players usually only move for one major reason and that is the money. He repeated his statement regarding the signing-on fees, before I intervened, asking him to get the club secretary to sign a statement regarding the issue. The club may have been ambitious, but to all intent and purposes it looked as if money was going to be extremely tight for any imminent signings. When the chairman discovered that signing-on fees had in fact been paid to quite a few players, he apologised.

I did make two signings in September, Michael Danzy, an aggressive centre-half from Aylesbury, who was joined by Steve West, a strongly built striker from Enfield. Justin Jackson, who had been our regular striker, was sold to Sam Allardyce at Notts County for £25,000, which more or less covered the West and Danzy moves.

As the season progressed, we hovered around the top of the league, without really hitting a run of convincing form. I made other signings such as defenders Eddie Saunders, Scott Smith and Richard Goddard, plus striker Andy Hayward on loan from Rotherham for a month, who went on to score five goals in six appearances. Despite these additions, we still struggled for genuine consistency. I set players high standards, as I expected the same from myself, never forgetting to lead by example regarding honesty and commitment. I never attempted to pull the wool over anyone's eyes.

One typical example was a Tuesday night home game against Stevenage Borough. The final score of 5-3 win in our favour will conjure thoughts of a football spectacular. Instead, it was a poor display from two teams who couldn't defend to save their lives. At the post-match press conference I confessed that at best Stevenage were slightly worse than we were.

Despite never achieving a satisfactory level of performance, we ended the season in third place, while losing in the final of the Spalding Cup to Morecambe in the last game of the season. I was rewarded for this competent first season with a two-year extension to my contract, having cut the wage bill and finished two places in the league better than the previous manager. I considered it a reasonable effort, with regulars Laurence Batty, in goal, striker Darren Hay and left-winger Scott Steele having all performed with some consistency, plus young Kevin Betsy proving himself with some bright displays. Our prospects looked decidedly rosy for the coming 1998/99 season.

However, as soon as we started back for pre-season training, a casualty list manifested itself. By the time we kicked off the season at Hednesford, my team could only be described as makeshift. I had desperately tried to find loan players of suitable quality, but with little success. We lost our first five games, albeit four of them by the odd goal.

Following a 1-1 home draw against Forest Green Rovers, and then a 3-2 home loss to Barrow, the atmosphere at the club was tangibly oppressive. The one-on-ones with the chairman Jon Davies were frequent, his outlook becoming decidedly gloomier following our disastrous start to the season. I firmly believed our results would change, because the players' attitude was good. No one hid or avoided responsibility, and that in turn gave me justifiable optimism as the man in charge.

Our next fixture was at Leek Town on 12th September. During the week preceding the game I sold Kevin Betsy to Fulham for £90,000. For Bill Sutton our financial director, it proved to be an eye-opener. He was party to my final discussion with Kevin Keegan, the Fulham manager. Bill was in my office trying to reassure me of his confidence in my ability to turn our results around. When Keegan came on the line, I motioned for Bill to sit down opposite me, in order to catch the proceedings.

"If you make it £90,000, it will give them enough money to pay me off when I get the sack," I said to Kevin. Bill jumped out of his seat waving his hands wildly, while mouthing the words, "No, no!"

Eventually Kevin agreed to the fee, so the phone went down.

"What the hell was all that about getting the sack?" Bill shouted. I told him plainly that, had he been party to my recent discussions with the chairman, he would understand my sincerity.

"They would have to vote on it," he said, "and we're not all like the chairman."

I calmed Bill down and thanked him for his genuine support. I then informed him that with the injury problems clearing up we would probably win at Leek even without Kevin Betsy.

Our trip to Leek was certainly bizarre and, caught up in a traffic jam, we arrived over an hour late at the ground. Not the finest preparation for a team under pressure. We played confidently, running out 3-0 winners. I was of course relieved, while hardly surprised. I let Brian Finn, my assistant, talk to the press, while I as normal discussed some tactical points with the players. As Darren Hay our striker passed me on his way into the showers, he smiled.

"Boss, why don't we turn up late for all our games?'

I turned and shouted for them all to hear.

"We might as well, but some of you didn't turn up for the first six games anyway!"

There was a pause before the laughter, making me realise that they were all delighted to have lifted the gloom.

Following a pleasant weekend at home, I travelled back to Woking on the Monday, had a brief meeting with the chairman, who told me I was sacked! Immediately I received a call from Bill Sutton to offer his regrets, and then he told me what had happened. Apparently it had been a four-against-three vote which went against me. I am sure Bill will always recall my phone conversation with Kevin Keegan.

For better or for worse, Woking had big ambitions, without the finance to fulfil them. They professed to wanting a full-time professional club, which at the time they blatantly could not afford.

Did I deserve the sack? One thing which never alters in football management is that you have to get results and quickly. My first season had been pretty good, finishing third. My second season was blighted by injuries, loss of form to key players and the intangible rub of the green. Being sacked after eight matches still hurts, despite the reasons.

It is always difficult to get back into the management game, as most positions are already filled long before they become public knowledge. Most other appointments are made through contacts, or previous working relationships. This had been the case in my Plymouth and Rotherham positions, working with ex-team-mates. My next football involvement was somewhat different, as I ended up working for a former player whom I had managed in my first job at Bolton Wanderers.

CHAPTER NINETEEN

A WEEK, A MONTH, A YEAR . . .

"**A**re you doing anything at the moment?" asked Warren Joyce.

Warren's father Walter had been my assistant at Bolton and Warren himself had played under me at Plymouth Argyle, during which time he'd amply demonstrated his honest, hard-working nature. Having given Warren his debut as an 18-year-old at Bolton, it was good to hear from him again.

"I've got the player-manager's job at Hull City," he continued, "I need some help off the field. It could be for just a week, a month, or a year . . ."

Hull were struggling for league survival, so it looked to be a fire-fighting job for sure. Warren told me his chairman, Tom Belton, was a genuine good guy, who offered him the job with a view to a permanent position, but this all depended on Hull remaining in Division Three. Mark Hateley had been sacked following some poor results, which gave me the distinct impression that this was mission impossible, but knowing Warren as well as I did encouraged me to sign a simple agreement from 20th November, 1998, to June 1999. The terms were £500 a week plus petrol expenses.

Having been a player-manager myself, I knew how much time was required, so I began talking Warren through the perils of trying to do too much. His enthusiasm for the job was infectious, coupled with his limitless energy, which all good midfield players possess.

Warren had a really solid working relationship with Tom Belton, which augured well for the future, an absolute necessity for any manager's survival! With Hull City lying at the bottom of the league, results were needed quickly, and a change of players essential. The biggest hurdle to overcome was how do you attract players to join you at the bottom of the league? Warren's friendly persuasion, coupled with the offer of decent wages, enabled him to wheel and deal with a fair degree of success. His contacts were numerous, resulting in a quick turnover of players, and enabling him to somehow obtain two Jamaican international players: Ian Goodison, a defender, along with Theodore Whitmore, a skilful midfield player. One player Warren asked my opinion of was former Doncaster midfield hard man Garry Brabin, who was at Blackpool. I endorsed his opinion on trying to sign Garry, which he eventually did.

Being Warren's assistant, I wasn't party to the deal bringing him to the club, which was concluded through the chairman. I was told by Warren that Garry was on the biggest contract at the club.

"It doesn't matter how much you pay him," I told him. "As long as he performs out on the pitch."

Garry Brabin was built like a concrete outhouse, which made him a fierce competitor in the tackle. His passing ability was limited to say the least, yet his all-round physical application made him a fine example for those around him. If the ball was there to be won, he won it.

When you are bottom of the league you need tough men, and Warren recruited them in abundance. Not quite like the "dirty dozen" in the movie, but pretty close. Subtlety was limited in the relentless scrap for survival. At one stage in that battle, we were five points adrift of safety behind Scarborough. During December we lost all four league matches, yet retained a surprising belief and enthusiasm throughout the club.

After matches we would normally discuss the performance in the manager's office. These post-mortems included me,

Warren, Rob Arnold, the goalkeeping coach, the reserve-team manager plus Billy Russell, the youth-team coach, who I helped recruit from Rotherham. When there are positive actions, bringing results out on the field, these post-match discussions are wonderful times. With any signs of negativity from outside the club starting to disappear, from January we won 10, drew eight and lost only four matches. For Warren it was indeed a job well done, considering he had played in most of the games himself.

Hull City ended up fourth from bottom (Scarborough were relegated) enabling everyone at the club the luxury of enjoying the summer break. Because we'd survived, I was given a new two-year contract, after negotiations with the new "power" men at the club.

Nick Buchanan and Stephen Hinchcliffe were installed as the incoming ruling chiefs of Hull City. Departing chairman Tom Belton had somehow been moved aside as the new administration took control. Never being privy to board meetings, I learned only what Warren told me regarding his conversations with the two new men in charge. We would compare thoughts and general opinions regarding the new regime. Warren seemed to give them the okay, while I had reservations regarding their manner, which appeared to me pompous as well as pretentious at times.

The 1999/2000 season could have been a springboard to better things, instead of gradually evolving into a grinding slog for survival. The change in attitude from the ruling element seemed to filter through the club, affecting even the players. It was common knowledge the club was in dire straits financially. Despite two enormously lucrative cup fixtures against Chelsea in the FA Cup and Liverpool over two legs in the Worthington Cup, the situation seemed to accelerate when our employers informed us that the signing of striker Colin Alcide had been an utter waste of money which we would never recoup.

Their opinions were expressed more and more abrasively

to the point of becoming counter-productive. In trying to improve the quality of the squad, Colin Alcide was then sold to York City for a profit, which was also deemed lucky by our less-than-genial employers.

It came as no real surprise when in April Warren and I were sacked. True to form, I wasn't informed face to face by either Buchanan or Hinchcliffe, but by one of their lackeys who had the cheek to opine that we had spent too much money. Taking into consideration our cup runs, which were televised, he obviously wasn't too good at arithmetic either.

With 14 months of my contract outstanding, I knew getting compensation would not be easy. After one payment of £10,000 the club went bust, leaving me out of work once again to consider my options.

My future considerations were somewhat interrupted as I had visits from the CID to my house in Sheffield, plus an interview with a Mr Bean from the FA at Bramall Lane about, surprise, surprise, large sums of money going missing from Hull City Football Club. When I gave my frank opinion on who I considered to be responsible, I was politely stopped, then informed that tangible evidence was necessary before a prosecution could begin. In the end there was no prosecution brought with regard to this particular incident.

I'd enjoyed working with Warren and helping to keep Hull City in the Football League, but that was one job I had no real regrets about leaving.

My problem was what to do next. That question was answered when Les Bradd, who was Nottingham Forest's commercial manager, called to ask if I would like to work as a match-day host at the club. I agreed immediately to his offer, which also led to my covering all the Nottingham Forest matches for BBC Radio Nottingham.

Being a match-day host is really a meet-and-greet role, involving being around the sponsors and generally talking about the club and the match. It allowed me to start working on radio because the only time the sponsors don't need me is during a match, while the only time the radio people don't want me is before and after a game. I wasn't required to do any commentary, but give my opinions on the game as and when required. Despite these jobs being enjoyable and giving me some financial reward, they certainly couldn't sustain the McGoverns totally.

CHAPTER TWENTY

BRINGING
THE HOUSE DOWN

A couple of days after attending a Sportsman's Evening at Forest's ground in 2001, I told Ann I thought I would become an after-dinner speaker.

"You can't do that," she replied quickly.

Undaunted by my other half, I went to other functions, studying the presentations of Gordon Banks, Nobby Stiles, Duncan McKenzie and my former manager Peter Shilton. I put together a script and learned it while rehearsing in front of a mirror until I could more or less remember it all. I didn't consider using prompt cards placed in front of me, as it seemed a little unprofessional.

Once I'd memorised and felt comfortable with my routine, I began to look for the numbers of agents who I thought might be helpful. I felt a bit like Yosser from the TV series *Boys From The Black Stuff*, spouting "Giv' us a job, I can do that."

"What experience have you got?" was the typical agent's opening line, repeated monotonously like a harbinger of doom as I struggled to capture an opening gig. Then one day Dave Watson, the ex-Manchester City and England centre-half, called to ask if I would host two couples at Market Rasen Races. It basically entailed chatting about my career throughout the race meeting plus having a flutter if necessary. I wagered and lost very little due mainly to my ignorance of gambling, but after mentioning that I wanted to do some after-dinner speaking, one lady gave me the telephone number of an agent who lived in the North East called David Greener. I subsequently phoned David, who said he would be happy to find me some work.

"How many people have told you that, with no reply? You've got no chance," Ann insisted.

Ten minutes later, David phoned me back with a booking at Lumley Working Men's club near Chester-le-Street.

A little nervous, I delivered my speech followed by the comedian's stint, which is the normal format of a sportsman's evening. I was given a polite round of applause, which gave me a real buzz of excitement. The comedian Dave "Grizzly" Adams then performed, receiving a similar warm round of applause, and to round the night off a fight broke out at the back of the room, spilling forward as glasses smashed and tables overturned.

Quite an eventful debut, then, but I enjoyed my first experience of after-dinner speaking and believed I could be good at it. I knew I would have to work hard at the job, but that was nothing new to me and, just as I had always done, I decided that I would aim to be the best I could at this new venture. David Greener phoned me the next day.

"I heard you brought the house down," he joked, and then added that the organisers had been pleased with my performance.

True to his word, he then recommended me to other agents, which has since helped to firmly establish me on the after-dinner circuit. At the suggestion of one comedian I began to imitate Brian Clough too. The impersonation was enthusiastically received so I've kept on doing it, and my after-dinner speaking has become an enjoyable part of my life.

A year or two after I took my bow on the circuit, I was phoned by an agent who said he had a booking for me.

"You'll never guess where it is," he told me.

"Where?" I asked.

"Elland Road!" he said.

He obviously knew I'd had a bad time there as a player, but a job was a job, and I certainly wasn't going to turn it down. Besides, if I did well there I thought I could probably do well anywhere. Just to add a bit of spice to the occasion, Brian Clough was in the audience with his son, Simon. I did my bit, including an impersonation of Brian, which seemed to go down really well. So well, in fact, that after I'd finished Simon came over to see me and said it was one of the better impersonations of his dad he'd heard!

My last foray into football management was a three-month spell at Ilkeston Town, where half my time was spent sorting through financial problems. It was so memorable that I have forgotten when this even was. The difficulty in trying to run a part-time business was being given part-time information. This resulted in a poor standard of communication between me and the chairman, Paul Millership, who could mostly only be contacted through chief executive Dave Pullin. This three-way communication lacked efficiency or discretion. Finding out from the bartender in the social club who you are trying to sign, during a post-match drink, was not my idea of professionalism. My parting was mutually satisfactory, however, with a firm handshake from the chairman.

Would I ever venture back into football management? The reason I would never say no is because experience has shown me how unpredictable life can be. At present I enjoy my radio work, match-day hosting at Nottingham Forest, plus the real buzz of speaking to people during sportsman's evenings. The applause or occasional standing ovation doesn't quite match the pure pumping adrenaline rush of running out in front of full houses at Old Trafford or Anfield. It does, however, give me sufficient nerves, thrills and enjoyment to appreciate how interested people are in my stories from the beautiful game. As time rolls on, I consider myself truly fortunate to have played in the greatest era – the '70s and early '80s – of British football, when that big shiny European Cup was retained in England for six consecutive years, courtesy of Liverpool, Nottingham Forest and Aston Villa.

Pelé rightfully named soccer "the beautiful game", which I always played with bundles of energy, heartfelt passion, total commitment and a sprinkling of skill. I, as one individual amid our massive national sport, always considered myself lucky.

Lucky to have had good health – excellent health in fact – enabling me to follow the dream I nurtured as a 15-year-old. Lucky to have met Brian Clough and Peter Taylor when I was so young, lucky to have won cups, medals and trophies, despite struggling to win over the fans at every club I played for. Lucky to still be with Ann, after 40 years, and luckier still to have our son Alek, who with his exciting rock band, Scrim, is striving to follow his dream. Most of all lucky that my mum, at 89 years young, is still around to tell me, "Deal with it!" if I ever feel sorry for myself.

The only way to sum up briefly all the good fortune I have enjoyed throughout my life is a quotation from Gary Player, the great South African golfer, who said, "The more I practise, the luckier I get."

Be lucky!

HERE WE GO AGAIN

By Ann McGovern

J ohn asked Alek and me to contribute to his book, as he thought readers might like to see another side of a footballer/manager, from the point of view of his family.

The title of my part of the book seemed appropriate, as John and I have moved house 10 times, mostly in the pursuit of the football dream. And as we have now lived in our present home for over 15 years, this shows how often we moved during John's days as a player and manager.

It has taken a long time to complete this book, as the computer died just before John had finished it the first time round, so everything was lost. We don't always do what we tell our children and others to do, when they are doing some vital piece of GCSE, A level or exam work, and back it up. So Alek and I set about typing it up from the manuscript again, and John wasn't allowed to use the computer, as it would have ended up being thrown through the window if something had gone wrong again. As you may have judged after reading this book, John likes to be in charge of everything he does in his life. It is also a measure of the man that he wanted to write the book in his own words, which he has done with the help of Kevin Brennan. He has given 100 per cent to this project, as he has tried to do in everything he has been involved with in his life.

I sometimes wonder why John went along with most of the

things that happened when he played for Brian and Peter, questioning very little his bosses told him to do, and just getting on with it. That wouldn't happen now. I suppose this is because he was part of a team and worked for the harmony and success of himself and others. When you are on your own and in charge of your life and other people's, having to think for yourself, it is a different matter.

He is a great taskmaster to himself and gets annoyed if things don't go right. He is a born perfectionist, to the point where even when he is washing up – yes he does wash up, cook and also iron, I don't do trousers – and drops something, Alek and I sit and listen to his shouts of rebuke to himself. In my opinion this part of his character has got him into trouble in management, making him strive for perfection, getting involved with all areas of the clubs he has worked for, and in the process ruffling a few feathers. I have learned that in life, and in football, people will always cover their own backs. This is why I think he got the sack at the clubs he worked for, as he didn't see some of the people involved doing their jobs for the good of the club. If he'd been given longer in the jobs, I am positive he would have pulled the clubs through. People panic, or can't stand the stick given by supporters when positive results don't pan out quickly, so sacking is inevitable.

I don't think supporters realise what heartache this brings to families, when your man has been sacked and becomes an object of derision because in the eyes of the powers that be he can't do his job. These men are human beings with feelings, and why they keep going for different jobs in the same profession (apart from the fact that they need to earn a living) is sometimes beyond me. But they love the game of football and want to be better than the next manager at their job, so that is why they keep trying, unable to supress their competitive spirit. People should be thankful for these men, not vilify them, or we wouldn't have any football managers at all in the Beautiful Game. I think it is one of the hardest jobs in the world, but also one of the most rewarding, if things go well, for them and their families.

Looking back on the 40 years we have been together has been a nostalgic walk along memory lane; not all good, but mostly exciting and interesting, and never dull. John is not the easiest person to live with, but he is a brilliant father and partner, and one who has always looked after us.

So here we go, my side of the story. I will first tell you a bit about myself and how we met. I was born in Derby in 1946 – a bonfire night baby – and I lived with my brilliant mum and dad, Vera and Wilf. I was an only child, and was probably spoilt as I never wanted for anything. I started as an apprentice hairdresser at my Uncle Billy's shop, next door to where my dad had his butchers shop in Abbey Street, and I then went on to college to do a full-time course in hairdressing, as I wanted to teach the subject. I was a child of the Swinging Sixties: Mods, Rockers, clothes boutiques, Mary Quant, Vidal Sassoon, the music, the discos (I was a Mod).

I started to make friends with a lot of journalists, fellow hairdressers, boutique owners etc, and this band of like-minded people evolved into a group of well over 20 people, all congregating in the week or weekend to have a good time. Most are my friends to this day.

It was a great era to be a teenager, as the whole world was changing, much to the fears of our parents. We were christened "The Tea Set", trend-setters in our town, as we were into everything modern and new wave. We had chrome-laden scooters or minis for transport, but for some reason I had a Hillman Imp Singer Chamois – just to be different I suppose. The other group in town was called "The Jet Set" as they were wealthy kids with Porsches and E-Type Jaguars. We congregated in Judy and Roger's boutique, Hilary's Boutique and Helen's card shop, all in Sadler Gate, and we were quite well known in Derby, as among the group we had members of bands and DJs.

It was with my Derby friends that I first started to go and watch my home team, Derby County. Amongst the group was Lin Frances, Roger Smith, Paul Hopewell, Paul Ham, John Barton, Roy Milton, Roy Hollingworth, Helen Vamplew and myself. There was something good happening to the Derby team, so like a lot of people who start going to see their local club when success beckons you are dragged along by friends or family to see what it's all about. You could tell something special was in the air as the Derby fans were buzzing. My favourite player was Les Green and I used to carry a picture of him in my purse. He used to come into the Kardomah, a coffee bar in town, with a few of the other players. My friends would shout "he's here" and I would go all wobbly!

I was going out with a journalist at the time called Trevor East who was also a local DJ. He was invited to the celebrations for Derby winning promotion to the First Division in 1969, and that was the first time I can remember being introduced to John. John also used to come and watch the press men play various friendly matches and as a dutiful girlfriend, with all the others, I was there home and away, often in the freezing cold. He always used to lend me his scarf and gloves (which had apparently belonged to his dad) to keep out the cold. Little did I know at the time that he used to go to these matches to see me, as he later admitted that he wouldn't have got up at the crack of dawn after a Saturday match just to see the press men play. At first I think he was impressed with my new car, a Spitfire, and he later told me that a girl with a car was something, but a sports car something else, as girls in Hartlepool rarely drove at all.

After I stopped seeing Trevor, who started seeing a girl called Pam, who is now one of my best friends, I was in my friend Helen's card shop when John came in and said he was taking his mum out for a meal and asked if I would like to come. Apparently he wasn't going out with his mum at all, but went home and said that she had to come as he was taking a girl out and needed moral support. He was quite shy in those days. We started going out from then, and he wooed me with the line, "Would you like to come up and listen to my Moby Grape album?" We did fall out for a short while, maybe a couple of months, and then Neil Hallam, a local journalist who we became friends with, took me to a Derby County celebration knowing that John would be there. I think it must have been a put-up job, as we started seeing each other from then on and have been together ever since.

Just before John and I started seeing each other I had started my first teaching job in Blackburn, so when we did start going out we only saw each other at weekends and holidays, but shortly afterwards I got a job as assistant lecturer at Clarendon College in Nottingham. It's strange how things pan out!

Given that a lot of my friends were well known in Derby, it was ironic that when we first started going out with each other people would say "Who is that with Ann Sharman?" rather than the other way around. People would ask John how he got into "the crowd". You didn't realise what people thought of you at the time.

When I started going out with John I had the privilege of free tickets for the stand. My friends Roger or Paul would sit with me, but we would still go to the Jorrocks pub first. I would always take a flask of coffee and a rug to the game, and Roger, being a good artist, made a birthday card for me once, which showed me throwing the flask at the supporters who were shouting at John during the game. Would I?

I used to pick my tickets up from the front door of the ground, and there was always something written on them, usually Moby Grape. I still have a few. One day John forgot to leave them, so the doorman said he would go and find him. I said "no" and went off in a huff, and John phoned me up straight after the match with humble apologies for the mistake, saying that they had been away on a trip and he had had a lot to think about and it had slipped his mind. He never forgot again.

Being new to the inner workings of a football club, I used to go into the player's wives and relations room, a small room below one of the stands, where we would get a cup of tea or coffee and maybe a sandwich, before and after the match. We would then wait for our spouses to meet us after the game. I must say I was very nervous about what they would think of a newcomer, and it was something quite new to me. I think, like a lot of people, I was a bit in awe of the wives of the seasoned professionals who had been in the game longer than John. I will always remember Val O'Hare being there and making me feel welcome, something I tried to follow when John was captain at Forest, trying to make new wives or girlfriends feel comfortable at their new club, as I knew how I had felt.

So I had got the football bug, going to all of the home and away matches, and it has remained with me ever since. In fact, I watch a lot more football on the TV than John does, doing my ironing on a Saturday as I watch Jeff Stelling & Co to find out all the results.

The main thing I remember at Derby was the game against Tottenham, which John has mentioned. In those days the crowds weren't segregated, and in the end the Tottenham supporters were cheering for Derby.

We also had gatherings with my friends at my mum and dad's to watch the FA Cup finals. As usual my mum would lay on a brilliant spread of food for us all and the odd drink or two. John was always away on the usual Mallorca jaunt, but we had some great times at our house, something we seem to have followed with our son, as our home is always an open house for his friends. I love it, and I can say that his friends have become ours: Alek's fiancée Lauren, Ben, Becki, Rob, Joe and Mike, Adam, Serena and their lovely baby Alexa, and his band members, John Clarke, John Lee and Dave Glasby, Joel and Alex. I have mentioned them by name in my part of the book, as I think they deserve to have their names in print. They have enriched our lives for being brilliant kids, all of them. They have been Alek's friends from the age of eight, since we have lived in Sheffield.

During the season 1970/71 I was at work at Clarendon College in Nottingham one night when I got a call from my friend Roger to say that Derby had won the First Division Championship and they were all going to celebrate. John was away again in Mallorca, and as I drove into Derby the crowds had gathered in the market place to celebrate. Off I went to do the same with my friends at the Broadway on Duffield Road, another of our haunts.

Back in the council house after the open-top tour of Derby I did my first and only interview for the radio with Val O'Hare. I suppose the wives and girlfriends had a certain amount of celebrity in those days, but nothing like the WAGs now, as we also did an article about ourselves for *The Ram*, the Derby programme. WAG has become a derogatory term for a footballer's wife or girlfriend these days, which I think is very unfair, as who knows what any of us would be like with all that money to spend?

So they were now in the big time, and it was brilliant to go to games and see the players you had only read about in the papers. The team winning the First Division Championship made all of us Derby fans so proud.

We went out after the matches, usually for a meal, sometimes to a disco or to Belper, where there were pubs with good jukeboxes to satisfy John's love of music. If the team lost, it was a bit iffy as John would take it personally and be in a bad mood, but on the whole it wasn't that bad – fortunately they didn't lose many matches. We also went to functions and supporters' clubs, where people would sometimes get you involved, but on the whole they only wanted a piece of your man. At times it got a bit annoying, as women would outrageously flirt with him (mostly older women who I think must have wanted to mother him, or something). I didn't say very much as I am quite easy going, but at times I threw in one or two barbered comments when it got a bit obvious and too much, especially when on one occasion a supporter pulled down her top and said "sign this!" They weren't very good boobs either.

Then the unthinkable happened, Brian and Peter resigned – and it wasn't all hunky dory after all. I remember going to a meeting at Brian's house with the other wives, girlfriends and players. Such was the charisma of the man that he got us fired up enough to go down to a meeting in Derby full of supporters protesting at them leaving the club. We girls marched in to a brilliant reception from the Derby fans, and that feeling was what I imagined walking out at Wembley must have felt like.

So John's days at Derby were numbered. Then Brian got the job at Leeds, so off we went there, with me having to give up my job. To be honest I didn't think twice about it as John's career always seemed more important than mine. Not from the financial side, though, as I was earning more money than him at one point. Whether this was right or wrong I don't know – we were young so we thought "what the hell". Going to set up your first home is an excitement in itself with everything it involves, and so off we went to live in our first house together. We found a cottage to rent in Batley, for £40 a week, near t' Variety Club, as they say in Yorkshire. It was a lovely cottage attached to an old house. I think the other players at Leeds couldn't understand why we lived there, not being the most salubrious part of the outskirts of Leeds, as they lived in far more up-market places than that, but I loved it. It was a bit of a waste of time, though, as John hardly played and was hated by the supporters. This was not new (I should have taken my flask to those games as well) but, as someone who cares for him, sitting in the stands and hearing the abuse was not a pleasant thing to have to go through. It brought me to tears on occasions when the abuse was very bad, although that didn't happen too often as I got used to it. I came to realise that a lot of supporters go to a match to watch their team and take it out on the players for a good crack, to get everything out of their system after their week's work. I don't think they consider that the players are people with feelings while they are doing this. There always seems to be one whipping boy in a team. I think it sums up this concept, when people have said to John over the years, "Were you John McGovern?", as if he is a different person to the one they once watched on the pitch.

There was never open animosity amongst the Leeds players towards us, as I remember being in a nightclub when a lot of the players turned up after a match. I thought that they were going to ignore us and felt like merging into the background, but the majority of them came over to speak or have a drink and were very friendly, particularly the younger ones like Gordon McQueen and Frank Gray.

After six months in the desert that was Leeds, we packed up and went to Derby, back to home territory, at first living with my mum and dad. We bought or first house in Borrowash on the outskirts of Derby. And you will know what happened next from reading the book. I also got my job back at Nottingham, and I must have been OK at it as I eventually went on to be in charge of the department.

When first arriving at Nottingham Forest I met the other players' families in the wives' room. Val O'Hare and I were the newcomers, and sometime after our arrival one of the player's wives said that they were all very wary of us as they thought we would be big-headed and full of airs and graces as we had come from a First Division club. Val and I did have fox fur coats at the time, which probably gave that impression. At a Christmas game some time later, though, there were a lot of people wearing fox fur coats, and it became something of a club outfit.

Again I went to most of the matches, initially going with John's mum and stepfather Stan. John's mum had married Judy and Roger's father after Judy and I had set them up on a blind date. Later we moved to Nottingham, where we made friends with our next-door neighbours Eileen and Graeme, so I started going to the match with them.

When John became captain at Forest I was sort of in charge of pouring the tea and serving the drinks after the match. I wasn't one of the young ones any more and was becoming a seasoned professional in the game. I don't know whether it was important or not for us to be at the games, but I wanted to go. I personally think I would have missed out on a lot of the success if I hadn't been there. I know some players' wives don't go to matches, but I didn't want to miss out on what was happening at the ground, along with the social side of the game.

Successful as they were, you may think that we were allowed to go to a lot of places with the players and be invited on trips, leading a glamorous life. No, we were not. The first time I can remember ever going with the players to a game was at Skegness – I think it was to open the floodlights. We were treated royally and it was the first time we all met Kenny Burns, with his long hair and bad reputation. I think we were all scared of him, which was silly, as he's a pussy cat when you get to know him.

Two trips we did go on, not with the players but the wives and families, were to Munich and Madrid for the European Cup Finals. The players stayed in a different hotel, and after each match they were not allowed to come and see us at all to celebrate. In Madrid we were kept company by the young apprentices, Stuart Gray being one of them, and had quite a good time actually. Some of the players did creep out of their hotel and come back to ours, as I saw Larry in the lift, but Sue Shilton and I both said our partners wouldn't. I nearly didn't go to Madrid, as after being informed that the players were not coming back to our hotel again I thought, "Blow you Mr Clough, I'm not going". Anyway, I changed my mind and got on the flight at the last minute – after all, it was only me who would have missed out.

I wish everyone could enjoy the feeling you get when you are travelling on the open-topped bus with thousands upon thousands of people lining the streets. It takes your breath away. You also get to go to places that you would never normally be asked to – to see the lord mayor's parlour, the sheriff's office etc. And of course, you have to have new outfits for these occasions!

I have been to the old Wembley five times (why they couldn't have kept the twin towers within the new design is beyond me). To see John lead out the team always made me cry (tears of joy this time). I was so proud of him, the team and everyone involved.

Then, as with all good things, they come to an end. The next move was to Bolton, as you will have read. I must say, I really enjoyed living there, as I could be near to my friend Elaine, her husband David and John's god son Marcus, and after living in Blackburn I knew the area well. As usual I went to most of the matches, but this time it was different as you were elevated to the directors' wives room, which was the same format as the players' wives room but amongst the bosses. The atmosphere was the same and we got on well, but what I didn't realise at the time is that these people's husbands can as easily hire as fire, which unfortunately happened to John. From an outsider it just seems good or bad that they got rid of him, and on to the next manager, but from the inside it was like someone or something had died. It was one of the most horrible times I have experienced; it was so upsetting for both of us. I don't know if this is how other people feel, but that was my experience. I got on very well with Maureen Warburton (one of the directors' wives) and her son Brett, and she very graciously phoned me to say how sorry she was and that they didn't want John to go. It made me feel a bit better to know that someone cared.

During his time as a manager or assistant, sackings happened again, and I began to realise this is par for the course and never let it upset me as much as the first time. But for John it felt the same, not being allowed to do the job that he loved. These times were hard emotionally as he would go into himself and not talk about how he felt. We got over it in the end though and just got on with life.

I began this piece with the amount of times we have moved and, well, there comes a time when enough is enough, and I put my foot down and said we are not moving house any more. Our son, who was born in Tenerife when I was 40, had been to three different schools in different parts of the country by the time he was eight, and we had him to consider now. So here we are still in Sheffield.

A football manager's family's life can be quite a lonely one, and I became something of a one-parent family, as it not only involves matches and training, but a lot of scouting also has to be done by the managers. So I went to a lot of school functions and out-of-school activities on my own.

Now John works for himself, I would hate him to go back into football again, but that is just me being selfish. I am sure he would love it, but I just like an easy, uncomplicated life, which I must say it has not been.

For all its ups and downs, though, I would not change my life for the world. Together we have experienced the best that football and life can offer – what a journey! We have met and made friends with some wonderful people along the way, and now we are invited to the best football stadiums in Europe as their guests. One was Wembley for the Champions League Final – Man United v Barcelona. Usain Bolt was sat in front of us and Paul McCartney was sat directly behind with his daughter. Not bad for an ordinary girl from Derby! Thanks John for a wonderful life together full of memories no one can take away. Thank you also for the best gift of all, our wonderful son.

Footnote

One last thing that I really wish for is that one day, when our son makes it in the music industry with his band, Scrim, is that people say to John, "Are you Alek McGovern's father?"

MY DAD

By Alek McGovern

"**W**hat's it like having a famous footballer for a dad?" I used to get asked that all the time, mostly by the old Forest and Derby County fans. The truth is that I don't know any different – I suppose I see him as "recognised" rather than famous, as I wasn't actually around to see any of his playing days. He does command a tremendous amount of respect from the "back in the day" fans, though. Nevertheless, I have agreed to write the epilogue in this book, so the following will be my views/experiences with the person known to me simply as "Dad".

I suppose I'd better start with what he's really like. I know that it's the main reason anyone buys a book about a person after all. I'll start with a few of his characteristics:

He is very stubborn; he often has an "I'm never wrong" type of attitude, which is probably due to his extremely competitive nature. I guess being wrong can often be viewed as losing, especially in arguments, which, annoyingly, he rarely loses.

Going hand in hand with his stubbornness is his determination; if something needs to be done he is very focused at finishing it. I remember when he was in a period of unemployment while living in Sheffield and looking for a source of income, he was so determined to get back to work that he took employment with a company selling personalised wine bottles. I had more than a few strange looks when people asked me what my dad was up to now, expecting it to be some football-related job. "Personalised wine bottles? What?"

Another side that people tend not to see is his more compassionate side, due to the fact that he has also always had to have the tough composure that football requires. I have chosen to follow my dream of being a musician and have had nothing but support from him. Whereas most parents would be looking for their kids to get a "proper job" instead of following something that would be considered a waste of time by most, my dad has stuck by me, having complete faith and allowing me to just get on with it.

Last but not least, he is honest. "Just remember son, you'll never be as good a football player as I was." Do I need to elaborate?

He's a bit of an old rocker. I'd probably go as far as to say he's solely responsible for my love of rock music. From an early age music was blasted out of car stereos, desktop speakers, anything really. I guess some subconscious part of me took notice because over the years I've become a big fan of AC/DC thanks to my dad. Mind you, something I'm not a fan of are his air guitar performances, especially not in full view of everyone at parties.

I did have the experience of accompanying him to work at football clubs such as Rotherham United and Woking FC. While it was weird hearing the players call my dad "boss" or "gaffer", I got used to it after a while. It was also obvious that he was respected by the players and staff at the clubs. I'm not sure that this was due to his previous experience or the fact that he was strict and could dish out a harsh bollocking (of all people, I should know). Looking back now, it is funny to recall how youth-team players he'd called over had exactly the same expression as a child who isn't sure if they are going to get a telling off or not by their parents.

While in the office at one of the clubs, I remember him telling me "sometimes you have to make the best of a bad situation". His stress was pretty apparent at times, but he always did his best to not let it affect his relationships with people. I developed a whole new appreciation for how much was actually put on you in a manager's position at a football club; the amount of pressure and work that you don't see makes the results appear all the more well earned.

While he was managing Woking I recall a not-so-fond memory of a fan shouting abuse at him at a match while I was sat literally two seats away. It made me pretty angry to say the least, even more so because I had an appreciation for what actually went on behind the scenes. For a person with a bit of a fiery temper at times, he is very calm under pressure and never seems to panic at all.

If I had to sum my dad up in a few words I'd say "hard working, honest, rocker at heart with an occasional Scottish temper". I'm sure people who have met him will know there's a lot more to him than that, but those are the things that stand out to me.

On a side note, I've recently been reminded of my dad's chart success at Forest with the club song *We've Got The Whole World In Our Hands*. So, many sarcastic thanks, Dad, you are currently a more successful musician than I am – as if I didn't have enough to live up to already.

John McGovern Career Roll of Honour

Playing Career

Hartlepools United

Promotion for the first time in the club's history: 1968

Derby County

First Division champions:	1971/72
Second Division champions:	1968/69
Texaco Cup winners:	1971/72
Watney Cup winners:	1970

Nottingham Forest

First Division champions:	1977/78
League Cup winners:	1978, 1979
FA Charity Shield winners:	1978
European Cup winners:	1979, 1980
European Super Cup winners:	1979
Anglo-Scottish Cup winners:	1977

Horwich RMI

Dairy Crest Floodlit League Cup winners: 1985

Managerial Career

Rotherham United

Auto Windscreens Shield winners: 1996